Crommelin's Thunderbirds

Crommelin's Thunderbirds

Air Group 12 Strikes the Heart of Japan

Lt. Cdr. Roy W. Bruce, USNR (Ret.)

Lt. Cdr. Charles R. Leonard, USN (Ret.)

Drawings by Roy W. Bruce

Naval Institute Press

Annapolis, Maryland

Library of Congress Cataloging-in-Publication Data
Bruce, Roy W., 1921–
    Crommelin's Thunderbirds : Air Group 12 strikes the heart of Japan / Roy W.
Bruce and Charles R. Leonard.
        p.   cm.
    Includes bibliographical references (p.) and index.
    ISBN 1-55750-509-8 (acid-free paper)
    1. World War, 1939–1945—Aerial operations, American.   2. World War,
1939–1945—Naval operations, American.   3. United States. Navy. Air Group
12—History.   4. Crommelin, Charles L.   5. World War, 1939–1945—Personal
narratives, American.   6. World War, 1939–1945—Campaigns—Pacific Area.
I. Leonard, Charles R., 1922–   . II. Title.
D790.B685   1994
940.54′4973–dc20   94-16277

Printed in the United States of America on acid-
free paper ⊗

9 8 7 6 5 4 3

✪ Contents

✪ Foreword

The pages that follow chronicle events in the course of a carrier air group during a short but historically significant segment of the Battle for the Pacific in World War II. The air group was Twelve—their aircraft carrier home was the USS *Randolph*—and the war segment was Kamikaze.

Following a doctrine of desperation, the Japanese Kamikaze Corps converted aircraft into suicide bombs. Among the military and logistic forces that brought on Kamikaze were the growing lopsidedness of American-to-Japanese aircraft loss ratios and the inability to replace those losses with trained crews and aircraft. The elite of Japanese air had been winnowed down to a precious few by January 1945.

Air groups by 1945 lived in a world of war equipment plenty. The U.S. industrial war machine was in high gear, and the U.S. was exploiting one-sided benefits such as radar. Kamikaze, however, entered into every facet of air-group life when in the combat zone. It dictated air-group composition, defensive tactics, operational priorities, theater strategy, and, of course, the task: to carry relentlessly the fight to the enemy's front door, and at the same time to prevent the enemy from successful suicide attacks against our floating airfields and all other naval elements.

Only the setting for this book, however, is Kamikaze. The story line is people—people anecdotes and the people side of the events of war. The chronology covers air-group buildup, training, deployment to the leading edge of war (without warm-up), combat action, targets, weather quirks, and enemy failure (and success) against the *Randolph*. The character of Twelve emerges—a montage of diverse

U.S. backgrounds. Like all combat recounting, there is a mix of fear, bravado, jubilation, peer pressure, and, clearly, a mutual respect among fighting teammates—those in the cockpit and those who support them. The success of any was shared through the efforts of all.

The reader will sense both admiration and veneration—those tributes that in a special way are set aside for heroes—as Commander Charles Crommelin's name appears in the text to follow. His leadership by precept continued to influence Twelve long after his untimely death removed him from our presence. I am privileged to provide the opening remarks for a book that bears his name and whose contents reveal his character as we knew it.

Frederick H. Michaelis
Admiral, U.S. Navy (Ret.)

✪ Introduction

In February 1945 when Carrier Air Group 12 and the USS *Randolph* (CV 15) first went into battle, the U.S. Pacific Fleet had started to batter open the very gates of Japan. To understand the situation these naval aviators faced, it is useful to examine how carrier war in the Pacific Ocean had developed over the preceding three years and two months. Each major phase of the naval war in the Pacific posed different problems for the fast carriers of the U.S. Pacific Fleet.

The 7 December 1941 Japanese surprise carrier strike on Pearl Harbor found the United States at a strong strategic disadvantage in the Pacific, initially outnumbered nine to three in carriers. Yet when committed to desperate battles in 1942 at Coral Sea, Midway, and Guadalcanal, the American flattops turned the tide of the war. Victory came at a terrible price. Only two of the fleet's six carriers survived 1942. Seasoned in battle, their naval aviators proved invaluable in training the vast numbers who followed.

Mid-1943, with the arrival of the first of what would ultimately be twenty-four *Essex*-class big carriers and nine *Independence*-class converted light carriers, brought a renaissance of carrier aviation in the Pacific. New models of carrier aircraft that outperformed their Japanese counterparts reached the fleet in numbers undreamt of only a year before.

The Pacific Fleet's fast carriers looked to the destruction of their Japanese counterparts, but with the United States firmly on the strategic offensive, the primary task of the carriers was to support the major amphibious operations being planned for the Central Pacific. Now irrevocably committed to the strategic defensive, the Japanese had to conserve their carriers until a favorable opportunity for counterattack existed or the position threatened was so vital it transcended preservation of the carriers. Until that time, the Japanese hoped their land-based air, shuttling from island to island—the so-called "unsinkable aircraft carriers"—would whittle down American carrier superiority before the decisive battle.

Warm-up carrier raids in the Central Pacific from August through October 1943 helped temper the new American air weapon. November air strikes against Rabaul showed that the fast carriers could hit hard and also stand up to a determined land-based air counterattack. That same month eleven fast and six escort carriers with more than nine hundred planes closely covered Vice Adm. Raymond A. Spruance's invasion of the Gilberts. In January and February 1944 the newly created Task Force 58 under Rear Adm. Marc A. Mitscher supported the Fifth Fleet's hugely successful assault on the Marshalls.

The new order in the Pacific really became evident later in February, when nine of Mitscher's carriers smashed the big Japanese fleet base at Truk. The Japanese lost 250 planes and 200,000 tons of shipping, as opposed to 17 American planes and torpedo damage to the *Intrepid* (CV 11). Breaking off from the main body, Mitscher took six carriers northwest against the Marianas. Although discovered by the enemy, he announced, "We will fight our way in." His air groups ripped Saipan, Tinian, and Guam, demonstrating that fast carriers could range deep into Japanese waters and rain destruction far from the actual invasion sites.

The long-awaited titanic carrier battle took place in June 1944 in the Philippine Sea. The latest American leap forward, this time by Vice Admiral Spruance's Fifth Fleet, aimed for the Marianas, which ultimately threatened the Japanese home islands by bringing them within range of the army air force's new B-29 bombers. To help defend Saipan, the Combined Fleet committed nine carriers with 430 aircraft against Mitscher with fifteen fast carriers and more than 900 planes. The Japanese hoped their land-based air, numbering some 530 planes in the region, would concentrate in the Marianas and cut down the odds. Mitscher's relentless attacks on key island bases dashed their hopes. The Battle of the Philippine Sea (19–20 June 1944) all but destroyed the Japanese carrier arm by costing them three carriers (two sunk by submarines) and nearly four hundred aircraft. No wonder some Japanese officers advocated suicide tactics; the alternative seemed no better. Mitscher would have dearly loved to sink all the flattops, but his aviators left them toothless.

In October 1944 Adm. William F. Halsey's Third Fleet supported Gen. Douglas MacArthur's return to the Philippines. Mitscher's Task Force 58 became Task Force 38, now stronger than ever with nine large and eight light carriers massing more than one thousand aircraft. Task Force 38 crushed the best of Japanese land-based air by destroying five hundred planes in a series of massive actions off Taiwan and moved to support landings on 20 October at Leyte. Until air units could be established ashore, the fast carriers joined the escort carriers in providing close support of the invasion area.

Desperate now that the Allies had a foothold in the Philippines, the Combined Fleet came out in full force. This time surface warships in combination with land-based air were to deliver the knockout blows. On 24 October after Halsey pounded one force of battleships, but lost the light carrier *Princeton* (CVL 23) to land-based air attack, he allowed himself to be diverted north away from the Leyte invasion beaches by a decoy force of four carriers with a token complement of aircraft. All four Japanese flattops succumbed the next day, but only the bravery of the escort carriers and their destroyers prevented disaster at Leyte.

The remnants of the Combined Fleet withdrew after gaining nothing of strategic value from the desperate gamble. Within a few months, the Japanese carrier fleet had disbanded, its aircraft sent ashore permanently and its few surviving flattops left idle in port.

In the Philippines the Japanese initiated a new tactic that would cause the Allies more trouble than did their carriers. This involved so-called "special attacks" of the kamikaze or "divine wind" volunteers. On 25 and 26 October Imperial Japanese Navy pilots executed deliberate suicide air attacks and sank one escort carrier off Leyte.

The employment of kamikazes in the Philippines set the tone for Japanese air strategy for the remainder of the war. Often flying in small groups and at varied altitudes, kamikazes succeeded in infiltrating through combat air patrols to dive on target. Bomb-laden special attackers ripped up carrier flight decks, setting planes, munitions, and gasoline aflame. Although no fast carriers ever succumbed to kamikaze attack, a suicider could put a carrier out of action for months.

Unlike the earlier island campaigns, the Philippines found Task

Force 38, now under Vice Adm. John S. McCain, confronting strong land-based opposition dispersed among many airfields difficult to interdict. By early November kamikazes had knocked four fast carriers out of service for either short or long duration. Yet until land-based air could relocate to the Philippines, the carriers had to remain there for the time being and fend off the kamikazes. Finally, after a bruising encounter with a typhoon, Halsey's fast carriers were loosed in January 1945 to conduct a massive rampage through the South China Sea before returning to the fleet anchorage at Ulithi.

By February 1945 both Admiral Spruance and Vice Admiral Mitscher had resumed command, respectively, of the Fifth Fleet and Task Force 58, the fast carrier force now joined by the *Randolph* with Carrier Air Group 12. Spruance's mission was the capture of two of Japan's inner strongholds in order to gain vital air bases to facilitate the direct air offensive against the home islands. Mitscher's carriers had the task of protecting the invasion forces by destroying enemy air power in the region and offering direct air support for troops ashore. Scheduled for 19 February was the invasion of barren Iwo Jima in the Bonin Islands, only 650 miles south of Tokyo. Set to follow on 1 April was the assault on Okinawa in the Ryukyu Islands, situated within easy striking distance of Japanese airfields both in Kyushu and Taiwan.

Mitscher's sixteen fast carriers, with more than 1,100 aircraft, carried pilots who had profited from more training than any before them had received, an average of 525 flying hours before being posted to a combat squadron. To meet the growing kamikaze threat, the air groups on big carriers now comprised seventy-three fighters (the latest-model Grumman F6F Hellcats or Vought F4U Corsairs) as opposed to fifteen Curtiss SB2C Helldiver dive-bombers and sixteen Grumman TBM Avenger torpedo bombers.

In February 1945 the Imperial Japanese Navy and the Imperial Japanese Army Air Force numbered perhaps 1,100 combat aircraft available immediately in the homeland and another 500 in Taiwan. However, by the end of April the Japanese high command expected to have a total of 4,500 planes (half of them trainers) in the battle area. For the most part, Japanese pilots were poorly trained, and their aircraft were obsolescent, if not already obsolete, but quantity rather than quality usually counted more with kamikaze tactics. It was decided that the Japanese army special attackers, considered less experienced than their navy counterparts, should concentrate on enemy transports, while the navy pilots took the warships.

On 16 February from only sixty miles south of Honshu, Mitscher's carriers opened the ball with the first of a series of massive air attacks in bad weather against airfields and other targets in the Tokyo area. His were the first carrier aircraft to violate the enemy's homeland, and this was the first carrier strike of any kind since the one-way Doolittle mission of 18 April 1942 from Mitscher's own *Hornet* (CV 8). The Japanese reacted savagely to this new affront, the tenor of their rage exemplified by the fate of one unfortunate Zero pilot who had to parachute on 17 February. Mistaken by angry civilians for an American pilot, he was beaten to death before he could identify himself as a Japanese. Thereafter, Japanese pilots wore a small rising-sun flag on their flight suits. With great bravery, the marines conquered Iwo Jima and declared the island secure on 26 March. Meanwhile, air strikes and CAPs against fierce kamikaze assaults between 16 February and 8 March resulted in claims by the fast carriers of 435 enemy planes destroyed in the air and 266 on the ground, in exchange for the loss of 138 aircraft to all causes.

For the fast carriers the Okinawa campaign began on 18 March with strikes against airfields and naval targets in western Japan. The actual landings on Okinawa took place on 1 April, and for a time the troops of the Tenth Army advanced deceptively quickly, until they bloodied their noses on the fortified southern third of the island. Thereafter, their gains were measured in yards. In the air the Japanese waited several days to regroup. Beginning on 6 April, they launched kamikaze and conventional air assaults with a ferocity hitherto unseen.

Required to support the Tenth Army until land-based air could be established ashore (an agonizingly slow process), Task Force 58, along with the rest of the Fifth Fleet, had to remain off Okinawa and take the punishment. For six weeks the fast carriers held station east of Okinawa in a sector 60 miles square and within 350 miles of Kyushu. Prominent carrier historian Dr. Clark G. Reynolds well described Task Force 58's ordeal: "Being held to the beach at Tarawa in November 1943 or at Saipan in June 1944 had been one thing, but Okinawa was murder!"

Some statistics can offer a glimpse of the ordeal of the fast carriers. More than 1,300 sailors died on the ten fast carriers damaged by air attacks during the Okinawa campaign. Mitscher himself had to shift his flag twice after the *Bunker Hill* (CV 17) and the *Enterprise* (CV 6) were hit, finally ending up on the *Randolph*. Between 18 March and 24 May 1945 Task Force 58 destroyed 2,252 enemy planes, while losing 437 aircraft to all causes. In actual air-to-air combat the carrier crews enjoyed a remarkable ratio of fifty-one enemy planes shot down for each of their own lost. April 1945 saw the peak flight performance of the war, with 16,052 action sorties from Task Force 58 and 5,033 tons of bombs dropped on target. The ten big carriers averaged an amazing 1,963 flights per ship per month. No wonder ship's company and air group alike became thoroughly exhausted long before Mitscher and Air Group 12 bowed out of the fighting on 27 May. Enemy resistance officially ended on 22 June on Okinawa.

What did the sacrifices by Task Force 58 off Okinawa accomplish? They certainly sealed the victory. The Japanese failure to destroy the American carriers, despite committing several thousand planes, and to repulse the invasion forces certainly shook their resolve, although few would admit it. Vice Adm. Toshiyuki Yokoi, chief of staff of the 5th Air Fleet, the principal headquarters controlling kamikaze and conventional air strikes against the ships off Okinawa, declared the wanton expenditure of Japanese pilots and planes there to be "sheer lunacy." He had vigorously urged that these aircraft be preserved to defend Japan itself.

Together these two campaigns, Iwo Jima and Okinawa, in which Air Group 12 played an important part, constituted a distinct phase of the Pacific War. Perhaps this period lacked the drama of the early battles and the glamour of the gargantuan 1944 fleet actions, but the first half of 1945 remains unmatched for the intensity and savageness of its fighting. Along with many others, the veterans of Air Group 12 and the *Randolph* can proudly say that they were part of "The Fleet That Came To Stay."

John B. Lundstrom

✪ Preface

This book has its origins in a 1987 navy air-group reunion. Former members of Carrier Air Group 12, meeting on board the USS *Yorktown* at Patriot's Point, Charleston, South Carolina, began swapping stories of their tour with the air group during World War II. Many of these members had not heard these sea stories before. Roy Bruce, organizer of the reunion, asked the newfound members to record their "most memorable event" concerning experiences on board the USS *Randolph* from January to June 1945.

The number and intensity of these stories far exceeded expectations. A half dozen were selected and presented to their authors during the reunion in the form of wood plaques commemorating the unique experiences.

After the reunion Bruce realized that these sea stories needed to be recorded before they were lost forever. As more members of the air group were located, they too were asked about their most memorable experiences with Air Group 12. The contributions continued to arrive for months and became the basis for this book.

The contributions appear with the current addresses of the contributors and not those of the original personnel rosters of Air Group 12, as listed in appendix A. Statistical details of the air group and Japanese activities (including kamikazes) during this period also appear in the appendixes.

In addition to the contributors, Tony Remkus, navy photographer for Air Group 12, provided an impetus with his collection of related photos. "The World War II Chronicle of the USS Randolph/CV 15" by Dr. Richard Williams, the ship's surgeon, provided a cohesiveness and timely personal account that keeps this book on track. Also, we acknowledge the assistance of James C. Elliott, NASA Public Relations spokesperson, whose advice and sharp editing pencil tried to keep us out of grammatical (and syntactical) errors. Our thanks also to the Naval Historical Center for air action reports and ship's histories. Lastly, our thanks to the National Archives for ship's logs and the Still Pictures Branch for photographs.

The period of operations, January–June 1945, involving the first carrier strikes on Tokyo and ground-support missions over Iwo Jima and Okinawa have been neglected or given only brief or passing acknowledgment. As an example, *The Pacific War, 1941–1945* by John Costello provides only three lines to describe one hundred seventeen combat ships that, while loitering less than one hundred miles off the coast of Honshu for three days in February 1945 and challenging the Japanese to retaliate, were capable of launching more than one thousand aircraft that struck at airfields and strategic aircraft-engine plants and removed more than four hundred aircraft from the Japanese inventory:

> . . . accompanying them in the *Indianapolis,* Spruance decided that the planned air strikes on Tokyo must go ahead on February 16 in spite of thick weather over the target. The Japanese capital was bombed, and over 300 planes were destroyed.

That was all for events that were the beginning of the end of the war with Japan. It is our desire that following Air Group 12 from its formation in 1944 through mid-1945, using personal sea stories, official narratives, and reports, will not only enlighten the reader about those events but will be entertaining as well.

Crommelin's Thunderbirds

 **Beginnings, June–December 1944**

One of the largest and most powerful naval forces ever assembled launched nearly 1,100 aircraft at the Japanese mainland early Friday morning, 16 February 1945. The surprise attack was the beginning of the final stage in the defeat of the Japanese war machine. The sudden appearance of low-flying enemy fighters and bombers spreading death and destruction in and around the Tokyo industrial complex must have been demoralizing for citizens of the capital city.

These naval air strikes were both a prelude and a diversion for the marines' amphibious landing on Iwo Jima four days later. The island contained two airstrips desperately needed by army air corps B-29s and their fighter escorts in bombing missions planned for the invasion of the Japanese mainland in the fall.

Tokyo Rose, Japan's most vocal radio propagandist, screamed like a wounded banshee and quit broadcasting as attacking aircraft smashed targets in the Tokyo area for nearly nine hours. Planes from seventeen aircraft carriers lying less than seventy miles off the coast of Honshu continued pounding targets for one and a half days before terrible weather intervened and forced withdrawal toward Iwo Jima. The surprise and success of the strikes could be labeled vengeance, payment for the devastating Japanese attack on Pearl Harbor three years and seventy-one days earlier.

Participating in these attacks was our new air group, launched from a new aircraft carrier, and we were eager to prove ourselves. We were like new kids on the block and threw ourselves into the melee with an aggressiveness pent up from months and months of intense preparations—preparations that led us to membership in the fast carrier task force, a common denominator of the two large war machines unleashed in the Pacific, Gen. Douglas MacArthur's Southwest Pacific Area forces and Adm. Chester Nimitz's Pacific Ocean Area forces. These forces were not only increasing in size but more importantly in experience and state-of-the-art equipment. Now that the conflict in Europe appeared to be winding down, the United States was able to increase its support of the Pacific war.

Composed of *Essex*-class carriers, light aircraft carriers, battleships, cruisers, and destroyers, the fast carrier task force, either Task Force 38 (TF-38) under the tactical command of Adm. William F. "Bull" Halsey, Jr., or Task Force 58 (TF-58) under the tactical command of Vice Adm. Marc A. Mitscher, was being used alternately to support invasion forces under MacArthur and under Nimitz. Each area commander had his own invasion fleet of aircraft carriers, battleships, destroyers, and amphibious landing forces. It is within this framework that Carrier Air Group 12 on board the USS *Randolph* (CV 15), a new *Essex*-class aircraft carrier, joined Task Force 58 at Ulithi Atoll on 7 February 1945.

The beginnings of this air group and the basis for our orders were hidden in the following plain-language dispatch, received in May 1944 as the USS *Randolph* was nearing the final stages of construction in Newport News, Virginia:

DISTRIBUTE GRADUATES OPERATIONAL TRAINING PERIOD 1 TO 15 JUNE AS FOLLOWS X COMFAIRWEST-COAST TEMDUFLY FFA DUFLY 8 VOVCS OS 2 UNCLE X 80 VTB TBF X 100 VF FOX 4 X COMFAIRWESTCOAST FFA DUFLY IN GROUP ABLE 60 VF FOX 6 FOX X 60 VSB SBD X 30 VTB TBF X COMAIRLANT TEMDUFLY FFA DUFLY 15 VB2 PV1 X 73 VPB PBY 5 X 75 VTB TBF X 11 VSB SBD X 40 VF FOX 4 X 24 VPB PBM.

Who needs elaborate wartime codes when such messages from the Bureau of Personnel to the Chief of Naval Operation Training are cryptic enough? However confusing they may seem, these acronyms signify something new in naval aviation training: Group Able.

As newly commissioned ensigns from the advanced training command at Pensacola and Corpus Christi, we had been ordered to training bases in Florida to join combat-experienced pilots for operational training. Upon completion, we were ordered by this dispatch to join the experimental Group Able. This message ordered sixty F6F- (Grumman Hellcat fighter aircraft) trained pilots, sixty SBD- (Douglas Dauntless dive-bomber) trained pilots, and thirty TBF- (Grumman Avenger torpedo-bomber aircraft) trained pilots to the Commander, Fleet Air West Coast for further assignment. The ensigns and experienced team leaders of experimental Group Able were to become Carrier Air Group 12, later nicknamed "Crommelin's Thunderbirds."

This new training concept was the brainchild of Cdr. Charles L. Crommelin, a battle-scarred veteran of the early Pacific campaigns. His plan was to assemble newly commissioned pilots and place them in a higher level of operational training under the tutelage of combat-seasoned pilots like himself. Group Able would provide three to four months of additional training in operational aircraft under team-leader pilots who had "been there"—"there" being the air raids on Truk, Rabaul, and Saipan, and the Gilbert and Marshall Islands campaigns in late 1943 and 1944.

Lt. Hamilton McWhorter, El Cajon, California, one of the team leaders, described the process:

> After we left Air Group Nine, they sent us down to Melbourne, Florida, to form combat teams. All of a sudden these high school kids show up. . . . They worked hard and did quite well during the first strike on Tokyo, but until I took them into combat I was very apprehensive.

And so were we.

McWhorter, as a member of Carrier Air Group 9 (CAG-9), had been in one of the first navy air groups to see action in both war theaters, Atlantic (North Africa invasion) and Pacific. CAG-9 was also the first air group to receive the F6F-3 Hellcat from Grumman Aircraft Corporation. The recipient of a Presidential Unit Citation, five Distinguished Flying Crosses, and seven Air Medals, McWhorter was the first Hellcat pilot to score five kills and then ten kills in that aircraft (while aboard the USS *Essex* [CV 9]) and is among the navy's top fifteen Hellcat aces with twelve confirmed kills. He was the type of naval aviator who could lead a bunch of "high school kids" into combat.

The advantages of having combat-seasoned pilots training the new ones are numerous. Flying together as a flight team and as a group of teams as early as possible encourages familiarity that benefits both flight leaders and wingmen. Commander Crommelin's theory was that the veterans could more readily teach us how to survive in combat: we young impressionables would more quickly absorb flying skills from the veteran pilots than from impersonal flight-training instructors, particularly since we would be flying together into combat. Crommelin's plan was more effective than the standard practice of collecting pilots fresh from operational flight training and lumping them together in squadrons for five to six months before deploying them to combat.

Some of Group Able's "buck-ass" ensigns or "nuggets," as the newly commissioned officers were often called, had been flying together as cadets at Pensacola, Florida. We already knew the important stuff, like one another's brand of whiskey, so we felt we were well ahead of the "old-timers," or so we thought. The "old-timers" were, of course, the team leaders from CAG-9 whose average age was about twenty-six or twenty-seven—some of the older ones perhaps thirty—as compared to the young ensigns' ages of twenty to twenty-three.

Experimental Group Able's pilots and enlisted men reported to San Diego in early July 1944 and were further assigned to advanced squadron combat training at Naval Air Station (NAS) Astoria, Oregon. Group Able was officially commissioned as Carrier Air Group 12 (CAG-12) on 20 July 1944, under the leadership of Commander Crommelin. Fighting Squadron 12 (VF-12) was under the command of Cdr. Noel A. Gayler; Dive-bomber Squadron 12 (VB-12), Cdr. Ralph A. Embree; and Torpedo Squadron 12 (VT-12), Lt. Cdr. Tex Ellison. These officers were all combat-experienced leaders.

Commander Crommelin, a 1931 graduate of the Naval Academy, "one of the navy's five famous Crommelin brothers, already had helped make naval aviation history in the Pacific, first as squadron skipper of Fighting Squadron One and later as commander of Air Group Five aboard the new carrier, USS *Yorktown* . . ." ("Memories, A History of Air Group Twelve"). He was awarded the Distinguished Flying Cross for action during his squadron's attack on Marcus Island on 31 August 1943 and was cited as follows:

As Commander of a Fighter Squadron . . . he led the fighter planes escorting the initial bombing attack at night on the enemy base [and] successfully carried out the difficult task of night-strafing anti-aircraft positions although the danger of collision and bomb blast was great. Following the bombing he remained in the vicinity until daylight. At that time, seeing seven enemy medium bombers on the airfield, he and his three wingmen commenced a series of low altitude strafing attacks until all seven planes were destroyed.

The following November, as commander of Air Group 5, he personally led air attacks in support of the occupation of the Gilbert Islands. He was awarded a gold star in lieu of a second Distinguished Flying Cross. The citation read in part:

> While leading an important reconnaissance flight over Mille Atoll on 21 November . . . in complete disregard for his personal safety and in the presence of determined anti-aircraft fire, he strafed one plane and was maneuvering to attack the other plane when his plane was struck by a shell which exploded within the cockpit, shattering the instruments and severely wounding him. With no vision in his left eye, his right wrist broken, a severe wound in his right chest, as well as many cuts and abrasions on his face, arms and body, and with forward visibility through the cockpit enclosure almost zero, despite loss of blood, he brought his plane back over one hundred miles and made a perfect landing aboard his carrier. . . .

His wounds would have been career-ending for the average pilot, but Crommelin was no average pilot. He was still recuperating from these wounds while coordinating and supervising the training of Group Able's pilots in Florida. Recuperation was complete by the time the group was commissioned at NAS Astoria, Oregon.

ATCS A. C. "Sparky" Fraser of CAG-12 Staff, Florham Park, New Jersey, remembered the following incident:

> NAS Astoria was having a War Bond drive which included a freebie movie called "Fighting Lady" showing continuously one day to help sell the bonds. In the movie about wartime life aboard the USS *Yorktown* was a clip of Commander Crommelin returning to the carrier after taking a hit in the cockpit canopy area, heavily slashing his face. He made the landing safely though virtually blinded. After the show was over, Commander Crommelin and I

walked out and caught up with two WAVES talking about the pilot who had been wounded. The commander reached over, tapped one on the shoulder, and asked, "How do I look now?" The poor girl looked bug-eyed, her mouth went wide open, and she almost collapsed. No doubt she has recounted the experience to her children and grandchildren.

The commander was already a navy legend, but to members of his air group he was a friend. He wasn't enamored of rank. The patch on his leather flight jacket read, "C. L. CROMMELIN, LT. CDR. USN." He had been a full commander for at least two years.

VF-12's skipper, Commander Gayler, also was a graduate of the Naval Academy.

With the United States on the brink of World War II, Lieutenant Gayler talked one of his classmates into swapping orders. As a consequence he was assigned to Fighter Squadron Three on the USS *Saratoga* (CV-3). Following the Japanese attack on Pearl Harbor . . . the squadron was transferred to the USS *Lexington* (CV-2) which soon sailed for the south Pacific. During this period his skills as a fighter pilot achieved for him the honor of becoming the first man in history to receive three Navy Cross Awards. (Gayler biography, Navy Department)

This biographical sketch alludes to his heroic actions in combat just months after the Japanese attack on Pearl Harbor.

His first award was for an engagement on 20 February 1942 during a planned attack on Rabaul in support of the Australian and New Zealand forces. Nine Japanese bombers challenged the attack. Lieutenant Gayler and his flight of F4F Wildcats intercepted the bombers and shot down eight. Gayler was credited with one kill and two assists. A virtual replay of this action later in the same day produced the same results, eight out of nine.

The first gold star in lieu of a second Navy Cross was awarded for action over New Guinea naval ports while attacking enemy ships. Flying escort for a group of torpedo planes (TBDs), "on 10 March 1942, in the distant enemy area, he intercepted and shot down an enemy seaplane fighter and later in the face of heavy anti-aircraft fire strafed and dropped fragmentation bombs on two enemy destroyers causing many enemy casualties," according to his citation.

Commander Gayler's second gold star in lieu of a third Navy Cross was awarded for his actions in the Battle of the Coral Sea on 7 and 8 May 1942. Again, after flying cover for friendly torpedo planes in a strike against an enemy carrier, the *Shoho,* which was sunk, four fighters took station nearby and encountered a group of Japanese Zeros. Three of our fighters failed to return after each had shot down one plane, and, as his citation explains, "Lieutenant Gayler shot down two of the Japanese planes, damaged two others and returned safely to the *Lexington.*" Unfortunately, Japanese torpedo bombers had attacked her, scoring two hits on the port side at 1120. Mortally wounded and racked by internal explosions, she was dispatched to the depths by our own destroyer, the USS *Phelps,* at 2000. The air group and most personnel had been evacuated to the *Yorktown* and other ships in the task group.

Lieutenant Gayler returned to the States and was reassigned in June 1942 as a fighter-plane test pilot at the Naval Air Test Center, Patuxent River, Maryland. In June 1944 he was ordered to Group Able at NAS Melbourne, Florida, bringing his experience in fighter aircraft to the future Thunderbirds. Later, during squadron training, his insistence on strict radio discipline, especially during combat, was "conspicuous in situations where others lacked discipline" ("History of Bombfighting Squadron TWELVE").

Commander Embree was a 1936 graduate of the Naval Academy. After several tours of shipboard duty he was ordered to flight training and was designated a naval aviator in February 1940. His first duty was with Bombing Squadron 4 aboard the USS *Ranger,* and he later transferred to Scouting Squadron 41 aboard the same ship.

He was awarded the Navy Cross "for extraordinary heroism as Acting Squadron Commander of Scouting Squadron Forty One, attached to the USS *Ranger* during the occupation of French Morocco, 8–11 November 1942." The citation continued,

> Leading five flights of planes in vigorous dive-bombing raids against hostile warships and coastal defense batteries, Lieutenant Embree, courageously pressing home his attacks in the face of tremendous anti-aircraft fire and fierce fighter opposition, aided greatly in the infliction of severe damage upon the enemy . . . [and] contributed materially to the reduction of hostile resistance in the area and to the successful accomplishment of vital objectives preliminary to invasion.

Lt. Cdr. Thomas "Tex" Ellison, skipper of the torpedo squadron, was a graduate of the University of Texas. After graduation he entered the U.S. Navy's V-5 Aviation Cadet Program, completing flight training in 1939. He was commissioned an ensign and designated a naval aviator in November of the same year. His first assignment was to Torpedo Squadron 5 aboard the USS *Yorktown* (CV 5). He saw action during the first few months of 1942 on strikes against the Gilbert and Marshall Islands to keep the supply lanes open to Australia.

The torpedo plane used by Ellison's squadron was the TBD Devastator, an obsolete aircraft armed with torpedoes that often failed to run true. Even more exasperating was that if they did run true, they often failed to detonate on impact, as the pilots in Torpedo Squadron 5 observed in the Battle of the Coral Sea on 8 May 1942. Although the battle had been indecisive, each side losing a large carrier, the Japanese had been prevented from taking the strategic Port Moresby on the southern tip of New Guinea, two hundred miles northeast of Australia. Lieutenant (junior grade) Ellison had been awarded the Navy Cross for participation in the attack on one of the largest Japanese carriers, the *Shokaku*.

He returned to instructor duty in the States as officer-in-charge of Torpedo Flight Training, NAS Fort Lauderdale, Florida. He was then designated commanding officer of Torpedo Squadron Group Able. "Things happened rather quickly after that," according to Tex. "Almost immediately six complete crews [one pilot and two crewmen each] reported to NAS Fort Lauderdale after a tour of duty with Air Group Nine on the *Essex,* all veteran airmen. Then six instructor pilots arrived, and shortly thereafter more than twice that many ensigns fresh from operational training. I had myself a squadron." Torpedo Squadron Able would soon head west and become VT-12, a vital part of Carrier Air Group 12.

These squadron commanders along with their combat-experienced flight-team leaders were now responsible for forming the newly commissioned pilots and enlisted crewmen into cohesive squadrons. Leading chiefs, aviation mechanics, electronics technicians, and ordnancemen rounded out the 320 personnel required to keep the aircraft of a carrier air group functioning.

The "nuggets" of Group Able had already completed familiarization and formation training in combat aircraft at Florida training bases. Formation flying—learning how to fly close together in a four-plane fighter or six-plane bomber division without colliding—had been stressed. Tactics in combat aircraft had been introduced but not emphasized; that job was left up to the squadrons, and the air-group commander was responsible for standardizing those tactics later.

Improving our communications skills was part of what our commanding officers emphasized. The strict discipline of plane-to-plane radio communications was stressed daily— "Stay off the air!" unless you are going to crash or have an emergency. This philosophy plus an elaborate system of visual in-flight hand signals would pay off later. Nonessential chatter over the operational radio channels can result in the loss of life and aircraft in combat.

We then trained in fighter-escort tactics—that is, how to protect the bombers when they were flying in a target zone. These maneuvers involved stationing the fighters five hundred to a thousand feet above, slightly ahead, and to either side of the bomber formation. Using their higher speed, the fighters would weave back and forth over the bombers, denying enemy aircraft access to them. Upon reaching the target, some of the fighters would precede the bombers in the dive on the targets to suppress antiaircraft fire.

The validity of effective fighter escort was tested time and again over Tokyo and Kyushu. Air Group 12 didn't lose a single bomber to enemy aircraft.

To emphasize this coordination, Commander Crommelin required all fighter pilots to ride as crew members in either the SB2C Helldiver dive-bomber or TBM Avenger torpedo planes so that they would understand the problems and limitations of those aircraft. Also, large groups of aircraft were sent on extended over-water navigation flights to teach the younger pilots a survival science—how to conserve fuel. These extended flights were also a confidence booster for the nuggets because we found out how far we could push our aircraft.

As combat training progressed, the advent of the kamikaze or "divine wind" suicide attacks by Japanese airmen in the fall of 1944 forced a tactical change in the air group's organization. The initial success of the first kamikaze attacks, directed primarily at aircraft carriers, elicited an immediate reaction: eighteen dive-bomber pilots from VB-12 were transferred to VF-12 and indoctrinated in fighter tactics. Their transition in the Hellcat was rapid and a credit to those pilots' versatility. The complement of planes and pilots was reduced in VB-12 and VT-12. The fighter squadron now had seventy-two pilots. The bombing and torpedo squadrons were reduced to fifteen aircraft and thirty pilots each.

For those pilots who transferred from VB to VF, the transition from the Helldiver (affectionately know as the "beast" because of its growling brakes) to the nimble Hellcat and fighter tactics was a rude shock. From flying very stable three-plane sections and six-plane divisions, they went to two-plane sections in four-plane divisions that included new and radical flight patterns. Especially challenging was adapting to the violent maneuvers involved in the "Thach weave" developed earlier by Cdr. John S. Thach when the Japanese Zero was still vastly superior to anything the U.S. Navy had in its aviation arsenal. The "weave," executed by two or more planes, enabled a lesser number of our own aircraft to survive attacks by superior numbers of high-performance enemy aircraft.

To execute the weave, the two sections of the division would position themselves abreast at a distance approximately equal to their aircraft's turning radius. When attacked, the sections turned toward each other, enabling one of the sections to meet the attacker head-on. They would recover in the direction of their original flight path and repeat this maneuver as often as attacked. The section wingman glued himself to his section leader, using any violent flight control possible, often slamming the stick from one side to the other as the sections reversed their position in the formation. This tactic was repeated again and again, and after returning from a practice flight, the newly indoctrinated dive-bomber pilots found their flight suits drenched with sweat and their necks stabbed with pain because of these new and violent maneuvers involving continuous "G" forces.

The "History of Bombfighting Squadron TWELVE" described another dimension of Group Able's training regimen:

> Much was accomplished at Naval Air Station, Astoria, but the weather also allowed time for play. August was good flying weather, September not so good and October impossible. Many mornings a pilot could roll over, see nothing but fog outside the window, roll over again and sack out for the rest of the day. Astoria and the Columbia River country are beautiful, but one rarely sees them. It is also to be noted in passing that John Jacob Astor here

founded a considerable fortune, but departed. Likewise, Lewis and Clark discovered the place, but departed. A monolithic monstrosity commemorates both events. Also, NAS, Astoria facilities consisted of juxtaposed clapboards, laughingly referred to as barracks, built on swamp and sand dunes. Naval Air Station, Tongue Point, nearby, luxurious and empty, was denied to the air group as a place to live, partly, but finally due to the "hallroom boys" and their friends. A locked ice box was something "hallroom boys" could not resist. As a consequence, they were always in and out of "hack," but they could fly an airplane.

One of the free-spirited ensigns, Ens. Carmen R. Hintz of VF-12, Ridgefield, New Jersey, explained what really occurred:

It is with a respectful note that I must take exception to the historical note that the restrictions imposed on the "hallroom boys" at Naval Air Station Tongue Point were the direct result of a locked icebox. Certainly the icebox is one of the events that played in what should more appropriately be noted as the Saga of the Fire Trucks.

We arrived very late at the Tongue Point BOQ, hot, thirsty, tired, and hungry. There were four or five two-story BOQ buildings located on a cul-de-sac. The center building, where we were quartered, housed the dining room with adjacent kitchen. The dining room and kitchen were secured when we arrived. Our hunger persisted, but fortunately we had arranged to have an adequate supply of thirst quencher available—beer. Our hunger did in fact compel us to send out a party of two to find food. The BOQ kitchen was secured with the food located behind a locked icebox door. The lock simply had to be removed. This was accomplished via the application of an appropriate first-class lever. Behind the door were a number of sides of beef. To bring this mass of meat to a size that could be handled, a knife was used. To hungry, tired people with a thirst reasonably quenched, this activity was far beyond the call of duty. An atmosphere developed that suggested that we, in fact, were heroes in our efforts to sustain ourselves in this strange environment. It was also incumbent upon us not to remain in the kitchen area too long, for obvious reasons.

The chunks of meat were therefore hastily taken to our room, where we found the sink to be a reasonable substitute for a barbecue grill. We did indeed satisfy our hunger—thus the mission was accomplished. During the course of this cooking operation, fat fell in the fire, pun not intended, and a degree of smoke and flames apparently aroused some nervous types who precipitously pulled a fire alarm.

Now the heart of the event: Two fire trucks approached the cul-de-sac, one going clockwise, the other counterclockwise. At the crest of the cul-de-sac they met, abruptly—demonstrated by steam from their radiators and a siren that involuntarily sounded. We witnessed this demonstration from the second-floor window and were appalled at this lack of professional driving.

The sink barbecue fire was brought under control, if it was ever out of control at all, by a blanket over the sink. The blankets were of the poorest quality as this one almost immediately developed a hole.

The incident developed to the point that the commanding officer of the base felt compelled to personally address two of the people from Astoria, one of whom was the senior officer of this hungry, tired group. The captain probably had been at this wasteland for a long tour as his demeanor was not cordial or friendly; in fact, it could be characterized as threatening.

We did return to Astoria, but it has never been revealed who was in that small kitchen party. However, they have always been the best at survival.

From the aforementioned historical report, the saga of Astoria continued:

Lest someone believe Astoria was a dreary place, let it be said that fifteen miles (all thumbable) away was Seaside. Now some might say that Seaside was a combination of Sodom and Gomorrah, but that is not true. It is simply that the more unconfined side of Seaside was more conspicuous, but married pilots and families lived nearby, and unmarried pilots lived nearby. Seaside showed a coat of many colors, and youth that must be served was. VF-12 closed the season and the entire incident with a final bang-up squadron party, and departed bag and baggage for the Mexican border.

The weather in early November had not completely stalled training but had reduced the flights to such short and unprofitable ones that on 9 November the fighter squadron moved south to Naval Auxiliary Air Station (NAAS) Ream Field, San Ysidro, California, a few miles south of San Diego. The move was so far south that the Ream Field traffic pattern actually extended into Mexico. The move was

> accomplished by plane and private conveyance, generally speaking. Those who, in this age of uncertain tires and facilities, motored the fifteen hundred miles over snow covered mountains and through desert valleys, experienced certain operational difficulties. The story never to be forgotten, however, was that of the Administrative Officer (Lieutenant Junior Grade Paul Husting), who, in an unguarded moment of generosity, offered to convey safely to final destination two young pilots' wives, happily or unhappily in a pregnant condition. ("History of Bombfighting Squadron TWELVE")

It was during this move, also, that the reality of this deadly flying game was brought home. During the flight south, VF-12 experienced its first casualty. Ens. William Murray was lost at sea en route to California.

The change in weather was like moving from winter to summer. Fair weather blessed the pilots with thirty to forty flights per month. It was not the number of flights or flight hours that generated difficulties, but as was so often the case, it was the nature of those flights. Air-to-air and air-to-ground gunnery drills and bombing runs were repeats of our activities at Astoria, but now an additional training phase was started—the field carrier landings. Unique to naval aviation, field carrier landings involve practicing on land a simulated approach to a carrier landing. The next stage was the actual carrier landings in December aboard the USS *Ranger* off the coast of San Diego. Both field carrier and actual shipboard landings were practiced day and night.

The carrier landing can be appreciated more when it is understood that the racetrack flight pattern around the carrier or landing strip was conducted approximately sixty to seventy feet above the ground or water surface, just above the aircraft's stalling speed, with landing gear and flaps extended. Flight in the landing pattern was controlled for the last three hundred feet by a landing signal officer (LSO) signaling the pilot with flags as to what was right or wrong with the approach. He had the final say as to whether a pilot would land on any approach or be "waved off" to make another approach. Needless to say, many approaches were made before a "cut" signal was given to allow the pilot to cut power and land. These two signals, the cut and the wave off, were mandatory signals that a pilot was required to execute.

On land these controlled crash landings were repeated by jamming on power, taking off, and continuing around the field for another try. On board the aircraft carrier, cables stretched across the flight deck brought the aircraft to an abrupt stop when the aircraft's tail-hook engaged one. Failure of the hook to engage a cable allowed the aircraft to continue up the deck and into a crash barrier (a cable fence); a barrier engagement tore up the aircraft and unnerved the pilot, squadron skippers, and flight-deck crew.

Carrier landings in daylight were an accepted phase of training in the qualification of carrier pilots. Night carrier landings were another story. Earlier, only the night-fighters were qualified for night carrier landings. That was to change. On 20 June 1944 Admiral Mitscher's Task Force 58 was pursuing the remnants of Vice Admiral Ozawa's Japanese Mobile Fleet during the final phase of the Battle of the Philippine Sea. The previous day Mitscher's fighter pilots had knocked down nearly four hundred Japanese planes in what Navy pilots termed the great "Marianas Turkey Shoot."

When the Mobile Fleet was finally located northwest of Saipan, a large strike composed of seventy-seven dive-bombers, fifty-four torpedo bombers, and eighty-five escorting fighters was launched very late in the afternoon. The nearly six-hundred-mile round-trip would get them back after dark—an unsavory situation as most of the pilots had never made a night carrier landing.

The strike attacked the Mobile Fleet a little before sunset, sinking one carrier and damaging two or three more in a brief encounter. The main threat next was the long flight back, low on fuel, to culminate in a night landing.

Admiral Mitscher, code name "Bald Eagle," knew the risks when he ordered all ships to "turn on the lights," an order that had been given only once before at the Battle of Midway by Admiral Spruance. That meant that running lights, truck lights, glow lights, search-lights beamed straight up as guides for homing aircraft, and what-ever else was available should be employed to help guide the pilots back to their carriers, at great risk to the fleet silhouetted by those lights. Mitscher could not afford to lose his pilots and aircraft. He also cared for his pilots. Rescue efforts recovered all but sixteen pilots and thirty-three aircrewmen out of eighty aircraft that went into the water that night. It could have been worse except for the compassionate admiral in command.

The Thunderbirds knew very little of those final moments, nor the details regarding those night carrier landings. What we did know now was that we were all to qualify at night carrier landings, and enthusiasm was not high.

Field carrier landings and carrier landings during daylight hours were difficult enough but were learned fairly quickly. At night, they were "hairy," as Ens. C. R. Leonard of VBF-12, Del Rio, Texas, testified:

> We were on night field carrier landing practice at Holtville in the California desert. I had just taken off and made a one hundred eighty degree turn downwind to make my first approach.
>
> For some reason I couldn't find the runway. It was lit by runway lights when I took off. I saw something skitter out from under my left wing light. It was a jackrabbit! I was considerably lower than the normal sixty to seventy feet for traffic patterns. I jammed the power on and climbed; sure enough, there was the airfield lit up just as I had left on takeoff. Seems I had been in a shallow land depression lower than the field. I haven't killed a jackrabbit to this day.

Where the field carrier landings were often forgiving of mistakes, the carrier landings were not, as Ens. Lowell T. "Barney" Bernard of VF-12, Breaux Bridge, Louisiana, explained:

> The most vivid impressions of naval aviation, one that will stay with you for years, are the night carrier landings. We were flying out of NAAS Ream Field to the USS *Ranger* off the California coast, December 1944. We chewed up their flight deck so badly and blew out so many tires that I believe the navy in its wisdom should have decided to forego any future night carrier qualifications.

The dive-bomber and torpedo squadrons, having transferred from Astoria to NAS Los Alamitos, California, also were perfecting the carrier landings, as were the fighters at Ream Field. As a consequence of this requirement and the inherent dangers involved, there were losses. Ens. Frederick A. Nittel of VF-12 was lost at sea during night carrier qualifications aboard the *Ranger* off San Diego. He apparently flew into the water and was never found. Another pilot lost several fingers when the cockpit canopy slammed shut on them upon landing. By the last days of December the Thunderbirds had completed both day and night carrier landing qualifications.

Earlier in the month VF-12 again had been augmented. This time twenty-one more fighter pilots from Fighting Squadron 5 destined to go aboard the USS *Franklin* (CV 13) were added to the fighter strength, along with two pilots from other squadrons. This expansion boosted the total number of fighter pilots to 106, including a night-fighter unit, VFN-12 (later detached, not deployed). The squadron was now so large it became a "group grope" rather than a well-disciplined and coordinated fighter unit. On 2 January 1945 the squadron was divided in half to become Fighter Squadron 12 (VF-12) and Fighter-Bomber Squadron 12 (VBF-12) for ease of coordinating flight schedules and administration.

Barrett Tillman's *Hellcat* (Naval Institute Press, 1968) addressed the same subject:

> An administrative change had occurred earlier in the month (January 1945) which bore directly upon CV fighter squadrons. With an average complement of 71 F6Fs and 105 to 110 pilots, it was decided to divide the enlarged fighter squadron into equal parts. . . . On those ships that operated all F6Fs (or later, all F4Us), it was no problem for both squadrons to fly the same aircraft interchangeably since maintenance could be performed on share-and-share-alike basis.
>
> . . . One of the first such [squadrons] to reach the fleet was Air Group 12, destined for the brand new *Randolph* (CV-15).

Continued pressure on the Pacific Fleet's air defenses by the kamikazes had forced this second increase in fighter-squadron strength. Kamikaze attacks by the Japanese Special Attack Force had begun in earnest in October 1944, sinking three escort carriers and damaging two large CVs that month. The increase in fighter strength was made all along the line from the fleet down to new squadrons being formed. The change reflected the seriousness that Admiral Nimitz,

Commander in Chief, Pacific, attributed to the deadly potential of this new tactic.

It was a fortunate and timely decision because the Special Attack Force was being consolidated and organized for the defense of Japan and the destruction of Allied forces. The destruction was to involve all military personnel in suicidal attacks to the last man and eventually was to include women and children. Defeat was being accepted, but it was hoped that the carnage from what was to become a national strategy would halt the Allied advance and end the war with a negotiated peace.

As fighter squadrons increased in size because of the need for increased air defenses, another choice for a carrier fighter appeared to augment the Hellcat. For almost three years the F4U Corsair had served the marines well as a land-based fighter-interceptor. It was good and had better performance at high altitudes than the F6F. The problem the F4U had aboard aircraft carriers was that its high profile with elongated landing gear and tail wheel raised the aircraft height above the deck that would accommodate specialized ordnance. This extended strut design induced a tail bounce that caused the hook to miss engagement, resulting in an unacceptable number of barrier crashes. The problem was finally solved through strut and oleo adjustments, and the Corsair was ready to take its place as a first-rate carrier-based fighter. Many would be needed because the war was moving ever closer to the home islands of Japan.

As to the differences between the two aircraft for Air Group 12, Lt. Cdr. Edward Pawka, La Jolla, California, the newly appointed commanding officer of VBF-12, stated: "It wasn't a question of our resisting conversion to F4Us, but the current allocation of VF (fighter) models at any one point in time. The Corsair had an edge in performance, especially at high altitudes, but that [factor] was far outweighed by the much better availability [percent of aircraft ready to fly], and the ability to take punishment by the Grumman Ironworks product," the Hellcat.

Dividing the oversized fighter squadron into clones had no effect on their missions. Both had been trained to provide escort protection for the slower, more vulnerable bombers, to make flak-suppression runs just ahead of them to eliminate antiaircraft batteries, and to fly combat air patrols (CAPs) for the increased fleet air defenses in the face of intensified kamikaze activity.

Lieutenant Commander Pawka confirmed the "no change of mission" policy: "There were no differences between VF-12 versus VBF-12 either in training methods or operational utilization of pilots." Commander Crommelin and his next in command, Commander Gayler, the original VF skipper, had ably set forth the criteria for the fighter combat training. The training had progressed too far and was too deeply ingrained in all fighter pilots to be affected by an administrative division of personnel. Doubling the fighter strength was critical to warding off an anticipated increase in kamikaze attacks on the fleet. The bomber and torpedo squadrons remained fifteen planes and thirty pilots each. It would appear that the decision to reduce bomber strength would have diminished the air group's offensive capabilities, bomb and torpedo tonnage, but that was not the case.

As a result of two one-sided victories in the Battles of Leyte Gulf and the Philippine Sea and the all-but-final destruction of the Imperial Japanese Navy, the few surface targets available did not justify as many SB2Cs or TBMs. They were more or less single-purpose aircraft, and they performed their roles well, whereas the fighters could deliver a considerable amount of offensive weaponry, then revert to their normal tactical fighter role. As if to reinforce this tactical decision, Task Force 58's ruthless destruction of the "last-resort mission" of the *Yamato* and her escorting vessels on 7 April 1945 demonstrated no lack of offensive capability.

The VBF squadron skipper, Lieutenant Commander Pawka, began his aviation training as a naval aviation cadet. Most of AG-12's "nuggets" had been aviation cadets also. There was one difference: he was required to fly as an aviation cadet one and one-half years with the fleet before being commissioned as an ensign in the navy. The newer aviation cadets were commissioned following final squadron training at Pensacola or Corpus Christi. His prewar experience in naval aviation was in demand to train new pilots until he joined the Thunderbirds.

Upon receiving his wings at Pensacola in 1938, he reported to VF-6 on the USS *Enterprise* (CV 6), spending the next three and one-half years flying Grumman biplanes (F2Fs and F3Fs) with their fabric wings, struts and wires, and crank-em-up landing gear. Pawka's most pleasant memory was perhaps VF-6's flying sequences in two World War II films: "Flight Command" (1940) with Robert Taylor and "Divebomber" (1941) with Errol Flynn and Fred McMurray. Pawka had a short speaking part in the latter film.

It was late December when the fighter squadrons began receiving their new "battle blue" F6F-5s. Until then they had been using war-weary F6F-3s with pastel-blue tops and white on their underbellies. The new -5s looked so potent it wasn't long before a wash and wax brigade was at work. One of the team leaders let it be known that a smooth wax gloss would give them another knot or so of airspeed. That was all the incentive the ensigns needed.

The -5s were a combination of give and take in performance. They gave up some rate of climb to 20,000 feet, accepting an increase in weight of 215 pounds. The take was far better, with an increase in speed at sea level from 312 to 318 mph and, most critical, an increase in range from 1,085 to 1,300 miles. Most favored was "WEP," War Emergency Power, for emergency use. The system provided an injection of a fine mist of water into the intake manifold, enabling a short boost in power to overtake or flee an enemy aircraft. It would increase speed slightly and provide a few minutes of advantage, often all that is needed between victory or defeat.

Familiarization and high-altitude flights were scheduled to get us comfortable with this new version of the Hellcat. Ensign Bernard, VBF-12, recounted one of his first flights:

> We had just received our new F6F-5s, and I was practicing some touch-and-go landings at Ream Field, which was very near the Mexican border.
>
> On the downwind leg I felt that the plane was a little sluggish, but I attributed that to the fact the F6F-5 had spring-loaded ailerons and was more sensitive than the F6F-3s we had been flying. Suddenly, the plane started to stall out, and I immediately nosed down and applied full throttle to gain airspeed. I then pulled back hard on the stick to flatten out the dive as I saw I wasn't going to make it. I skidded along the ground at 100 knots through mesquite trees, barbed-wire fences, and assorted debris and came to a grinding halt.
>
> When the dust and smoke had cleared, I groggily heard someone banging on the side of the devastated plane. It was a little Mexican boy saying, "Señor, you want to buy some Chiclets?"
>
> Stan McCabe was behind me and witnessed the crash: I had forgotten to lower the flaps.

The last week of December turned out to be the start of something big and prophetic. Arrangements had been made to "intercept" a carrier coming up the West Coast and conduct simulated attacks from high altitude (35,000 feet) and on the deck (50 feet). The target, the USS *Randolph,* unknown to us at the time was to be the new home for Air Group 12. This would be good practice for both ship and air group if they were to go into combat anytime soon—neither knew just how soon.

About ten days later the air group was ordered to NAS Alameda, California, for deployment overseas. The orders arrived none too soon, as there had been an invasion of privacy at NAAS Ream Field. The airfield's sparse lodging had been invaded by a small vermin called body lice, or more bluntly, "crabs." Continued applications of Absorbine Jr., Campho Phenique, and anyone's guess of what else couldn't stem the tide of these creatures. Isolation was a solution. Isolation it was, by navy edict: go aboard ship at San Francisco.

Some leave was granted during the last days at Ream and Los Alamitos, but by 16 January all aircraft were on the way to NAS Alameda except a few SB2Cs. One of the ensigns almost didn't make the trip north from Ream Field. Ens. Lee E. Furse of VF-12, Flushing, Michigan, had a problem:

Saturday night before we left for San Francisco, I had O.D. duty that day and I missed the last bus into San Diego. I decided I had to go to town for a final fling, so unlike my usual M.O. of strictly following the rules, I commandeered a base jeep and attempted to get out of the gate.

I told them I was on a recreation mission to check facilities for future use by the air group. The guard didn't really buy that, but I told him I had Commander Gayler's personal permission, and then I crashed the gate.

I went to the downtown USO and had a super time until I returned to the jeep with several people whom I promised rides back to the base. There were two shore patrol in the jeep waiting for me.

I stuck to my recreation story, then they called for a lieutenant to back them up and deal with one officer. He arrived and got all the facts, including my serial number, and told me to return to the base and he would deal with me through my skipper.

Bright and early the next day, Commander Gayler called me in. He was really upset. After some discussions, he put his three fingers on the three stripes on his sleeve and said, "If you had three stripes you could probably have sold a wild story like this, but one stripe, you didn't have a chance." He said the shore patrol wanted to throw the book at me, and they even wanted me to miss going to sea with my air group. But the commander prevailed and, instead, restricted me to the base for two weeks, with the sentence to begin our first day at sea.

 **2**   **Guns at the Ready, January 1945**

A trained air group is like a cocked pistol without ammunition. It has to have a base of operation, be it on land or at sea, to become lethal. Air Group 12 was to become that lethal weapon, boarding an aircraft carrier under rather unusual circumstances.

The USS *Randolph,* an *Essex*-class fast attack carrier, was to be home base for our air group. "She was the first big carrier to go into combat without returning to the builder for re-check after the shakedown cruise, actually launching planes against the enemy four months and seven days after commissioning—a feat believed to be without precedent in big carrier history" (History of USS *Randolph,* Ship's Section, Office of Public Information, Navy Department).

The *Randolph* was commissioned on 9 October 1944 as the eleventh of the fast attack *Essex* class. She was built by Newport News Shipbuilding and Dry Dock Company, Newport News, Virginia. Her commanding officer at commissioning was Capt. Felix Baker, a 1920 graduate of the Naval Academy, who would take her into combat with Air Group 12.

Sometime after graduating from the academy, Captain Baker was ordered to NAS Pensacola, Florida, for flight training and designated a naval aviator in 1924. His first assignment was to Fighting Squadron 1 attached to the USS *Langley* (CV 1). For the next few years he participated in the development of dive-bombing tactics from carriers, later switching to patrol planes. Just prior to joining the *Randolph's* fitting out at Norfolk, he was in command of more than twenty squadrons involved in antisubmarine warfare on the Atlantic coast.

Captain Baker was tall, slim, with greying hair and black bushy eyebrows. To those of us whose only contact with him was a salute, he appeared quiet and reserved, but he got things done and ran a tight ship.

The *Randolph*'s namesake was Peyton Randolph, the first president of the Continental Congress. He was also a soldier and statesman of Colonial Virginia and was a close friend of George Washington. The first ship named *Randolph* was a Continental frigate, one of thirteen built for the Continental Navy, and was commanded by Capt. Nicholas Biddle.

Essex-Class Carrier USS *Randolph* (CV 15)

Weight (full load)	36,380 tons
Length @ waterline	820 ft
Length of flight deck	862 ft
Width of flight deck	108 ft
Speed @ 34,000 tons	33 kt
Endurance @ 15 kt	20,000 nm
Number of boilers	8
Armament	12 5-in/38-cal. on 4 twin mounts
	4 5-in/38-cal. on single mounts
	32 40-mm guns on 8 quadruple Mk 4 mounts
	44 20-mm Oerlikon guns on 44 single mounts
Protective armor plating:	
Hangar deck	1.5 in
Side belt below waterline	2.5–4 in
Steering compartment sides	4 in

Within a month after commissioning, this aircraft carrier was under way in an unprecedented accelerated schedule of fuel and ordnance loading for her shakedown cruise. By 22 November 1944 she was en route to the Gulf of Paria, Trinidad, British West Indies, with Air Group 87 (AG-87) aboard. Intense drills in battle preparations, damage control, fire fighting, and flight operations were conducted while operating out of Port of Spain, Trinidad.

A rude shock was awaiting the ship and her crew after getting under way on 17 December. Captain Baker announced that the ship was declared ready for action by Commander Fleet Air, Norfolk, and now was headed for the Pacific via the Panama Canal. The Pacific

Fleet needed aircraft carriers in a hurry in support of planned operations in that theater. It was a disappointment, as both the ship's crew and members of the air group had anticipated being home for Christmas. Instead, they would spend New Year's Eve in San Francisco. The expected return to Norfolk was thousands of miles and many months in the future.

The announcement may have been disappointing to the officers and crew, but not for Captain Baker. Cdr. Charles Minter, the assistant air officer, Annapolis, Maryland, recalled, "To say that Captain Baker was not disappointed at the news, is a gross understatement. . . . He was itching to take his ship into combat. In fact, he was very much afraid the war would pass him by before getting the ship out there."

Intense air operations and shipboard drills continued en route. The *Randolph* docked at Hunter's Point, San Francisco, on 31 December 1944 to add antiaircraft gun sponsons on the starboard side below the island, to rearrange the 20- and 40-mm gun mounts on the port side, and to make the necessary repairs always needed on newly commissioned ships.

Upon completing the modifications to the armament, she moved across San Francisco Bay to Pier One, NAS Alameda, on 10 January 1945 to take on stores and load Air Group 12's aircraft, all the new F6F-5s and some of the SB2Cs. Air Group 87 had been disembarked. VT-12 inherited AG-87's new TBFs to replace the tired "turkeys" left at NAS Los Alamitos.

In at least one F6F there was some extra baggage. Ens. Hal Lindley of VF-12, Orford, New Hampshire, had purchased a case of bourbon whiskey and secured it in the tail section of his F6F just before he and the other VF-5 fighter pilots departed NAS Santa Rosa to join VF-12. He took very special care in his landing at Ream so as not to dislodge the prize cargo. The plane was eventually loaded aboard the *Randolph,* whereupon Lindley retrieved his "baggage" from the aircraft in the small hours of darkness and stashed it in his bunk. There it remained the entire cruise, except when he required a short snort of "courage," which was practically every combat mission. He needed it during the mission, not afterward, when all the pilots got a booster of brandy.

Most of our aircraft were new, and the *Randolph,* fittingly enough, was a new carrier. A new aircraft carrier, a new air group, and a group of new aircraft is hardly the ideal way to go into combat. The ship's crew was relatively green, and the air group's pilots were predominantly young ensigns, and we needed some time to be integrated into the ship–air group life.

Most of us and many of the enlisted men had only been aboard ships for a few days at a time. Now these steel decks and bulkheads would be our home for six months or more. A home with a labyrinth of passageways interrupted with hatches and combings that could simultaneously bark the shins and crack the skulls of the unwary who hurried too fast or carelessly through them. A home with the continual roar of blowers moving air through compartments that otherwise would be stifling with heat. A home with community "heads" with sinks, showers, and toilets.

The toilets consisted of "spaces," separated by vertical panels, with seats over troughs, through which seawater gushed every few minutes. The navy also provided a special soap that would lather (to a degree) in salt water.

While the young ensigns of the air group had little privacy in their bunk rooms, called "boys' town," the airdales (aircrewmen) had none. Their home away from home was one of a stack of four narrow bunks spaced vertically about two feet apart—just enough space to turn over from one side to the other. These were pulled up and secured against the bulkhead when not in use. Each man had a two-cubic-foot gear locker for his personal items, and it was inspected periodically—without prior notice. Their compartment was located on the deck next to the catapult-equipment area, so it was a very noisy place to be during flight operations. On the *Randolph,* flight operations were often a twenty-four-hour-a-day occurrence with a night-fighter unit aboard providing dusk-to-dawn CAPs.

The ship's plans indicated that the airdales would have their own chow line and eating area with tables. Unfortunately, the need for bomb-storage space consumed that idea, so aircrewmen found themselves in ship's company chow lines, getting a tray of food, then trying to find a place to eat on neatly stacked 500- and 1,000-pound bombs.

These airdales were a special breed of sailor but were not necessarily the heroic type. They were motivated by the money, as ARM1c Alfred Smith, Scituate, Massachusetts, put it: "The big reason was the pay—we received an additional 50 percent of our base pay as a combat aircrewman [rear-seat gunner] in the SB2C dive-bomber. We flew into combat facing backwards." Smith, a three-tour veteran aircrewman, compared their day-to-day lives to that of the ship's-company sailors: "We never stood watches, and when we hit port, we had more money and more liberty to spend it. It was definitely worth getting shot at."

On 20 January 1945 the USS *Randolph,* with Air Group 12 aboard, went to war. During the morning the last of the squadrons' aircraft had been loaded aboard, along with more than 230,000 gallons of aviation gasoline—reflecting the *Randolph's* growing tradition of loading up fast and getting on with the job at hand.

Six days later, docked at Pearl Harbor, the remainder of the aircraft were loaded, but not without incident. AMM3c Merrill E. Booth of VT-12, Nashville, Tennessee, was watching: "Ground crews proceeded to hoist our airplanes with a crane up onto the flight deck. While loading an SB2C Helldiver a cable broke with the aircraft suspended probably some forty feet in the air. The aircraft fell and crunched on the dock, pushing the main landing gear right through the wings. It looked like one sick aircraft."

Under way after three days in Pearl Harbor, the *Randolph* found herself transiting the Pacific in company with the illustrious old "Sara," the USS *Saratoga* (CV 3), ironically the home of another Air Group 12 of days past. She had been mended and was now armed with a night-fighter group. Strange company, these two carriers, a battle-scarred veteran—the oldest of the fleet carriers—and one of the newest, untried in combat, en route to join the fleet at Ulithi Atoll.

More effort was given to enhance ship–air group coordination and teamwork. It took some adjustments of both elements to achieve operational combat readiness during the ten days it took to cross the Pacific to Ulithi. A few familiarization flights were made en route to give each pilot at least one landing on our new carrier before going into combat.

On 1 February near the International Date Line Ens. Stanley H. Davidson of VF-12, Franklin, Massachusetts, had a close call and an unplanned trip to Ulithi:

> We were on a combat air patrol over the ship. I was on Lieutenant Benson's wing. "Dawg" Detter and Rich Davis comprised the second section of the division.

CIC called and said they wanted some vectoring practice. Benny and I were instructed to fly away from the ship and come back on another heading. CIC would then vector Detter's section out to intercept us just as they would under combat conditions. Our section headed back towards the ship, was intercepted, and naturally a dogfight ensued. During the melee my engine suddenly quit—no sputtering or anything—it just died!

After checking the obvious instruments, I swallowed my heart and hollered, "Mayday! Mayday!" Benny promptly joined up and began offering advice, including the fact that I'd better drop my auxiliary [belly] tank, which I'd forgotten.

It was a beautiful sunny day with few whitecaps, so I decided to land into the wind. I touched down and must have hit a swell because it felt like hitting a brick wall. In spite of pulling my shoulder straps as tight as possible, my head hit the gun sight, and I was knocked out. For how long I'm not sure, but when I came to, my plane was up on its nose, and beautiful green water was pouring into the cockpit. That really aroused me!

I had unbuckled my chute on the way down and intended to take my raft and survival pack with me. But after the violent landing, I didn't have enough strength to wrench them free of the parachute as the plane dove for the bottom, taking me along. I thought, "To hell with it," released the fastener that held the survival pack and life raft, pulled the toggles on my Mae West, and after forever popped to the surface into a mess of gasoline, some of which I swallowed.

I then realized that what I had seen as a calm sea was actually tremendous swells . . . one of which I had slammed into.

Good ol' Hoosier Two was circling overhead, so I pulled out one of the dye markers, which promptly sank—carefully pulled out the second. That worked OK. Up until this time only my head was out of water, but after seeing the yellow dye, Benny and the other section made a couple of passes over me, waggling his wings. I waved, then they flew back towards the ship.

Sometime later a TBM came over and dropped a life raft within twenty-five feet of me, and although I swam toward it, I never saw it again. The pilot made another pass and almost hit me on the head with another one. I promptly opened the valve, it inflated, and I gratefully pulled myself aboard.

The gasoline I'd swallowed made me sick, and as I was kneeling over the side to get rid of everything I owned, a shark's fin cut the water near the raft. It circled lazily, then disappeared only to reappear about a foot away before ramming my raft, almost upsetting it. Backing off a couple of feet, he looked at me with his cold eye. We were so close I could detect the sandpaper texture of his skin, and I knew the raft couldn't take much more ramming. As he backed off and rammed the raft again I reached out and hit him as hard as I could on his head with my fist. It must have startled him because he darted away—all seven or eight feet of him. Another one circled a couple of times before departing.

A short time later me and my home floated up with a swell, and there was the most beautiful destroyer ever built, the *Harrison,* coming to save me. The crew threw a line towards me, which I was able to grab, then strong hands pulled me up and into a cargo net.

The captain, Commander W. V. Combs, offered me his cabin for the remainder of the voyage to Ulithi, where I rejoined my squadron. DD 573 treated me, possibly the oldest flying ensign in the navy, like a king for ten days!

En route, pilots and aircrewmen when not flying played acey-deucey, bridge, or poker. However, the airdales seemed to prefer the riskier game of craps, in which a month's pay could change hands on a single roll of the dice. Others would spend hours in hanging over the catwalks, watching the flying fish scamper just above the bow wave as they matched the ship's twenty knots. At night the ship's wake provided a dazzling array of sparkling green lights as our carrier constantly churned up fluorescent sea life.

Several days after Davidson was rescued, land-based B-26s from Eniwetok in the Marshall Islands flew by the *Randolph,* towing a sleeve, or banner, to provide a moving target for the ship's gunners. Air-group personnel observing gunnery practice for the first time received a jolt from the concussions that almost knocked them down. Shock waves from the 5-inch antiaircraft guns had aircraft toe-dancing on the flight deck despite their being tied down securely.

These gunnery drills bred a competitive spirit not only among the ship's divisions but extended into an intership rivalry. S1c Stan Moreland, Shadyside, Maryland, related one incident. Moreland's battle station was in the upper handling room of the second 5-inch turret aft of the island. He recalled:

> The *Randolph* didn't have a particularly good score on the target sleeve that day. The other ship competing in the firing practice rubbed it in on us hot and heavy on TBS [talk-between-ship radio circuit]. We responded by reminding them that at least we hadn't hit and damaged the B-26 towing the banner. There was no more rubbing it in on us that day.

The younger Thunderbirds had now been aboard just over two weeks and were beginning to feel at home on the floating, ever-in-motion airport with three thousand officers and men. We scarcely noticed the constant roar of the blowers any more and had learned to maneuver, on the run, through the narrow hatches without barking our shins or cracking our heads. Most of the time we could get to and from wherever without having to ask the ship's company for directions.

Shipboard drills and flight operations continued as the *Randolph, Saratoga,* and escorting destroyers drew near the fleet anchorage at Ulithi Atoll. A respectable ship–air group team effort had been developed. The seriousness of the drills, with the ship's company in full battle gear during every fire, damage-control, and abandon-ship drill, was an indicator of the near future. Tension was beginning to build as the *Randolph* entered Mugai Channel to Ulithi Atoll on 7 February.

When Captain Baker left the ship to pay official calls on Commander, Task Force 58 (CTF-58), Commander, Task Group 58.4 (CTG-58.4), and Commander, Carrier Division 1 (ComCarDiv 1), the *Randolph* and her air group officially became part of Vice Adm. Marc Mitscher's Task Force 58 (TF-58). The *Randolph* and Air Group 12 felt prepared. The pistol was not only loaded, but cocked and ready to be fired.

However, one air-group pilot was not going. Commander Gayler, leader and preceptor of the original fighter-squadron doctrine, was detached on 9 February for duty with Commander, Fleet Air Pacific. His experience was to be utilized above the squadron/air group level.

Lt. Cdr. Frederick H. Michaelis, Alexandria, Virginia, became the new commanding officer of Fighter Squadron 12. He was a 1940 graduate of the Naval Academy and had been attached to the battleship USS *Pennsylvania* when she was hit at Pearl Harbor. Fortunately, he was not aboard at the time, as his stateroom was demolished. When the *Pennsylvania* was returned to the West Coast for repairs, Michaelis was detached and sent to flight training. After completing flight training in 1943, he joined Air Group 12 at Astoria, following a tour as an advanced training instructor.

TF-58 sortied from Ulithi Atoll on 10 February, and rumors as to its destination were rampant. Lt. (j.g.) Richard T. Williams, Sarasota, Florida, the ship's surgeon, logged the event in his "Cruise Chronicle of the USS *Randolph,* WW II":

> Shoved off from Ulithi for a strike at the Jap—probably the homeland. Force comprised of the five groups: our group is the *Yorktown, Randolph, Langley,* and *Cabot, Washington, North Carolina,* about three cruisers and 16 cans [destroyers]. The entire force comprised of 11 CVs, 6 CVLs, 8 BBs, 9 light cruisers, 5 heavy cruisers, 2 battle cruisers, 73 cans. We can launch approximately 1100 planes.

For weeks speculation had been high as to what the Thunderbirds would do first. It had been a secret. In fact, the target objective had been so well concealed that we hadn't been issued winter flight gear so as not to give any clues as to our destination.

The "History of Bombfighting Squadron TWELVE" confirmed:

> And it was in truth a secret. The A.C.I. [Air Combat Information Officer] was for once the most popular [guy] in the squadron as most pilots knew that the A.C.I. office had been working over the Operation Order for some days. All pilots had been briefed on certain phases of the Iwo Jima support operations, but operations scheduled prior to that had not been revealed, not even to squadron skippers.
>
> On 13 February 1945, Commander Crommelin, Air Group Commander, assembled all pilots in the wardroom and announced in a manner only he knew how. "Well fellows," he said, "We're on our way to Tokyo." There was a moment of silence, and then applause that Tokyo Rose herself must have heard. One pilot, sitting next to this humble historian, after applauding loudly, suddenly stopped, turned, and said, "My God, why am I clapping?"

The reaction was typical. With five large task groups all out for no Japanese good speculation had been rife, but few had considered Tokyo a possibility.

Considered to be a major offensive, this action was to be the navy's first attack on Japan since it launched Gen. Jimmy Doolittle's raid on Japan on 18 April 1942. That strike had been launched from the aircraft carrier USS *Hornet* (CV 8) but involved the army air corps's B-25 Mitchell Bombers. They were launched 650 miles east of Japan on a one-way trip to bomb Japanese facilities around Tokyo and continue on to China. No navy aircraft were involved in that operation. TF-58, now under the strategic command of Adm. Raymond Spruance and the tactical command of Admiral Mitscher, was no small operation. (It seemed appropriate that Mitscher would be in tactical command because he had been the commanding officer of the *Hornet* during the Doolittle raid.) The magnitude of such a force now on its way toward the Japanese mainland was difficult to envision except from high above this fleet of ships. One of the most spectacular scenes we saw at sea was the coordinated movements of this task force of more than one hundred ships. From twenty thousand feet the ships' telltale wakes appeared as short-tailed comets. Then, as if choreographed in slow motion, all ships would reverse direction simultaneously, their wakes leaving white hooks on the ocean's surface as they turned. So precise was the maneuver that it appeared the vessels were linked by some invisible force in a magnificent display of seamanship.

Conversations with landlubbers about flying off aircraft carriers inevitably comes around to the subject of "finding" the ship upon returning from a flight. With an immense group of ships such as in this task force stretching twenty to twenty-five miles from one end to the other, the problem isn't "finding" the carrier but determining which one is yours.

Before the *Randolph* and AG-12 joined TF-58 at Ulithi Atoll, the main thrust of MacArthur's forces had been in the Southwest Pacific. Their objective was to retake the Philippines, then, in coordination with British, Australian, and New Zealand forces, gradually approach Japan from the south, with Kyushu the first island to be assaulted.

Nimitz, in the Central Pacific, literally was driving directly at Japan, bypassing nonstrategic islands on his way. Together, these forces were pushing hard to meet a timetable for an invasion of Japan in the fall of 1945.

The army air corps's bombing of Japan's industrial complex preliminary to that proposed invasion had begun from bases on Saipan and Tinian that the marines had secured in June–August 1944. When plans for invading these islands were formulated, the decision was also made to take Iwo Jima and, six weeks later, Okinawa. Both were to be used for the preinvasion aerial bombardment of Japan. Originally, the scheduled invasion of Iwo Jima was planned for the latter part of January. However, MacArthur's progress in the Philippines from Leyte northward to Luzon was delayed by the onset of an earlier-than-normal monsoon season, and Admiral Halsey's TF-38 was held over in support of that campaign. This delay was transferred to the invasion of Iwo Jima. Once released, Halsey returned to Ulithi and transferred command to Mitscher late in January. The Iwo Jima invasion was rescheduled for 19 February.

This delay and postponement resulted in less intensive prelanding shelling of Iwo Jima. Where the landing force had requested ten days of preinvasion bombardment, only three were provided. This was to be a costly change because there were hundreds more reinforced concrete bunkers than originally estimated, many constructed during the delay. The reason for taking Iwo Jima and Okinawa was the necessity of bombing Japan prior to the planned fall invasion. The result of bombing strikes from Saipan and Tinian were unsatisfactory. The B-29s' ability to haul nearly ten tons of bombs was reduced to three on the three-thousand-mile round-trip that required climbs to twenty-eight thousand feet. The Japanese were always alerted in advance of the strikes by their units in the Volcano and Bonin Islands lying along the path of the incoming bombers. There were no surprise bombing raids on Japan. High-altitude bombing was less than satisfactory and was not accomplishing the objective of preinvasion destruction. Thus the need for air bases closer to the Japanese mainland.

Iwo Jima and Okinawa had been thoroughly reinforced. The Japanese had correctly guessed the U.S. strategy of invading these islands and were well prepared.

However, no one, not even the Japanese, suspected the navy would preempt both of these objectives with a massive strike so directly or so soon. The raids on the Tokyo industrial complex on 16 and 17 February seemed to have surprised not only our own pilots but the Japanese as well. What happened on those two days was hairy and scary to our people but, more importantly, very damaging to Japanese industry and to the morale of Japan's citizens. More than half of the pilots and crewmen flying from seventeen carriers never had seen combat before. How they performed in a hostile environment would be the result of the training they had received from team leaders who had "been there."

On 15 February the *Randolph* topped off three destroyers for two and one half hours, a prebattle procedure being repeated throughout TF-58 during the morning hours. Afterward, the task force resumed antisub zigzagging courses in a generally northwest direction, maintaining CAPs until the *Saratoga* and *Enterprise* night fighters (VF-N) took over at dusk.

3 Pearl Harbor Avenged, 16 February

The hundred plus ship armada plowed through stormy seas ever closer to the Japanese mainland. Low-hanging clouds, rain and snow squalls, and strict radio silence masked the approach. Contributing to the stealth of the raid was the Japanese mind-set underestimating the ingenuity and daring of the Americans, in spite of the fact that they had demonstrated this same ingenuity and daring at Pearl Harbor. Defense of Iwo Jima they comprehended and were well prepared for its invasion. The eventual invasion of their homeland they also understood, accepting the inevitable by returning their decimated fleet to the relative safety of the Inland Sea and the majority of their aircraft to airfields on Honshu and Kyushu. However, the strength and boldness of Mitscher's raid on their capital city was not anticipated, at least not so soon.

As TF-58 proceeded toward Japan, tensions among those in command must have increased as a result of the events noted in the USS *Randolph*'s action report of 15 February:

> After sunset altered course to NW. During the night several Jap picket boats located ahead of the Task Force and were destroyed by gunfire. A lone Betty [twin-engine Japanese medium bomber] attempted to trail the force and was shot down. . . . It was hoped that tactical surprise could be effected, but size of the task force militated against it. It was assumed that Japanese reaction would be quick and heavy with air and submarine attacks. Preparations within the ship[s] were made accordingly.

The speed of the force was increased to twenty-three knots, and the resulting heaving, lurching, and creaking of complaining expansion joints made sleep almost impossible. Ens. Roy W. Bruce of VF-12, Fairfax, Virginia, recalled that night:

Our stateroom was starboard side forward of the hanger deck. My bunk was bolted to the sloping side of the ship's hull. A loose cable or chain clanked against the hull with every lurch and heave of the ship as it sliced through the stormy seas. Even in the darkness I could sense that my three roommates weren't asleep either. Like me, they were wondering what was in store for us. I must have finally dozed off for a while, being suddenly awakened to the blare of "General Quarters. Man your battle stations." This was what we'd trained two years for.

By 0600 Admiral Mitscher had maneuvered the task force about one hundred miles off the coast of Honshu southeast of Tokyo, and the first planes were launched at 0646. The *Randolph*'s log for the 04-08 watch recorded the events following the approach: "0646— First plane catapulted. 0730—Completed launching aircraft, a total of 47 VF's." For the ship and air group, the war was on.

The first flight launched off the *Randolph* was a group of sixteen fighters. Lieutenant Commander Pawka was the group leader. Similar launches occurred on many of the other carriers assigned different targets in and around the Tokyo area.

Ens. Hal Lindley of VF-12, Orford, New Hampshire, was "tail-end Charlie," the last plane in this group:

I can remember there was approximately a two-hundred-foot ceiling that morning. We took off about 0645. We climbed through fourteen thousand feet of overcast without running lights on planes, flying off each other's exhaust. I was on the extreme right-hand end of the line of sixteen planes, and I can remember using full throttle to no throttle, trying to stay in position.

We broke out of the overcast, and as we hit the coast of Japan it became clear, from dense clouds to absolutely clear.

Once the weather was reported, we made a run on Choshi Airport [a fighter landing field seventy miles due east of Tokyo]. On that field there was one multiengine plane that turned out to be a fake. I remember strafing that and firing some of my rockets at one of the hangars. There was at least one line of fighters in front of them, and other guys were strafing those. I also remember seeing what I thought must have been individual rifle shots sparkling all over the hangar area, like they were shooting at us.

Ens. Jack Schipper of VBF-12, Redwood City, California, was Pawka's wingman on this flight:

We took off in the dark and flew in the clouds all the way to the coastline. The first land we saw was Japan.

Pawka had told me earlier, "I don't care what else you do, you stay on my tail. If you lose me, you're grounded."

We didn't see any planes in the air, so we started down. On the way down to strafe planes on the ground, a Jap plane goes sailing across underneath us, and I was so scared I pulled the trigger. We pulled right up from our strafing run, and this Jap got right on Pawka's tail. I had them both in my gun sights. So I claim to be the first in our group that shot—hit a Jap plane, but Pawka was in my gun sight too.

I fired because I thought I had to, and as soon as I did, the Jap plane peeled off.

When we got back to the carrier there were holes in Pawka's tail section. We never did figure out whose they were.

Don't think you really want to know.

At first, air opposition was light, with little or no effort to intercept the incoming raids. It took several hours that first morning before the Japanese realized the seriousness and magnitude of the strikes. Then out came many aircraft with skilled pilots who were being held for the anticipated invasion of Kyushu in the fall.

The F6Fs issued to the fighter squadrons were the latest off the Grumman Aircraft production line. This fifth modification of the aircraft contained some new equipment. One was a "G suit." A pump forced compressed air into the abdomen and lower-leg compartments of the pilot's flight suit. The pump was activated when G forces were encountered in tight turns or when pulling out of steep dive-bombing runs. The device allowed pilots to put more stress on the aircraft without "blacking out." They could make tighter turns than the famed Japanese Zero at high speeds.

A more controversial piece of new equipment was the Mark 23 gun sight. This gun sight was similar to the older Mark 8 that contained a pipper and rings for computing the lead and deflection angles of a moving target. The Mark 23 also contained movable reticles operated by twisting the throttle handle. Outlining the target aircraft with these reticles and flying the movable pipper onto the target, the F6F's six .50-caliber machine guns were then aligned with the correct lead ahead of the target. The bullets were set to converge at 1,500 feet. This computation was done with gimbals and gyros. This gun sight became almost useless in aerial combat requiring continual twists and turns, climbs and dives, so much so that many pilots of VBF caged the gyro and used the sight as they would have used the older Mark 8.

Lieutenant McWhorter had one success with the new gun sight:

As for the Mark 23 gun sight, I was very surprised to hear that some of the other pilots didn't like it. I found it to be a tremendous improvement over the old fixed-reticle sight. It certainly functioned beautifully the first time I used it in combat.

On our first Tokyo strike as we were nearing the target above the overcast, I saw a Zero about a mile or so distant at my ten-o'clock position and about the same altitude. I turned into him, and he immediately commenced a dive down under me and towards the cloud tops. As he came underneath me, I rolled into an overhead attack and simply put the pipper on his nose and waited to get into firing range. I was inverted on my back most of the time through the run, only reaching the vertical dive position as I got into firing range. Our ammo-loading sequence was for an armor-piercing incendiary [API] every fifth round, and they make a nice bright flash when they hit. When I fired on this run, I immediately saw a whole bunch of these bright flashes all around his nose and wing-root area, exactly where I was holding the gun-sight pipper. Surprisingly, he did not explode or burn immediately, as most of the earlier Zeros had when I hit them.

Just before he reached the clouds, a long flame appeared from the engine area, and he was burning as he disappeared into the clouds. Also, as I recall, someone else from the squadron was down below the clouds beneath us and saw the Zero spinning down in flames out of the clouds near them.

I also found out many years later that they were putting self-sealing fuel tanks in their later planes—which would explain why this one didn't explode or burn immediately.

Some dive-bomber crews had a few chilling moments that first day. ARM3c Paul E. Nugent of VB-12, Silver Spring, Maryland, gave some ideas as to what could go wrong for a rear-seat gunner in the SB2C:

The day of the first Tokyo strike, Ensign Hammonds and I flew in the second strike at Tachikawa Airfield. On reaching the target Ensign Hammonds announced he was going to bomb steep and fast, using no or partial dive brakes. As he nosed over, the twin .30-caliber machine guns I had deployed came lose from their mounts and flew straight up over my head. Luckily, I held on to them, but as we pulled up, the G forces of the dive forced them downward, and they hit inside of the rear seat very hard, causing one or both to fire a single round through the fuselage and tail. Hammonds, on hearing the shot[s], assumed we were hit and asked if I was okay. I informed him what had happened. We landed on the *Randolph* without further incident. As I unlocked my chute and seat belt, I glanced down and, to my surprise, found I had flown the mission without a Mae West, and believe me, I'm no swimmer of any great distances!

Distractions could get pilots and crewmen in trouble sometimes as quickly as the enemy. Ens. Harold W. Wegener of VB-12, La Mesa, California, explained: "One of the most memorable moments of the Tokyo raids was during a strike north of Tokyo. I was admiring Mount Fujiyama off my right wing tip when the plane ran out of gas on one of the tanks."

Nothing like an engine sputtering out over enemy territory to get your attention.

In destroying enemy aircraft, sometimes a little ingenuity had to come into play. On his second flight of the day, Lt. Lou Menard of VBF-12, Jacksonville, Florida, and his division (Ensigns Manhold, Glasser, and Barr) were covering returning strike aircraft off the Japanese coast:

When one strike group was returning to the carrier, a submarine called us and said to check out the last plane following the group of returning aircraft. We turned in that direction, and when the Tony saw us coming towards him, he full-throttled it and dove for the water and headed for the beach.

We started chasing him, and he was outrunning us. Manhold was trying to shoot him down, but the bullets were falling short. I slid in beside Manhold and said, "Hey, I'll just try to shoot him down with a rocket." I fired one rocket, and it missed him. It went right over the top of his wing and landed in the water. When it hit, the shell went off and made a huge geyser of water. He flew into it, and his plane disintegrated.

The dive-bomber squadron lost a crew on this first day of action. Ens. Charles H. Brown, Kingwood, West Virginia, and his aircrewman, ARM3c J. D. Richards, Ft. Lauderdale, Florida, flying an SB2C, were "hit by anti-aircraft fire while in a dive bombing run, but made a successful water landing in Lake K. [Lake Kasumiga-Ura]." This quoted VB-12 aircraft action report (AAR) pales in bluntness when compared to the full story. Brown and Richards were listed as missing in action, as were most losses when the outcome was uncertain. They lost contact with each other soon after the war but were reunited as a result of AG-12's reunion publicity in 1990. They recalled some of their experiences:

Brown: Commander Embree maneuvered the VB squadron into position for the attack on the alternate target [Kasumiga-Ura Naval Seaplane Base] because Oto, the primary target, was completely overcast. We were at ten thousand feet, and as I nosed the plane over into my dive, I felt a shudder through the SB2C, and I noticed that my bomb-bay doors had closed and the engine was, to say the least, not working properly. I knew I was in trouble and that I wanted to be rid of the bombs. It was difficult to reopen the bomb-bay doors while in the dive, but finally managed to accomplish it. I looked in the bomb sight, and all I could see was the roof of a large building. The altimeter showed three thousand feet as I released the bombs and began recovery from the dive. Commander Embree had pulled out of his dive with a turn to the left, and through habit, training, or lack of a better place to go under the circumstances, I started to follow him. The tracers were passing behind his left wing and very close to the rear cockpit. The flames from my dead engine passing my open cockpit caused me to look for a more plausible course of action.

I was then at one-thousand-feet altitude with decreasing airspeed. I decided to bail out, but with increasing loss of altitude and my inability to release the harness, I changed my mind and called on the intercom to Jack Richards in the rear cockpit that I was going to ride it in for a water landing on the lake that was just ahead. The tips of the flames were in and out of the rear cockpit. Jack had released his harness and was crouched on his seat with hands on the radio cord at his helmet ready to unplug it and bail out when I called. He decided to ride it in too, and sat down, pulled the life raft from its storage tube between the cockpits, and placed it across the cockpit in front of him. He didn't have time or was unable to refasten his seat belt or shoulder straps.

It became apparent that the plane would not reach the main body of water, and I would have to settle for a narrow neck of the lake. I hit the flap lever to lower the landing flaps, using the last of the hydraulic pressure. The plane almost stopped its forward motion—the dive flaps had opened because I had failed to change the selector lever from the dive-flap to landing-flap setting. I immediately shoved the nose over in a dive and then pulled back on the stick as hard as I could. The plane responded nicely, and we splashed down with very little forward motion. I unfastened my harness, took the chart board out, and threw it as far as I could. The plane was starting to sink. Neither of us suffered any injury as a result of the crash landing, and I only got wet up to my knees.

Richards: I remember the pull-up. Looking over the side, I saw the smoke coming from the front. I turned my head to look around to the engine, and a big burst of flame came flying down the fuselage, and, of course, I heard the engine spitting and coughing and everything during that time. I called and asked, "Are you all right, what's going on up there?" I wasn't getting any answer. I don't know whether I forgot to push the [mike] button or what. I climbed up in my seat after a while. I remember it was like another hit or explosion, I don't know what it was. I was up in my seat, and I yelled, "Brown, if you don't answer, I'm going over the side," and you yelled, "Hang on, I see water." I was standing up in the cockpit. I looked over the side—we were right off the water. I put my arm up over the radar set and had my head against it. That's when we hit the water. Of course, it was the most beautiful landing he ever made in his life. At that point, I rolled out the life raft, threw it out in the water. For some reason I remember them always teaching us that if your landing doesn't hit hard enough, there was a button to destroy the radar—DESTRUCT. Well, I hit that and got out. The life raft had drifted away a little bit. I jumped in the water so it wouldn't go any farther, pulled the toggle—it popped right open, and I pushed it back to the plane.

Brown: I had taken the chart board out and thrown it as far as I could and was trying to get rid of stuff out of the cockpit while the plane was sinking.

Richards: The water came up real fast, I remember that, it really came up fast.

Brown: When I looked around you were sitting in the life raft.

Richards: I remember in the life raft—I think we were talking about trying to make it to the mountains inland. We could see people up that way; then decided to go another way, and there were people that way. I do remember there were some potshots being taken at us. We were sitting there. There is no sense letting them keep shooting at us. They signaled that we were to surrender. The first guy that got out there was a real old man in a boat. Do you remember him?

Brown: A farmer, I think, came out very cautiously in a rowboat, picked us up, and took us to the shore. He was about afraid of us as we were of him.

Richards: He kept making a motion with his fingers—you got a gun? When he got there he said get over in his boat from the life raft. Pretty soon these other boats got there. Our hands were tied behind us. They took us up to a little dock like, and they half-pushed me, half-stood me up to get up there because I had my hands tied behind me. A little Jap came over to me and said something, then he said, "Are you Russian or American?" I was surprised to hear that. I said Americans and turned around to see that you were not out of the boat yet. There was a guy with a big club standing up on the wharf, and he starts shouting around us, and he swung his club down as you stepped forward—the damn thing would have killed you—it just missed you.

Brown: He missed, thank goodness.

Richards: Then all of a sudden everybody let out a yell. I looked up, and there comes this guy with this big rope. I thought, "Oh my God, it's a lynching." They wanted to put us on the end of a long rope. I found out later that it was a disgrace to be pulled through the streets like that.

Brown: There were some other civilians waiting in front of a building, and several doves were sitting on the roof. I remember thinking—doves of peace?

An automobile with a big red star on the driver's door came speeding into the area. Two Russian officers got out, looked us over, got back into their car, and left without saying one word to anyone. Russia had not yet declared war on Japan. Shortly thereafter, some Japanese soldiers arrived.

After retying our hands behind our backs and blindfolding us, they marched us down a road, stopping every now and then to let women kick our shins with their wooden clogs or "geta." Finally, we were thrown into the bed of an army truck and driven a short distance.

Richards: I remember a flatbed truck pulled up, and there were Japanese soldiers on it. Somebody hit me with a club or something right on my legs and knocked me ass over tin cups, and I went down. When I got up, soldiers beat them off. They had thrown you up on the truck. They just picked me up like a sack of potatoes and threw me up on the truck the same way they did you. Then they put a blanket over our heads, old army blanket, tied it around the waist.

They took us to an old building—I assume it was old, I don't know—there were wooden steps, and they took us upstairs.

Brown: I was taken into an office, made to sit on the floor with my back to a wall, hands still tied, and still blindfolded. The interrogating officer spoke some English, and his first question was, "What is spruance?"

He was insistent that I tell him the meaning of the word "spruance." He stood on my thighs, balancing himself with a staff, one end of which was in my groin. Each time I refused to answer or pleaded ignorance, he would shove down on the staff with sharp jabs. After considerable time and pressure on the interrogator's part, he must have been convinced of my ignorance. With all due respect to Admiral Raymond Spruance, who was in fact strategic commander of the Task Force 58 carrier attack on the Tokyo area, I had never heard of him. His next question was, "Why did you bomb the school with all the children in it?" From there on it was all downhill.

Richards: The soldiers had tied my elbows too. Not only that, I know it was pulling back on my shoulders real bad. They picked me up and took me inside the office. I remember there was a Jap sitting at the desk. They paid no attention to me for a few minutes, and then the guy from the other side of the desk picked up his club and said, "Do you see that, American?"

I said, "Yeah, I see it."

He said, "You tell the truth or you're going to die. Do you understand that?"

I said, "I understand that."

He said, "Where are the carriers?"

I said, "I don't know."

Bang—he hit me right over the head.

I remember saying I didn't know nothing.

Somebody says, "Then you are not the pilot."

I said, "No, I'm the crew."

Brown: Thanks, you laid the groundwork for me. After a while I was taken outside. It had turned extremely cold. There were many sharp commands or exchanges among the soldiers. I was pushed down on my knees, and a hand on my shoulder shoved me so that I was forced to kneel with my head extended parallel with the ground. I envisioned the photo of the pilot kneeling and about to be beheaded by a samurai with his sword. I accepted imminent death and waited. After a moment that seemed an eternity, a hand shoved me back to a sitting position upon my heels. A short time later I heard a train come to a stop, and we were put aboard and taken to Kempi Headquarters in Tokyo.

Richards: It seems to me I had more trouble—they had my elbows so tight they were pulling my shoulders. But I know I got on the train, and I don't know what it was, but I got real sleepy. I couldn't stay awake anymore, and I would keep dozing off, and they were pushing me and hitting me, and at one point I tumbled down a flight of stairs. I think they led me to it and let me walk over. I remember getting into a car. One of the guys got in and threw me down on the floor, and I guess it was you they piled in on top of me.

Brown: I spent the next two weeks in an unheated cell with a young Korean and another Oriental whose nationality I could not determine. The cell was not quite wide enough for all three of us to lie down at the same time. I acquired body lice, which remained with me for the remainder of my time in Japan. The weather was below freezing, with snow on the outside, and during the questioning by the army intelligence officers, "school and spruance" were brought up repeatedly.

Richards: Yeah, it was very bad, I remember. I had two Jap civilian prisoners in the cell with me, two blankets, and the bathroom was a hole cut over in the corner. Then the questioning. I remember there was a guy, he really knew Washington. He said he used to be the naval attaché in the Washington Tokyo Embassy. I think he may have been because he wore civilian clothes.

This guy was sort of like a—I called him the good boy, but he knew Washington. He asked what part of Washington I was from, and I said, "Up northwest," and he said, "Near Walter Reed Hospital."

I didn't answer the first time, and the next morning they took me up to see him, and I asked him, "Was my family notified I'm alive?"

He said, "No. You are not a prisoner of war."

I said, "Well, what am I doing here?"

He said, "You are a special captive of the Japanese. We're not going to let anybody know you are alive."

There were a couple of other sessions over the next couple of weeks. There weren't too many times they had them. I did see the "slugger" more than the other guy. I called him the slugger because he always wanted to bang me around some.

Brown: At the end of two weeks we were taken by train with other prisoners, blindfolded, on the way to what turned out to be a naval interrogation camp at the city of Ofuna. After getting off the train, we walked quite a long distance along dirt roads. At one time when I tilted my head back and looked under the blindfold, I saw this huge statue at the top of the hill, which I later found out was the Kannon of Ofuna, or Goddess of Mercy.

I had no sooner been locked in my cell when an American prisoner served a bowl of barley. He whispered that I was not to recognize Pappy Boyington. I spent the next six weeks in solitary confinement but was taken for interrogation each day. The next two and one-half months I was still not permitted to talk, but my cell door was allowed to be open, and I could at least see the prisoners in the adjoining cells and the cells across the corridor. We were given a cup of boiled barley and bowl of soup that usually consisted of hot water with a few greens in it. On one occasion a rather large green worm was floating on top of my soup. I flipped it out into the corridor with my chopsticks. Two prisoners had a head-on collision as they each grabbed for the worm. I might add, that was the last worm I discarded!

Richards: But up there [Ofuna], if you wanted to go to the bathroom, you used to bang on the door and say, "Benjo, benjo." They'd come in and would blindfold you, tie your hands, and take you down to the end of the hall. Mostly, you would have to bow to the guard when they came in. Half of them would punch you in the jaw, slap you, or something if you didn't.

They would set the food in front of your door, knock, and only then could you open the door and pick up your own bowl. There were only two blankets in the cell. I think there was a little mat, wasn't there?

Brown: Yeah, there was what you call a tatami, a straw mat. It was the bed, and that is what you slept on.

Richards: Then there was a little table.

Brown: You could put your food on it. We had to learn to eat with chopsticks. If they caught you even thinking about using your fingers, you got clobbered.

Richards: Yeah, wasn't neat. I remember the first time they gave me a lunch was a bowl of water with a fish head in it. Mama never gave me this before! Other times it was worse because you got the tail. That was worse. There wasn't enough meat on that.

Brown: There was more meat on the fish head than there was on the tail.

Richards: That's right. I also remember getting just cucumbers in the soup, the peelings. Not the cucumbers, just the peelings.

Brown: The worst I remember was the marigolds. That might have been after you left. They would boil marigolds, and that was our soup. Marigolds! That soup tasted just like marigolds smell, and that's not good.

Richards: It took me longer to get to eat the cucumbers than it did rice. I didn't like the smell.

Brown: Do you have any idea of how many of us were taken to Ofuna? That was about March 1st, I think. I know Dave Puckett, you, and I were, and so was McCann.

Richards: I think there were about eleven or twelve.

Brown: In the cell next to mine was Major William H. Walker from Utah who was an observer on a B-29 shot down on one of the Tokyo raids. On 29 August when we were repatriated, Bill was brought from Ofuna and taken aboard the hospital ship, the USS *Benevolence*. He died that night.

Bill's widow later sent me a poem written upon a gum wrapper that was found in his effects. It expresses how much we all looked forward to nightfall:

> The day is ending,
> > There's the call "Sing Foy."
> The Holy Book I close
> > and start with joy
> To spread my blankets
> > on the floor, and fold
> Each tuck, complete with care
> > to stem the cold.
> The Shepherd's words have
> > lulled my mind content.
> The guards, their spiteful
> > verbiage spent,
> Recede until their awkward
> > steel shod tread
> Is all I hear within
> > my humble bed.

All of the fliers and submarine men were treated as captives and not prisoners of war. We were informed that the Geneva Convention did not apply to us. At one time during the early interrogation I was requested to draw a diagram of the USS *Randolph,* which was a new carrier in the fleet. After persuasion, I finally drew the picture and had enough guns in place on the island and around the outer edges of the flight deck that the *Randolph* would have been top-heavy and rolled over! I thought this was a clever way of getting the subject changed. I had been on the *Randolph* only thirty days, and I certainly didn't know where the guns were placed, nor what caliber they were. I had ten 5-inchers on the superstructure, and the drawing looked more like a destroyer. About three months later I didn't feel so clever when the interrogation officer insisted that I redraw and relabel the caliber of each gun emplacement.

Ensign Brown and Aircrewman Richards were declared missing in action. Also missing on Air Group 12's first day in combat were Lt. Bleeker P. Seaman, Jr., of VBF-12, "last seen following a Zeke into clouds," and Lt. (j.g.) Sabe Legatos of VF-12. Legatos "was lost while engaging two Zekes. He had shot down one and was running head-on toward the other when both he and his opponent crashed in flames" (VF-12 Narrative, 20 July 1944–20 July 1945; VBF-12 Narrative, January–July 1945; VBF-12 AAR#3, 16 February 1945).

Ens. Jim Meacham of VF-12, Buckeye Lake, Ohio, a member of Legatos's flight, related what happened:

Our flight was led by "Sam" Legatos, with Ensign Rafferty as wingman, Ensign Ball, section leader, and myself as his wingman. We were scheduled to participate in the second attack group shortly after daybreak. Rafferty's plane was grounded, so Legatos, Ball, and myself flew a three-plane flight in rather cold, inclement weather. We were instructed to fly to the target area on our belly tank, then jettison it. For some reason I forgot to switch to it after takeoff until we were over halfway to the target area.

When we reached the target area, an airfield just north of Tokyo, I opted to keep the belly tank and made the first pass, a steep diving approach with a sharp pullout. I marveled at the smooth and "quiet" operation of the F6F and then realized I'd lost the belly tank and quickly switched to the wing tank. I finally caught up to my flight, and we gained some altitude to head for the next target.

At this time Legatos spotted a fighter and went in hot pursuit. We were both firing at the Zeke, which exploded. We then realized that we were under attack by other Jap planes. Our flight broke formation and engaged in a dogfight in which Legatos's plane was hit. I observed it in a gradual, straight-and-level descent—

smoking very badly. I suspect Legatos was killed in the action as there was no maneuvering of his plane.

I then became aware of a head-on run at me by a Jap plane, which I luckily survived. Ball and I then joined in a scissoring maneuver [Thach weave] for a time and then proceeded to the next target area.

After our mission was accomplished, we headed back to the carrier. My foolish error had cost me a lot of fuel, and as we approached the task force, both tanks were registering empty. I attempted to land on the first carrier recovering planes. After one bad pass I was taken aboard. As I climbed out of the plane, they told me my tail section had been shot up a bit. I didn't respond and headed for the wardroom, hoping to find a cup of coffee.

I had landed on the USS *Lexington,* which was identical to the *Randolph,* but I couldn't find the wardroom, much less a cup of coffee. Finally, someone caught up with me and told me I had to report in. I believe I was in a state of shock. Three days later my plane was repaired, and I flew back to the "Randy."

The loss of three pilots and one aircrewman the first day in combat was tragic. The Japanese paid dearly for those losses. Pilots of VF-12 and VBF-12 were credited with forty-one aircraft shot down, many destroyed on the ground, and extensive damage to military facilities by the bombers.

Aircrewman ARM1c Alfred Smith, ringleader of VB-12's enlisted aircrewmen, commented about what happened after the Tokyo strike:

After the attack on Tokyo, Commander Embree visited the enlisted ready room, accompanied by a doctor. He asked how many men took part in the attack, and I said there were sixteen to eighteen. He then told the doctor that I was the only person authorized to give the Upjohn Brandy for issue to any gunners for this or any other upcoming missions. Then he said, "There are twenty-four to the case," winked, and on his way out remarked, "Smith, don't give it to any sailors under twenty-one."

Bucky Walters, ARM1c, said later, "Commander Embree just made Al Capone a bank guard."

4 More Hostilities, 17 February

The second day of strikes on the Japanese mainland, 17 February, was reminiscent of our October flight days at Astoria, Oregon—lousy weather. The similarity ended there, however. Here, we couldn't just roll over and sack out for the rest of the day: there was flying to be done, regardless of the weather. Targets again were to be airfields with strange and exotic names such as Konoike, Hokada, Mito, Mawatari, Hyakurigahara, and facilities at Kasumigaura and Tachikawa Aircraft Engine Plant. All were east of Tokyo except Tachikawa; it was twenty-five miles west of the capital and eighty-five miles from the coastline at Hokada.

The briefing for this flight provided an insight to Commander Crommelin's positive attitude and confidence. ATCS A. C. "Sparky" Fraser of the AG-12 staff related, "At the briefing on the seventeenth he told the pilots, 'In the Task Force we have about two thousand planes. The Japs have about five thousand, but we're four times as good as they are, and that's going to leave them about three thousand planes short.'"

Crippling known fighter airfields early on 16 February had been critical in conjunction with the tactical surprise that had been achieved. This mission offered an additional opportunity to destroy a huge supply facility (Kasumigaura) or an aircraft-engine plant (Tachikawa). Damaging the latter would interrupt the flow of new aircraft for us to contend with in the future.

Commander Crommelin was strike leader, employing "all available VB and VT from Task Group 58.4 plus suitable escort (VF)," according to the VBF AAR for this mission. That entailed drawing aircraft from the *Yorktown* and from one of the two CVLs in the task group, the *Cabot:* approximately sixty VB and VT, plus at least an equal number of VF for protection.

The same action report provided the following narrative:

All aircraft launched and rendezvoused without incident. Tachikawa Aircraft Engine Plant was the primary target and Kasumigaura Supply Base the secondary target. Weather from Base (TG 58.4) to the coast of Japan was particularly bad with heavy rain and ceiling from 300 to 700 feet. While enroute to the coast, weather reports from planes over the primary target area influenced the flight leader to announce Kasumigaura as the primary target to be attacked. Upon approaching the coast the weather opened up considerably and Strike Group climbed to 16,000 feet. A short distance inland it could be seen that the weather was clear as far south as the primary target. 301 Cobra (from USS *Yorktown*) announced that some of his planes were having trouble and that he would pull out all his VT with 4 VF and strike Kasumigaura. Permission was granted.

The extreme cold at higher altitudes was freezing oil in the propeller control domes. This difficulty had been experienced on 16 February also.

Ens. John Morris of VB-12, Haverhill, Massachusetts, provided a first-hand look from the dive-bombers:

On the flight to Tachikawa Engine Plant on the seventeenth, Crommelin led. . . . The weather was lousy. It was terrible milling around through the clouds. It was a wonder there weren't midair collisions.

We climbed up to about twelve thousand feet atop the overcast. The minute we hit the coastline of Japan the weather cleared. We were a little north of Tokyo. We were jinking left and right and up and down, and the AA fire was all over the place on the way to the target. There were Jap fighters on either side of our formation, calling out the altitude for the AA fire, and Crommelin was telling the VF, "Don't go after the fighters, protect the bombers and torpedo planes."

Commander Crommelin ordered the attack on a westerly heading, with dive and retirements toward the south. Morris recounted the dive-bombers' attack:

> I remember the torpedo planes made their glide-bombing runs first. As we made steep dive-bombing runs, the AA fire from Tachikawa became intense, but the Jap fighters left us alone as we dove. We pulled out and rendezvoused, and went south down Tokyo Bay at low altitude, jinking left and right and up and down. We strafed any ships that happened to be along our flight path, but we didn't go out of our way looking for something.

One other member of the attack group hadn't released all of his bombs, according to Ensign Morris:

> When we left, Charley Jaep of the torpedo squadron had made his run with the rest of us, and didn't release all of his bombs. I don't know whether he was carrying 500-pounders or not. So while we left, Charley climbed back up like he was practicing in training and made another run. He took pictures with his gun cameras of the damage that had just been done, dropped his bombs, and straggled back to the ship.
>
> I don't think he knew whether he was going to get a medal or a court-martial. I believe he got a Navy Cross on that mission, the rest of us got DFC's.
>
> When he had returned from this flight his remark was, "I must do something outstanding on each hop."
>
> He'd learned to fly before he got into the navy. Every time he took his plane back to the hangar, there would be a deputy sheriff waiting for him for some outstanding flight.

Commander Crommelin's division remained over the target to observe and take photographs for damage assessment, then dove on the target, releasing rockets and retiring.

From the same VBF-12's AAR#12:

> Three planes in the Strike Leader's division, including the Strike Leader's plane, had trouble, as did planes in other divisions, in that prop controls froze at 2000 to 2200 rpm. . . . On retirement from target the Strike Leader's division, strung out in a line before

join-up after dive, was attacked by three Tonys. The strike Leader, whose prop had frozen . . . at 2120 rpm, called for help. Lieutenant A. G. Bolduc [Crommelin's second section leader], in front of the Striker Leader's plane, made a high speed turn at 260 knots indicated, pulling six 'G's throughout, and shot the Tony off the Strike Leader's tail.

Although Bolduc's G-suit prevented him from blacking out, he "greyed" out in the turn.

Lieutenant Bolduc described Crommelin's call for help:

It was difficult to believe he was in trouble when he called, "I could use a little help" with little or no sense of urgency. It was then I got a glimpse of two or three Tony's raking his plane with gunfire. It was just his way of doing things.

What the VBF AAR did not address was how Ensign Mangieri, Bolduc's wingman, reacted quickly enough to shoot down the second Tony off Bolduc's tail. Nor did it address the loss of Ensign McAdams. As Crommelin's wingman, he had ended up last in the tail chase on retiring south. He was having prop-control problems, and his prop was seen to freeze. He headed for a water landing at the southern end of Tokyo Bay.

Upon landing after a five-and-one-quarter-hour mission, Commander Crommelin displayed no evidence of fatigue or stress. Not so his aircraft. After inspecting his Hellcat, the plane handlers and flight-deck crew were astounded that he'd made it back to the *Randolph,* let alone landed it in one piece. It was riddled with holes from cowl flaps to stabilizer. Lieutenant Bolduc was among those who inspected Crommelin's plane: "I counted fifty-four holes in one wing tank, and the fuselage appeared as though it had been used for target practice, target practice for the Japs."

Tachikawa Aircraft Engine Plant was described by Bolduc:

It was an immense structure—must have covered five acres— and looked untouched by the B-29 bombings. It was so large that, when I looked through the gun sight on my rocket run, I could only see a portion of the building at one time. No way we could miss it.

The enlisted men who flew as aircrewmen in the dive-bombers and torpedo planes saw combat from a different perspective. ARM1c

Alfred R. Smith of VB-12 provided some thoughts on his job as gunner:

> Our main job was to get that plane over the assigned target and return to the carrier for future missions. You take off on a mission, fly many miles over water or jungle, get shot at, occasionally shoot back, and there's always the carrier landing.
>
> One of the most critical responsibilities the airdale has, especially in dive-bombing, is to call out the altitudes during the bombing run. Most pilots wanted a mark at fifteen hundred feet, and at twelve hundred they would begin their pullout and level off at two or three hundred knots and streak for the rendezvous position. We had fighter escorts most of the time except on antisubmarine or search hops. Zero pilots liked to get us alone on a dive or on pullout. They never would attack en route to the target as we would have a tight formation and twin .30-calibers staring them in the face. Most gunners strafed on pullout, if possible, always on ships, making sure to save a couple of hundred rounds in case we got jumped on the way back to the carrier. We had a good view of the bomb hit and reported it to the "jockey" on the intercom.
>
> The SB2C tail was very large, and we lost a lot of angle of fire power trying to shoot around it. It [the rear cockpit] had no flight controls, just an altimeter and a turn-and-bank indicator for this "rumble-seat rider."
>
> When you fly with the same pilot every day, you can tell what he is doing and thinking just by his movements—fishing for a smoke, switching gas tanks, getting weary, or ready to land.

Another reason these aircrewmen saw combat from a different perspective was that they were among a small group of warriors who went riding backward into combat. For one of these backward-flying crewman, 17 February began routinely enough. ARM2 M. Ray Schultz, Catonsville, Maryland, a radio-gunner in VB-12, recounted one of his missions:

> 0623—"General Quarters, man your battle stations," blared the PA system. Aircrewmen wolfed down a breakfast of steak and eggs astraddle bombs. "Aircrewmen, man your planes." Last words between Lieutenant Al Lindstrom, my pilot, and me. "Start your engines." Our plane captain gives us a thumbs up, and the "beast"

lumbers forward towards the launch point just aft the island. Within minutes we're up and leaving the *Randolph* as we rendezvoused with the dozen other bombers heading north. So much for routine on this, my second combat mission.

The target, Tachikawa Aircraft Engine Plant northwest of Tokyo. While climbing to about fourteen thousand feet we fitted oxygen masks and opened the cockpit cowls of our "rumble seats" to ready our twin .30-caliber guns for action.

Cold. My God, it was frigid back there, and we "coolies" envied our jockeys and their heaters in the closed cockpits. My rubber oxygen mask felt as if it were bonding to my face. Later, after landing, aircrewman Bucky Walters showed us his snow-white frostbitten hands, which took two weeks to regain their normal flesh color.

I tried clutching the twin .30s with one hand while banging the other against the scarf ring or stomping both feet against the decking. Anything to increase blood circulation—nothing helped very much at that point. Then Mr. Lindstrom informed me on the intercom, "Thirty minutes to target." Hours later, it seemed, "Twenty minutes to target." His reports continued until, "We're over target, commencing dive."

We began a high-speed run to twelve thousand feet, nosed over straight down with dive brakes extended. That really got my blood boiling as we dove down through a concentrated cone of AA fire. I watched the gunfire all around us as he held the plane right on target [machine shops] and suddenly realized, those glowing traces are only every third bullet!

Ordinarily, I stood in the small, forward area of the scarf ring while preparing to strafe on pullout. For some strange reason I planted my feet and leaned back behind the cowl-covered area. As we pulled out of the bombing run to level flight I sensed, or saw with peripheral vision on the port side of the SB2C, the exploding shell. Its blast laid up to the side of my head like a baseball bat as it knocked me to the deck.

Strangely, I remember seeing page one of the Boy Scout Handbook section on first aid: "Think. See what is wrong. Don't panic!" I just wanted to go to sleep, to be left alone.

The concussion blasted through the space between the cowl and the guns, knocking them muzzle down, but apparently still intact. The gun sight had been flipped sideways. Had I taken my normal firing stance I might well have been cut in half.

Lindstrom turned southeast over Tokyo Bay, alone at low altitude, all the while executing violent evasive-action turns and looking for friendly aircraft to join up on. Sixth-sensing a flying meatball at four o'clock, I was jolted alert and immediately righted, then swung my weapon around to firing position. It will never be known whether the "rising sun" veered off because of my sudden movements or by our fighters' approaching.

Tokyo Bay slowly gave way to the blue salt water of the North Pacific before I finally began to relax. There's something spiritual and healing about the sea—it never looked so good to this sailor!

Neither of us had spoken since the attack. It wasn't necessary. When my right ear felt as though a wet fluid was draining into it, a brush of my hand confirmed the cause—matted blood. I considered a call on the intercom.

Why complicate the situation? Lindstrom had more than enough to do, scanning the grey skies for bogeys or friendlies. The latter appeared just as we crossed the coastline and shortly thereafter entered the pattern over the *Randolph,* making our landing in turn.

After touchdown and hook release, the aft elevator took us below to the hanger deck, where each of us was handed a cup of hot "joe" as we climbed out onto the wing. Inspecting SB2C for damage, we were amazed at how minimal it was, one small round shell hole through the leading edge of the right wing, along with another razor sharp slit in the rubber strip around the rear-seat cowl at head height—my head height!

In sick bay a corpsman cleaned my head wound, removed some fragments from the AA fire, methodically sterilized it, then went about writing up his report.

Welcome back to routine duty.

Returning planes tested the nerves of the ship's flight-deck crew at times, and some unsung heroes stepped forward to be counted. On the flight deck these men scurried around, moving planes to take-off positions, releasing tailhooks from arresting cables, and directing planes forward after landing. This group, recognizable by the yellow sweaters they wore, included ABM2c Glen W. Putney,

Lake Jackson, Texas, who was a flight-deck director and in a position to see plenty of action topside: "I remember the many times, we were always forewarned, that aircraft would be coming in with guns not on safe or a bomb hanging by one strap or a rocket that did not fire. Sometimes nimble and fast footwork was required to get out of the way."

"Sparky" Fraser recalled one such incident:

When the planes were landing, the ice wagons [torpedo bombers] were coming in first, and Buglione [an ACOM from VT-12] was doing a flight-deck-ordnance check up forward. I was in flight-deck radio/radar. I was kidding him about ordnancemen being brainless, and he was saying, "damn reserve," things like that.

The first torpedo bomber came in and landed. It opened its bomb-bay door and, bam, a 500-pounder dropped down and armed itself. There was about two feet between us, and I froze. I wasn't an ordnanceman. I didn't have an arming/disarming wrench, and there was a "hot" propeller just ahead of me. But Buglione, he slid forward like a slide into second base in a baseball game, flat on his stomach. When he got there he had the arming/disarming wrench off his belt and had it on the percussion cap in nothing flat. He buttoned the thing [fuse] off—never got up—laying flat on his stomach, took the thing and threw it backhand. It hit the flight deck once, splashed into the water—bam, it went off, all in less than ten seconds.

As this was happening, the second torpedo bomber had landed. So he saved two torpedo crews, me, himself, and no telling how much damage to the ship.

When I told Commander Crommelin what had happened, he said he was only doing his job. If he hadn't been there, I wouldn't be telling this.

ARM3c Marcus Cummins of VT-12, Goleta, California, remarked about the same incident: "How about the time a TBF landed, opened the bomb-bay doors, and a 500-pounder fell to the flight deck. The little fan started to rotate (keeping it cool?). Everyone left the scene rather quickly except one brave (or flaky) soul who removed the fuse and tossed it into the drink."

The ship's log for 17 February addressed some other flight-deck incidents in a direct and unemotional manner:

1244—Commenced landing aircraft.

1245—Plane type TBM, Bureau No. 20317, piloted by Lt(jg) G. L. Lucas while attempting to land aboard, failed to engage arresting gear and crashed into barriers. Plane was completely demolished and jettisoned; no injury to personnel.

1257—Commenced landing aircraft.

1307—Plane type SB2C, Bureau No. 20831, piloted by Commander R. A. Embree, while attempting to land aboard this vessel, failed to engage arresting gear and crashed into barrier. Plane severely damaged and caught fire. Fire extinguished in about two minutes. Commander Embree suffered second degree burns about the face. His burns about the face and neck were not serious.

They were only serious enough to keep him out of a plane for several days. Commander Embree later became commander of the air group.

Pilots whose planes crashed into the barrier aboard ship had a very high survival rate. At-sea rescues did not have so high a success rate, but every effort was made to save pilots and airmen who could not make it back to the carrier, for whatever reason. We knew that submarines were available to pick us up close to the Japanese coastline. That fact was reassuring as those intrepid souls were often seen on the surface within sight of land. The operations of 16 and 17 February were supported by a rescue submarine off Cape Nojima at the southern end of Tokyo Bay. However, whatever rescue measures were in place, rescue efforts were sometimes inadequate as Mother Nature foiled the best of plans.

Lt. Lou Menard of VBF-12, Florida, was in the vicinity of one rescue attempt. Ens. William T. McAdams of VBF-12 got hit over land on the Tachikawa strike. He made it to the outer reaches of Tokyo Bay and announced, "I'm going to ditch."

According to Lieutenant Menard,

I told him the sub is out there ready to pick him up. Just get out as far as you can.

He ditched about a mile or mile and one-half off the beach right where he was supposed to, except he didn't get out far enough. The submarine started in for him and began churning mud. Someone on the submarine called and said, "I'm running aground. I can't go in any farther."

McAdams landed, had gotten in his life raft, and was fine, but he couldn't buck the wind, and it blew him onto the beach. We flew down low, and I could see people running out of a wooded area and taking hold of him and pulling him back into the trees along the beach.

Lt. Cdr. Frederick Michaelis, the commanding officer of VF-12, was strike leader when Lt. James E. "Buck" Toliver was hit by AA fire that afternoon. The VF-12 combat-action report described what happened:

At Hokada air field Lieutenant James "Buck" Toliver was leading his division in a strafing run when medium caliber anti-aircraft fire disabled his engine. He recovered from his dive, gained altitude and headed for the sea when his power plant failed about five miles offshore due east from Hokada.

He made a successful water landing, broke out his life raft and climbed in. His division continued to orbit, making the prescribed rescue transmissions on VHF and MHF [very high and medium high frequency].

Meanwhile Lieutenant Toliver struggled against the wind and current from the enemy beach. He was too close in, however, to permit entry to a surface vessel or submarine, and too far from the Task Force, which had turned away by this time, to permit a seaplane launch.

Lieutenant Commander Michaelis was, of course, upset that a very fine pilot had been lost when it appeared that he had ditched in an off-the-beach area characterized in the prelaunch briefing as appropriate for rescue. Knowing that basic fleet policy was to do everything possible to rescue downed flight crews, Michaelis drew attention to the loss of Toliver in his report covering this action. A few days later the air-group commander and Michaelis were summoned to report to the task-group commander as soon as operationally possible. Both flew to his flagship, the *Yorktown,* immediately.

The VF-12 skipper explained his concern about the apparent lack of coordinated rescue effort on Toliver's behalf. Crommelin listened in silence, nodding affirmatively occasionally. When he was finished, Admiral Radford, the task-group commander, handed them a shocker. The area in which Toliver had ditched was heavily mined.

A rescue attempt by either a surface ship or a submarine was out of the question. Admiral Radford further reported in succinct and unmistakably clear language that fleet policy with regard to the rescue of flight crews had not changed. He firmly charged his two listeners to personally convey to all flight crews the emphasis that he, Admiral Radford, attached to that policy.

Both Crommelin and Michaelis were impressed with the fact that a small comment in a war-operation report, among hundreds, that could be construed as critical of rescue policy had so quickly reached the attention of the task-group commander and triggered an immediate personal response. The warm feeling of concern was quickly transmitted to all ready rooms. (Many pages of this book carry positive proof of the sanctity of the fleet rescue policy and the morale benefits it engendered among air-group personnel.)

Commander Crommelin's AAR summary for the period covering this incident expressed his concern and recommendation: ". . . I merely feel that any time the parent squadron's pilots can participate in a rescue mission, that there will be no question in the minds of the squadron personnel that everything possible was done to effect a rescue." This recommendation would materialize later for AG 12.

Submarines gave many rescued pilots and aircrewmen a short tour of sea duty under the surface. Destroyers also rescued many airmen in their role as either plane guard during flight operations or as radar picket on the outer perimeter of the task force. Both types of vessel were stationed between the Japanese mainland and the task forces to warn the fleet of approaching enemy aircraft and to pick up airmen of navy and army air corps aircraft forced to ditch at sea.

The destroyer skippers had a number of means they used in this rescue business. If the operation area was considered void of hostile submarines and aircraft, the captains would stop their ships and put a small boat over the side. If they could get close enough to a downed airman, they could use a swimmer to carry a line to the victim. Also at the commanding officer's disposal were line-throwing guns, and in rare instances the destroyer's cargo net could be used to dip pilots out of the water. Whatever the means used, at-sea rescues were hazardous and, when successful, one of the greatest contributions to morale among fleet personnel. Admiral Mitscher was beloved for his daring and tenacity in recovering his downed airmen and for his sincere concern for the naval aviators in the forces he commanded.

Lieutenant Menard, having participated in one rescue attempt that day, became the subject of rescue himself:

The hop on the seventeenth was one in which we started in to hit the Tachikawa Aircraft Engine Factory. Charles Crommelin was leading this flight that, for me, ended in the water when I had to bail out after being hit by AA fire over Yokohama four hours later.

I was around six or seven thousand feet when I got hit. It knocked me into a spin. I got out of the spin and started heading out east over Tokyo Bay, and I spun again. I got out of that about two thousand feet. As I started climbing out, I noticed every time I let my airspeed get below 140 knots, the plane would vibrate and wanted to go into another spin. When I pushed forward on the stick and picked up speed, I managed to stay level.

Then I started to survey my aircraft damage. When I looked out at my right wing, two of the .50-calibers [machine guns] were sitting straight up in the air through a jagged hole in the wing. Ammo was hanging out of the cans and dangling off the wing and breaking away. My right aileron-control rod obviously was broken and causing the plane to veer hard right. If I got below 140 knots, that aileron would flop up, making me go into a severe turn. I came to realize that if I could keep above 140 knots, the aileron would stay streamlined and I could fly fairly well. Also, I got to thinking that I could not come aboard at 140 knots, nor could I land in the water at that speed with the sea as rough as it was.

It was obvious I was going to have to bail out. My radio was knocked out, and I couldn't communicate with anyone. I was also by myself.

I got out over the fleet; somebody joined up with me. I don't know who it was. He could see my problem with those two .50-calibers sticking up in the air.

The reason I'd gotten this way was when we were going out over Tokyo Bay I passed another F6. His right elevator and stabilizer was shot off. (I later found out his name, Jim Cain. He made it back to ship OK.) A couple of Zeros were beginning to come in, so I made a three-sixty [full circle] to kinda escort him out. In that three-sixty is when I got hit by AA fire around the Yokohama Naval Base.

When I got out over the fleet, the guy with me gave the word by hand signals that the picket ship [destroyer] closest to land was standing by for me to bail out, and they would pick me up. I started to get ready to get out of the airplane.

I cranked the canopy back, but it would only open about eight or ten inches. I tried to crank it open a half-dozen times, then I realized that the back side of the fuselage must have been hit and jagged metal was sticking out, so I couldn't open the canopy. Then I rolled it open about an inch and tried to jettison it with the two emergency slide jettisons on the sides of the canopy. The left came out, and the right one didn't. The canopy was flopping in the breeze on the left side. I took my knife and stuck it through the little loop on the right jettison handle and hammered it off with the handle of my pistol. It finally came out that way.

When it finally released, the canopy flew off the right side of the plane, slamming against the fuselage, and the steel cable from the left mechanism pinned me to the seat. I couldn't get out! All this time the plane was going all over the sky as I was trying to fly it with my knees with the stick held way over to the left-hand corner.

I wondered how I was going to get out of this situation. I put my gun back in the holster and took my knife and started scrapping the cable right in front of my chest. One strand would break, then another, and then, finally, all the strands started popping, and the whole cable broke loose. All this took a lifetime of five minutes.

Now I was above the overcast at three thousand to thirty-five hundred feet, and the other pilot was still with me. I sat down and opened my canteen and took a drink of water. My mouth was like a ball of cotton. Well, OK, now I could get out.

I undid my safety belt and got rid of my shoulder straps, and I just barely stood up in the cockpit and dove over the left side. I cleared the plane, then I opened my chute and came down through the clouds. I was about two thousand feet when I broke out under the clouds. I looked around, and I could see the destroyer there at a distance. I started looking down to see how close I was to the water and went through my water-landing procedure of getting out of the parachute harness.

In the process of getting out of the airplane, one CO_2 toggle of my Mae West got pulled and inflated half the vest. It made the harness so tight I couldn't get my thumbs in back of the chest strap to get it undone. I had also tightened my leg straps before I bailed out, and that was a mistake because I couldn't get my fingers underneath the buckles on my leg straps to get those undone either.

All the time I had been flying, I got the parachute riggers to tack my seat cushion to the risers in the pack so my cushion would be in my harness. That was a mistake because when the chute opened, the cushion was between those risers up above my head and prevented me from getting my arms around those risers in back. The standard procedure to get out of the harness, when you are ready to hit the water, is by throwing your arms back and slipping out of the harness. I couldn't do that. The wind was so strong the chute didn't collapse when I hit the water, and it kept pulling me downwind through the water.

I was so heavy that I would go through a wave, then I would come to the trough, then I would skip along again. I thought, well, if I time my breathing and get in sync with the trough and the waves, I might last long enough for the tin can to pick me up.

I did that as long as I could, and then my timing, my breathing, got out of sync with the waves, and the last thing I remember was I was looking up at the surface of the water about four or five feet above me, and I had to take a breath. I took a breath, and it was just like a rheostat turning the lights out. It was the way I went out.

The destroyer USS *Taussig* (DD 746), commanded by Cdr. Josephus A. Robbins, was on radar-picket station when Lieutenant Menard's problems began. An eyewitness on the *Taussig* described the rescue:

We were cruising with carrier Task Force 58 some one hundred miles east-southeast of Tokyo, marking time, awaiting the return of our planes. It was just a very ordinary afternoon. The temperature was about fifty degrees, wind twenty-two knots was coming from the northeast, water temperature was sixty degrees.

Then the radio on the bridge opened up: A fighter pilot was about to parachute from his plane directly ahead of the task group. All destroyers were to standby to rescue.

It wasn't hard to spot the plane. It was flying broad circles several miles ahead at an altitude of about two thousand feet. For long minutes the circling continued. Was he unable to get out, because of the high speed he was maintaining, or was he taking his time, screwing up his courage a bit before he got out and walked?

Then, it happened. The plane was about a mile away, broad on our port bow, when the shiny white parachute burst open ahead of us. The plane headed in our direction, then turned away in a graceful bank that soon became a spin, and crashed into the water.

Already we were on our way. Assuming that the pilot would be able to unfasten the parachute when he landed and, therefore, would remain fairly stationary in the water, we headed for a point slightly upwind from where he would hit the water, expecting to let the wind drift us to him after we stopped.

The pilot was falling fast, five hundred feet to go, a hundred, then he hit, and hit hard. Immediately it became apparent that he was unable to free himself of the parachute because it was pulling him away from us. "Left full rudder," ordered the skipper. In an instant he realized that the situation had reversed itself. Instead of drifting downwind to the pilot, the pilot would have to drift to us. Instead of going to a point upwind from where the pilot was, we would have to reverse course and head for a point downwind from where he was. It was roughly equivalent to "man bites dog."

The pilot was a pitiful sight, completely helpless behind his parachute, held under by over fifty pounds of equipment much of the time and apparently lifeless the rest of the time. The equipment consisted largely of survival gear, tinned foods, an inflatable rubber boat, fresh water, etc. It was ironic that those articles designed to save his life were now threatening to take it.

Though it seemed like hours, it was only a matter of minutes before we were to leeward of the parachute fifty yards ahead of it. "All engines back full," the skipper ordered, and with almost uncanny seamanship he brought the ship to a stop just at the instant when the parachute reached the most advantageous spot from which to make a rescue, amidships.

In a few seconds the pilot was hoisted aboard, lifted up by the shrouds of the chute to which he was still securely buckled. He was unconscious and had ceased breathing, his heart action was feeble, his face and fingertips were already blue.

The medical officer of the *Taussig,* Dr. Blankenship, lost no time. Without delaying even long enough to remove the flying equipment, the doctor right on the deck began applying artificial respiration.

Lt. (j.g.) George Blankenship, the ship's physician, Neosho, Missouri, had come on deck as Lieutenant Menard was hoisted aboard. He immediately began artificial respiration, but the maneuver was futile, as Dr. Blankenship expressed it, "because of all the groceries he was wearing."

He continued:

The pilot was technically dead. There was no respiration, no pulse, and his face and hands were blue. I directed the rescue crewmen surrounding him to cut away the parachute harness. This was done expeditiously with sharp knives that sailors always seemed to have about them.

I began working on the pilot, again. After about five minutes his color had begun to return, and he managed some breathing on his own. A little later, he opened one eye, and I told him he was on board the destroyer *Taussig.*

Another five minutes, and Menard had regained consciousness. The crisis had definitely passed. He was carried to an officer's stateroom, his wet clothes removed, and he was placed in a bunk. A half hour later he had regained control of his faculties and identified himself.

The next morning over a cup of strong navy coffee Lieutenant Menard was describing how Tokyo looked from a Hellcat, and that afternoon he was returned to the *Randolph.* Then he met with Commander Crommelin and the air group's flight surgeon, Lt. Rees Anderson, Salt Lake City, Utah. According to the latter: "When Lieutenant Menard, Commander Crommelin, and I met in sick bay several days after his dramatic rescue, he was still shook up, confused, and not the least bit enthusiastic about returning to combat! He was physically OK, but I recommended that he be returned to the states for R & R. Commander Crommelin outranked me (by several stripes), but he never ever questioned my medical opinion and had orders written up for Menard pronto." Menard had used up all of his good luck accumulated in two previous tours of combat and returned to the States.

Further tribute must be made to these destroyer crews. A rescue of another pilot by the *Taussig* the day before Menard's is another perfect example of the determination of these people to save downed pilots. Seaman First Frank H. Applegate, Manasquan, New Jersey, a member of the *Taussig's* rescue team, having described Lieutenant Menard's rescue, recalled his rescue of Ens. George Salvaggio of VF-17, USS *Hornet* (CV 19), the day before:

The morning of 16 February 1945, two days before my twentieth birthday, was cold and blustery. The sea was extremely rough as I stood at my battle station aboard the destroyer. Just after daybreak, in spite of the rough seas, our planes began taking off from their carriers.

All morning our ship plunged in and out of intermittent snow squalls. My station was at mount 41 on the wing of the bridge.

Just before I was to be relieved from duty at noon, we left the aircraft and submarine screen and pulled behind a carrier, which was recovering aircraft returning from their strike over the Tokyo Bay area. I stood on the wing of the bridge, watching the carrier land planes, when there was a minor accident on deck, which made it necessary to wave off the next planes attempting to land.

We were monitoring conversations between the pilots and the carrier, and I heard one pilot say, "I'll never make it around again because I'm out of gas!" He climbed some, then his engine stopped, and he glided to a landing in the water between our destroyer and the carrier.

Our skipper alerted the plane-crash party, which included me, and attempted to maneuver our ship close to the downed pilot. The approach was not good, but it was the best he could do under the circumstances.

As I climbed over the face of the bridge I started dropping my foul-weather gear. I arrived on deck, wearing a Mark II navy knife and an engineer's life belt, not a life jacket. Word was passed down to put a swimmer in the water when we were close.

The chief boatswain's mate handed me a swimming lifeline so they could pull me back to the ship. I put it over my shoulder and stepped into the sea. The windchill that day fluctuated between twenty-nine and thirty-nine degrees.

After I swam about two hundred yards I was numb with cold, exhausted, and had lost all sense of direction. I tried to inflate my life belt only to find that someone had stolen the CO_2 bottles.

I raised my body out of the water as far as I could and spotted the pilot approximately forty yards away. I hollered to him to swim toward me. He responded, "I can't, I'm hurt." I uttered a simple prayer: "Dear Lord, give me the strength to reach that man while he's still alive."

Immediately, my muscles began to respond to command, and my limbs began to propel me through the water. With increasing strength and speed I reached the young flier and told him to roll over on his back. I never saw a naval officer so anxious to take orders from a seaman, for he responded instantly.

I signaled the ship to pull me back alongside. The *Taussig* was lying dead in the water and rolling heavily from side to side. Because of his injuries, the pilot could not climb out of the water under his own power. When the ship rolled to the starboard side, I got him across my shoulders and caught the bottom rung of the Jacob's ladder with my feet. I had one arm between his legs and the other arm between his arm and neck. In this fashion when the ship rolled back the other way I was able to lift him out of the water and climb the six or eight rungs up the ladder until the men on deck could grab hold of him.

I climbed out of the water under my own power. The ship's doctor took the pilot to the wardroom to undress and care for him. He ordered the chief pharmacist's mate to tend to "Applejack," my nickname. The sick bay, located right above the engine room, was too hot for me, so I retreated to the companionway, where there was heat from the firerooms, yet the wind was blowing through there. My friends rubbed me with towels, wrapped me in blankets, and supplied me with coffee. The pharmacists's mate took my blood pressure, then went into sick bay and got a bottle. He returned and said, "Applejack, drink all of this you can drink comfortably." I drank about a pint of hard whiskey, which warmed me up and raised my blood pressure.

After this I went below deck and got into a shower under the supervision of a pharmacist's mate. I started off with cold water and increased it slowly to warm. As my body temperature rose I became woozy, dressed, and went to the mess deck. The pharmacist's mate ordered the cook of the watch to fix me something to eat, but he refused. However, both the medical officer and the commanding officer soon changed his mind.

I ate a big steak and four or five eggs. I went down to my bunk and fell asleep while the pharmacist's mate periodically checked my body temperature and blood pressure. I slept until the following morning, when I awoke, suffering no ill effects.

This, in itself, was miraculous because in such cold water a human is supposed to be able to survive for only five minutes, and I was in the water at least eight.

Secretary of the Navy James Forrestal awarded Applegate the Navy and Marine Corps Medal for his performance on this rescue. His citation read,

For heroic conduct in rescuing a downed Pilot of a carrier-based plane which had landed in the water near the USS *Taussig,* during operations against enemy Japanese forces off the Coast of Japan, February 16, 1945. Despite extremely cold weather and great danger involved, APPLEGATE jumped into the rough seas and carried a line over two hundred yards from the ship to the dazed and exhausted pilot, thereby saving the man's life. His courage and unselfish concern for the welfare of another were in keeping with the highest traditions of the United States Naval service.

Applegate was a natural for rescuing downed pilots at sea. He grew up learning to cope with the cold Atlantic water off the New Jersey coast and frequently swam out a mile or more to test his stamina. When asked if the navy provided the man-overboard detail something resembling modern-day wet suits, he smiled and replied, "My Mark II knife and engineer life belt was it." Then after a slight pause he added, "Including my own personal jockstrap, of course."

Many pilots did not make the trip home. So often no one knew what happened to them. They were listed as missing in action and later declared dead. On one occasion, Lt. (j.g.) Dan A. Carmichael of VBF-12, Columbus, Ohio, did see what occurred in the loss of Ens. William N. "Mac" McConnell, on a flight of fighters covering the bomber strike on Tachikawa:

On 17 February Mac was assigned as a standby pilot for our mission. My wingman aborted due to a malfunctioning engine, and Mac was put in the air to take his place as my wingman. He was an excellent pilot; he held his position easily and smoothly, and I was completely comfortable with him on my wing.

Our approach to the target was quite uneventful, except for the extreme cold, with many fighters reporting frozen prop governors. As we reached the coast there were enemy fighters rolling around our formation and lining up, but in no large numbers and well outside our strike group. It soon became apparent that they would probably attack us after our pullout at low altitude, where the enemy fighters had their highest performance and were at their best. I believe there was another strike group near us, and we were never certain which group they would attack.

Our mission plan called for the low-cover fighter-escort group to attack the target-area antiaircraft gun emplacements with rockets and strafing. They were to dive down just ahead of the dive-bombers in order to both suppress the AA fire and also to draw the AA fire away from the dive-bombers, which, with dive brakes out in their dive, were a much slower and easier target.

As the lead dive-bomber approached the dive point, it became quite apparent that the low-cover escort was in no position to lead the dive-bombers down, due to either frozen prop governors or bad positioning. We were in excellent position, so I requested and received permission to lead the bombers down. We passed the bombers in their dive just after they had pushed over, so by luck we were in perfect position to run interference for them.

Mac was close on my wing when our dive began. I continued down to a very low altitude, using rockets and strafing against the AA gun positions, which were easily identified at that low altitude. Due to our extremely high speed at pullout, I knew we were going to be too far ahead of the dive-bombers to help them after their pullout, so I began a gradual "S" turn in order to drop back to the bombers. At this time enemy fighters were making contact, although most of them seemed to be engaged with another strike group rather than ours.

I looked around for Mac and found that he had become widely separated from me; he was off to my right about two to three miles and ahead of the leading dive-bomber. This separation is understandable because he probably selected his own targets during our rocket and strafing run. Also, he may have taken evasive action to avoid AA ground fire after pullout from the dive. I was not immediately concerned because the distance was not much at the speed we were moving.

However, just as I started to call Mac to join up on me, I saw an enemy fighter go by him at very high speed. The enemy plane had evidently made a run on a dive-bomber and was pulling ahead in order to climb back for another attack. He did not seem to fire at Mac, and I don't know why, it's possible that he just wasn't looking and didn't see Mac until it was too late.

As soon as I saw the enemy plane I told Mac to break left toward me, but it all happened so fast that the enemy fighter was passed before he could react. The enemy fighter pulled up into a vertical climb right in front of him, and Mac pulled up after him. I immediately called and told him to break away and not follow the enemy plane. I was at full throttle in a hard right turn, trying to get there in time.

Perhaps Mac did not hear me, perhaps my transmission was garbled by another, perhaps he felt he was committed and would be in a more difficult position if he broke off, or perhaps he was just determined to see it through. Whatever the reason, Mac continued the high-speed climb and pulled through nicely toward the inverted position on top, probably thinking to roll out in an Immelmann turn. The enemy pilot had reached the inverted position well ahead of Mac, whereupon he rolled out one-third and into a tight right turn and pulled around behind Mac just as he reached the inverted position. The enemy pilot's turn appeared to be so tight and the radius so short that he undoubtedly had dropped his flaps as he started his rollout.

The enemy pilot continued to roll into the nearly inverted position and opened fire, very close in. He was flying a plane that was code-named Frank. It was a derivative of the German Focke-Wulf 190 and according to the book *WW II Fighter Aircraft*. In postwar analysis it was rated at least equal to any Allied fighter. And make no mistake, this was a highly skilled and experienced pilot—he knew exactly what he was doing.

Mac's plane was hit by a hail of what appeared to be both cannon and machine-gun ammo. There was no fire or smoke, but small pieces of the plane did break away. I was sure then and still am sure that Mac died instantly. There was simply no possible survival in that cone of intense gunfire. His plane fell off on one wing and began to drop earthward. There was no attempt at recovery.

I could not continue to watch because I was now close to the incident, and the enemy pilot had spotted me. We were coming into a head-on firing run. There followed a somewhat long and difficult dogfight that wound up literally at tree-top level. I finally managed to get on his tail very, very close, and I unloaded with everything I had. I remember being quite surprised that there was no sign of smoke or fire from his plane, although some pieces did break off. The fight ended abruptly when my gunfire apparently caused almost the entire tail assembly to separate (narrowly missing me when it broke away), and the plane disintegrated into the ground on the outskirts of Tokyo.

This was the twelfth enemy plane that I had shot down and the only one toward which I had any strong personal feeling.

The Thunderbird's tally for this day was not as good as the sixteenth. We lost three pilots while only shooting four Japanese planes out of the air. However, many parked aircraft and ground facilities were destroyed.

Commander Crommelin, commander of Air Group 12, pins the Distinguished Flying Cross on Lt. Hamilton McWhorter. These two, and other experienced veterans "who had been there," provided combat leadership for the younger pilots of Fighting Squadron 12. McWhorter was the first Hellcat pilot to shoot down ten Japanese aircraft and was among the top fifteen Hellcat aces in the navy. (U.S. Navy)

Cdr. Charles L. Crommelin, commander of Air Group 12. (U.S. Navy)

AIR GROUP 12

Cdr. Noel A. Gayler,
commanding officer of Fighting
Squadron 12. (U.S. Navy)

FIGHTING SQUADRON 12

Cdr. Ralph Embree,
commanding officer of
Bombing Squadron 12. (U.S.
Navy)

BOMBING SQUADRON 12

Lt. Cdr. Thomas "Tex" Ellison, commanding officer of Torpedo Squadron 12. (U.S. Navy)

TORPEDO SQUADRON 12

Lt. Cdr. Edward Pawka, commanding officer of Fighter-Bomber Squadron 12. (U.S. Navy)

FIGHTER-BOMBER SQUADRON 12

The USS *Ranger,* as seen from the rear cockpit of an SBD Dauntless shortly after takeoff. More SBDs and F4Fs are ready for launch. This veteran of the North Africa Campaign was the first ship built from the keel up as an aircraft carrier. Pilots of Air Group 12, having qualified in day landings aboard her, finished night-landing qualification in December 1944, less than a month before deploying to combat. (National Archives)

Ensigns Lew Colin, Bud Hintz, and Jack Schipper and Lt. (j.g.) Bob
Green (left to right) give one of the new F6F-5s a washdown prior to
waxing at Naval Auxiliary Air Station, Ream Field. They had heard the
procedure would add a few extra knots of airspeed to the Hellcat, and
they wanted that. (U.S. Navy Photo by Tony Remkus)

Capt. Felix Baker watches flight-deck operations from the USS
Randolph's bridge. To judge by the heavy bridge coat Captain Baker is
wearing and the murky weather conditions, this photo was probably
taken during the first Tokyo raids starting on 16 February 1945.
(National Archives)

FIFTH FLEET
Admiral Spruance in Heavy Cruiser Indianapolis
TASK FORCE 58
Vice Admiral Mitscher in Carrier Bunker Hill

CARRIER TASK GROUPS

	58.1 Clark	58.2 Davison	58.3 F.C. Sherman	58.4 Radford	58.5 Gardner
Commanders					
Carrier	Hornet Wasp Bennington	Lexington Hancock	Essex Bunker Hill	Yorktown Randolph	Enterprise Saratoga
Light Carrier	Belleau Wood	San Jacinto	Cowpens	Langley Cabot	
Battleship	Mass. Indiana	Wisconsin Missouri	S. Dakota New Jersey	Washington N. Carolina	
Battle Cruiser			Alaska		
Heavy Cruiser	Vincennes	San Francisco Boston	Indianapolis		Baltimore
Light Cruiser	Miami San Juan		Pasadena Wilkes Barre Astoria	Santa Fe Biloxi San Diego	Flint
Destroyer	15	19	14	17	12

Task Force 58, composed of five task groups for the first time, provided CAPs at night and night-heckler TBMs for the carrier raid over Tokyo. (Source: Samuel Eliot Morison, *History of United States Naval Operations in World War II*, vol xiv *Victory in the Pacific, 1945*. Boston: Little, Brown and Company, 1960, 1975, p. 21)

This view from the *Randolph* at anchor in Ulithi Atoll reveals part of Task Force 58's carriers, often referred to as "Mitscher's Row." The *Essex*-class carriers can be distinguished by the pyramid-looking islands, as compared with the square or block-looking island structures of the *Saratoga* and *Enterprise*. (U.S. Navy)

Lt. Cdr. Frederick H. Michaelis, commanding officer of VF-12, succeeding Cdr. Noel A. Gayler. (U.S. Navy)

Strike results on Konoike Airfield, a medium bomber base forty miles east of Tokyo, photographed after a raid on 16 February 1945. The plumes of smoke are from burning aircraft. The wavy patterns near the runways are truck tracks on the lightly snow covered field. (National Archives)

VB-12's dive-bombers lined up for a deck launch. The SB2C Helldiver carried its bomb load internally, as opposed to its slower predecessor, the SBD Dauntless of Midway fame, which carried the bomb load externally. (National Archives)

VB-12 aircrewman ARM1c Alfred Smith, ringleader of the enlisted "airdales" in their ready room, was charged with the responsibility of rationing postflight "tension reliever" to the flight crew members after combat missions. (U.S. Navy)

Lt. James E. "Buck" Toliver of VF-12 was listed as missing after ditching his damaged Hellcat, following a fighter sweep east of the Tokyo area on 17 February. He survived the ditching but drifted ashore and was taken prisoner. (U.S. Navy)

A jammed and malfunctioning canopy-jettison system compounded Lieutenant Menard's problems with his damaged Hellcat while orbiting over the *Taussig*. Ironically, his survival gear also brought him perilously close to death's door. (Drawing by Robert A. Keeton)

Lieutenant Menard's parachute dragged him through the waves. The seat cushion (circled) prevented his leaving the chute upon entering the rough water. His survival gear is just left of the circle. He is several feet underwater. (U.S. Navy, courtesy USS *Taussig*)

Survivors Ensign Salvaggio of VF-17 (left) and Lieutenant Menard (right) with Seaman First Class Frank Applegate, on the deck of the USS *Taussig* following their rescue, on 16 and 17 February, respectively. Applegate was awarded the Navy–Marine Corps Medal for his heroic swim to save Salvaggio the previous day. (U.S. Navy, courtesy USS *Taussig*)

Lt. Cdr. Tex Ellison, commanding officer of VT-12 (left foreground), and pilots present Ens. Floyd E. Hall (standing) with a cake commemorating the 3,000th landing aboard the *Randolph,* made on 13 February 1945. This ceremony was observed as the ship was heading into combat. Ensign Hall and his aircrewmen, AOM3 Glenn J. Frazier and ARM3 Marve Mershon, were shot down five days later during a raid on Chichi Jima and declared missing in action. (U.S. Navy, courtesy Tex Ellison)

(Top) Commander Embree's SB2C Helldiver just moments before crashing into the (cable) barrier on 17 February. The impact separated the engine and the prop. Ruptured fuel lines spewed fuel over the hot engine, and the aircraft burst into flames. (Bottom) Within seconds the fire-rescue crew was on the starboard wing, extracting the pilot and aircrewman. The SB2C was completely engulfed in flames, but the pilot suffered comparatively minor burns to face, neck, and wrists. (National Archives)

Lt. (j.g.) Bud Hewlett (left), VF-12's air combat information officer, debriefing pilots from a support strike on Iwo Jima in February 1945. They are (left to right) Lt. Lane Bardeen, Ens. Tex Hardin, and Lt. Hal Vita. All three pilots were wearing G-suits, which reduced the risk of blacking out in tight turns. (U.S. Navy, courtesy John Franks)

The *Saratoga*'s forward flight deck (top) was a jumble of fire and debris sustained from a half dozen kamikaze attackers. One hundred twenty-three crew members were killed, and 192 were wounded. The near-fatal attack that blasted the huge hole in the starboard hull (inset) put the ship out of commission until August. (National Archives)

The ship's medics gave assistance to wounded personnel within minutes of the explosion and fire from the bomb-laden kamikaze on the evening of 11 March 1945. Fortunately, most of the ship's company and air-group personnel were just leaving the forward hangar deck area after the movie and were several hundred feet from the impact area. (National Archives)

Admiral Spruance (left), strategic commander of Task Force 58, inspects the *Randolph*'s kamikaze damage. He concurred with Captain Baker (center) in the decision to keep the *Randolph* at Ulithi for repairs rather than return the ship to Pearl Harbor or stateside. The officer to Baker's left is Commander Neblett, executive officer of the *Randolph*. (National Archives)

The repair ship USS *Jason* is moored alongside the *Randolph* to replace the flight gallery and deck damaged by a kamikaze on the night of 11 March 1945. The aerial photo (top) was taken early in the cleanup stage. Only moderate damage to the flight deck was sustained, as compared with the complete destruction of the hangar deck (bottom). The arrow and broken line indicate the flight path of the kamikaze as it struck just below the flight deck. (National Archives)

On 19 March 1945 the *Franklin* disgorged flaming gasoline and torrents of water (top) from the hangar deck as her captain turned the ship hard starboard, a turn that very well may have saved his ship. Several days later the *Franklin* managed to get under way on her own power (bottom) en route to Ulithi. Twenty-one pilots of Air Group 12 were former members of Air Group 5 aboard the *Franklin* and lost many friends in the holocaust. (National Archives)

The USS *Intrepid,* in her first day of combat after rejoining the task force, was hit a glancing blow by a kamikaze on fire. In spite of the apparent fierceness of the fire and smoke, she controlled her fire damage and was operational within an hour. (National Archives)

A smoldering mass of metal, this aircraft engine and prop are all that remain on the hangar of the USS *Wasp* after a kamikaze attack on 19 March 1945. Intense heat from fires also warped the number three elevator shaft, thereby limiting flight operations. However, the carrier remained on line for another week, supporting the Okinawa campaign prior to returning to Pearl Harbor for repairs. The *Wasp* was the fifth *Essex*-class carrier damaged in two days of combat. (National Archives)

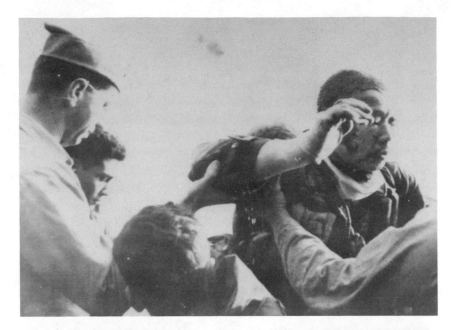

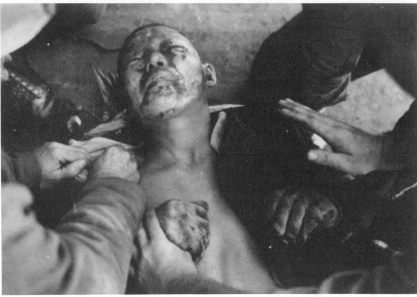

On 6 April 1945 kamikaze pilot Sata Omaiti (IJN) bailed out of his aircraft when damaged by antiaircraft fire and was pulled aboard the USS *Taussig*. A crewman removes his revolver (top). He was treated for superficial wounds (bottom) and then transferred to the *Hornet* for interrogation. The pilot bragged of an impending attack on 11 April—a claim that proved to be true, but on 12 April. He was later reported to die of injuries. (U.S. Navy/USS *Taussig*, courtesy Pat Repoli [top] and Geo. Blankenship [bottom])

The USS *Hancock*'s damage-control crew fights fires started by a kamikaze. The fires were under control in time to recover the carrier's returning aircraft. However, the damage limited the ship's operations such that she was ordered to Hawaii for repairs. (U.S. Navy)

Lt. C. Hamilton and crew exit from their downed TBM after engine failure on takeoff. The USS *Erben* picked the crew up and had them back aboard in just over two hours. This procedure was repeated thirteen days later—again, they were picked up by the *Erben*. (National Archives)

Ens. Jay Finley of VF-12 spent five days on a wild rubber-raft ride before being rescued in the open sea by a VPB-18 Martin Mariner, fairly close to where he was shot down. (U.S. Navy, courtesy Jay Finley)

Commander Embree, commanding officer of VB-12 and later commander of the air group, poses with an antiaircraft hit he sustained on a bombing run. He was later lost to another antiaircraft hit over Okinawa while leading a close-air-support mission. (U.S. Navy, courtesy Tony Remkus)

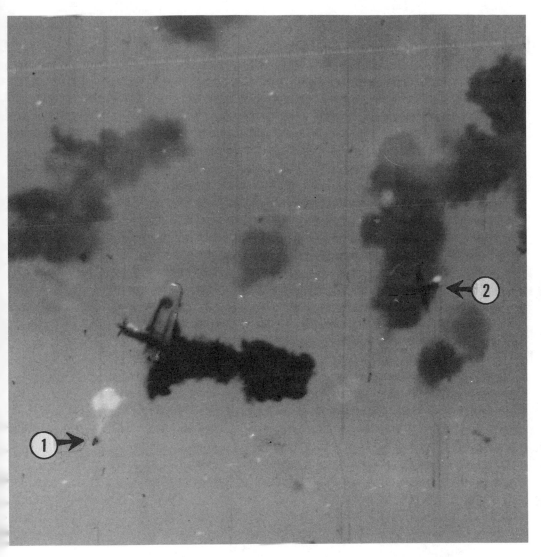

In this first confirmed "kill" by the *Randolph's* gunners, a direct hit was scored on one wing and tail section. What was unusual about the kill was that the pilot bailed out and was photographed (circle 1) just prior to entering the water. Supposedly, kamikaze pilots did not wear parachutes. The bright streaks (circle 2) were the tail section blown off by a killing burst of shrapnel from a proximity-fused 5-inch shell that hit the aircraft. The lethal range of this shell was approximately seventy-five feet. The vertical streaks were falling, still-smoldering shrapnel. The white dots were portions of the exploding shell. (U.S. Navy)

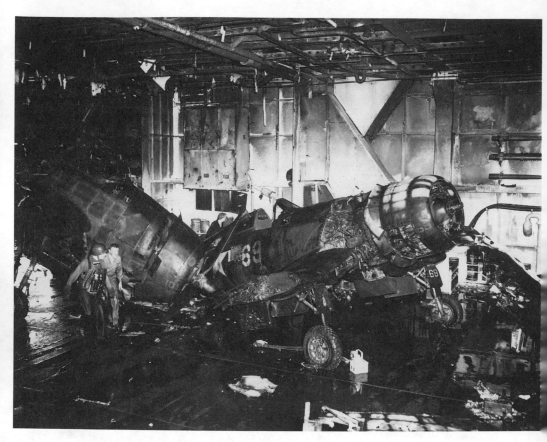

Damage-control personnel work their way past a TBM that has collapsed
onto the tail section of an equally damaged F4U on the hangar deck of
the USS *Intrepid* on 16 April. Once more, heat generated from the
burning aircraft severely warped the number three elevator shaft,
knocking the ship out of action for the third time during the war.
Kamikaze pilots were instructed to dive on the forward or aft elevators
because damaging them would prevent our carriers from operating
aircraft. (National Archives)

AIRCRAFT ACTION REPORT

I. GENERAL

DECLASSIFIED   CONFIDENTIAL

(a) Unit Reporting __VF-12__   (b) Based on or at __USS Randolph (CV-15)__ (c) Report No. __VF-12-26__

(d) Take off: Date __17 April 1945__ Time (LZT) __0616 (I)__ (Zone); Lat. __26-40N__ Long. __129-32E__
Scramble CAP & Sweep of TOKUNO SHIMA & KIKAI
(e) Mission __SHIMA, AMAMI GUNTO, NANSEI SHOTO__   (f) Time of Return __1013 (I)__ (Zone)

II. OWN AIRCRAFT OFFICIALLY COVERED BY THIS REPORT.

TYPE (a)	SQUADRON (b)	NUMBER TAKING OFF (c)	NUMBER ENGAGING ENEMY A/C (d)	NUMBER ATTACKING TARGET (e)	BOMBS AND TORPEDOES CARRIED (PER PLANE) (f)	FUZE, SETTING (g)
F6F-5	VF-12	8	8	-	-	-

III. OTHER U. S. OR ALLIED AIRCRAFT EMPLOYED IN THIS OPERATION.

TYPE	SQUADRON	NUMBER	BASE	TYPE	SQUADRON	NUMBER	BASE
None							

IV. ENEMY AIRCRAFT OBSERVED OR ENGAGED (By Own Aircraft Listed in II Only).

(a) TYPE	(b) NO OBSERVED	(c) NO ENGAGING OWN A/C	(d) TIME ENCOUNTERED	(e) LOCATION OF ENCOUNTER	(f) BOMBS, TORPEDOES CARRIED; GUNS OBSERVED	(g) CAMOUFLAGE AND MARKING
FRANK	8	8	0830(I) (ZONE)	South of Kikai Shima	--	
OSCAR	6	6	0830(I) (ZONE)	South of Kikai Shima	--	
			(ZONE)			

(h) Apparent Enemy Mission(s) __Attack vs either OKINAWA or Task Force 58__

Did Any Part of
(i) Encounter(s) Occur in Clouds? __No__ (YES OR NO) If so, Describe Clouds _____ (BASE IN FEET. TYPE AND TENTHS OF COVER)

Time of Day and Brilliance
(j) of Sun or Moon _____ (NIGHT. BRIGHT MOON; DAY, OVERCAST; ETC.) _____ (k) Visibility _____ (MILES)

V. ENEMY AIRCRAFT DESTROYED OR DAMAGED IN AIR (By Own Aircraft Listed in II Only).

(a) TYPE ENEMY A/C	(b) DESTROYED OR DAMAGED BY: TYPE A/C	SQUADRON	PILOT OR GUNNER	GUNS USED	(c) WHERE HIT, ANGLE	(d) DAMAGE CLAIMED
FRANK	F6F-5	VF-12	Lt.Cdr.F.H.MICHAELIS,USN	6x.50	Eng., 3, level	Destroyed
FRANK	"	"	" " "	6x.50	Eng., 12, level	"
GEORGE	"	"	" " "	2x.50	Fus.. 6, above	"
FRANK	"	"	Lt., H.B. VITA, USNR	6x.50	Fus.. 6. level	"
FRANK	"	"	En., T.J.NORTHCUTT,USNR	6x.50	C'pit,6-8,level-above	"
TOJO	"	"	" " "	6x.50	Fus..wing,6, level	"
FRANK	"	"	EN., E.RAFFERTY, USNR	4x.50	Eng., 12, level	"
OSCAR	"	"	En., E.S.MASSEY, USNR	6x.50	Fus., wg.roots, 6, level	"
OSCAR	"	"	Lt., H.E. Vita, USNR	6x.50	C'pit, 6, Hi above	"
OSCAR	"	"	" " "	6x.50	Eng.&C'pit,6, 90° dive	"
OSCAR	"	"	Lt.L.E.THOMPSON,Jr.USN	6x.50	Wg root, 4, level	"
OSCAR	"	"	Lt(jg)R.D.GATLIN, USNR	6x.50	C'pit,7 6, level	"
OSCAR	"	"	Ens.E.RAFFERTY, USNR	4x.50	Tail,Fus., 6, above	"
OSCAR	"	"	Ens. E.H. BALL, USNR	6x.50	Fus.,tail, 6, above	"

ALLSET — MFB. BY THE EGRY REGISTER CO., PATENTED

Aircraft Action Report No. VF-12-26 for 17 April 1945, as originally filed by Lt. Cdr. Frederick H. Michaelis, commanding officer of VF-12, and Lt. (j.g.) H. W. Hewlett, the squadron's air combat intelligence officer. It is page one of a five-page report and includes enemy aircraft destroyed or damaged in the air, the amount of ordnance expended, and a narrative of the action. These reports were required of the flight leaders. In this instance, eight VF-12 Hellcats destroyed fourteen enemy fighters south of Kikai. (U.S. Navy Historical Center)

Ens. W. L. Mason of VF-12 lost control of his Hellcat while landing. As he veered left, the right wing tip struck the barrier, and the aircraft became inverted as it flipped over the port side, sinking immediately. A tailhook failure (arrow shows it missing) caused this unfortunate operational loss on 18 April 1945. (National Archives)

A motley crew of Crommelin's Thunderbirds thoroughly enjoying the fact that they'd just tossed Crommelin (left, squatting) into the surf at Mog Mog, Ulithi Atoll, during a brief rest and recreation time following the Tokyo raids. Even during the dunking, Crommelin could not be separated from his proverbial cigar. (U.S. Navy, courtesy Tony Remkus)

Ens. Lowell Rund was only slightly burned when his 150-gallon belly tank exploded after being projected through the prop blades during an arrested landing (1). He was still in the cockpit (2). The *Randolph*'s fire fighters assisted him after he was extricated and the fires were under control (3). (U.S. Navy)

USS RANDOLPH
CV-15

Essex-class carriers were all basically the same. The USS *Randolph* was
number eleven of the series. These ships could accommodate up to one
hundred aircraft but usually carried about ninety. (Courtesy of Antony
Preston, *Aircraft Carriers,* Brompton Books Limited, 1979)

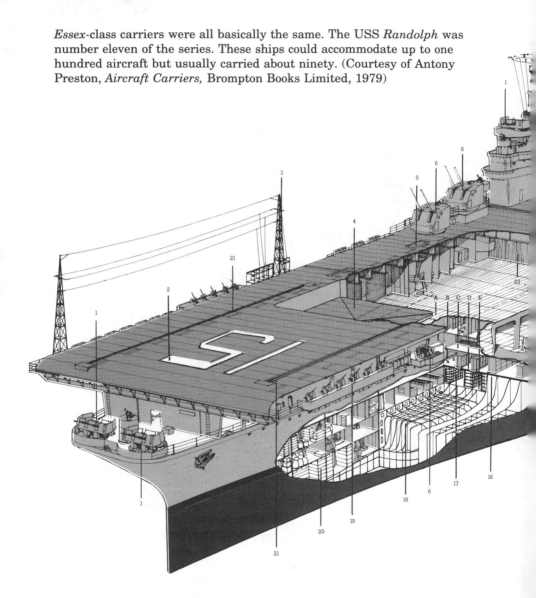

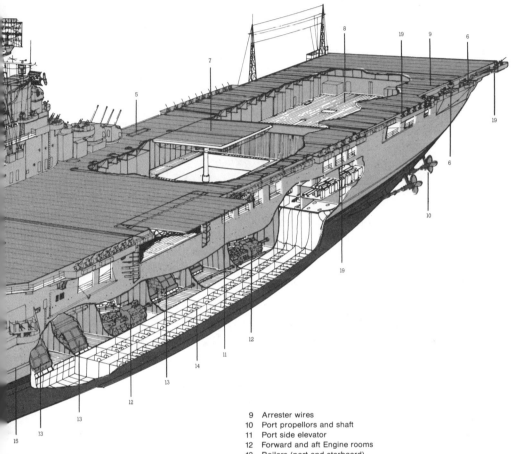

GEND:
   Quadruple 40mm Bofors AA guns
   Deck recognition number (also aft)
   Radio masts (horizontal during flying)
   Forward aircraft elevator (lowered)
   Bomb lift
   5-inch dual-purpose guns (twin and single)
   Aft aircraft elevator (raised)
   Aircraft hangar deck (full length)

awn from the original plans by John A. Roberts.

Twenty-four Hellcats prepare to deck launch for a fighter sweep over Kyushu as the *Randolph* turns port into the wind. Two F4U Corsairs, which found a temporary home, are included. It was standard operating procedure to land aboard another carrier with a "ready deck" when low on fuel or in an emergency. (National Archives)

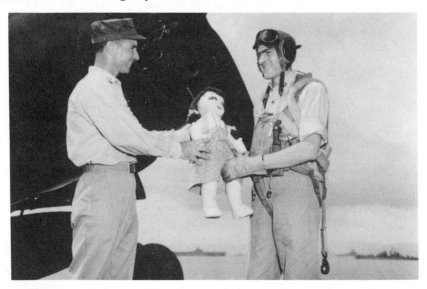

Lieutenant Bureau, the ordnance officer of VB-12, presented this tongue-in-cheek doll award to Lieutenant Bolduc following Bolduc's five kills in one flight, although only four were confirmed. Bureau's work on the napalm problem enabled pilots to realize the full potential of this deadly weapon. He had already been commended for his improvements in the ring-tail aerial torpedo used successfully against the *Yamato*. (U.S. Navy)

With huge clouds of black smoke erupting from amidships, the USS
Bunker Hill writhes in agony, turning 180 degrees away from the task
group's course to control fires on her hangar deck. This photo was taken
from the *Randolph* just minutes after the *Bunker Hill* was struck by two
kamikazes. The *Randolph's* 20-mm gunners gaze skyward to see if any
more kamikazes lurk in the clouds overhead. The Hellcat in the right
foreground is manned and ready to be catapulted if needed. (National
Archives)

Pilots evacuating their ready room suffocated in the adjoining
passageways. (U.S. Navy)

At 0642 on 14 May 1945 the USS *Enterprise,* abeam the *Randolph,* received a kamikaze near the forward flight-deck elevator. The bombs penetrated through to the hangar deck, causing massive explosions. The force of the explosions (upper photo) catapulted the elevator four hundred feet into the air (circle). It just missed the ship on the way down. Many survivors blown over the side used it to stay afloat while awaiting rescue. The damage to the elevator and hangar decks was so extensive as to require her return stateside for repairs (inset). (U.S. Navy [upper], National Archives [inset])

Upon return to the *Astoria,* Lieutenant Tanner and Lieutenant (j.g.) Comb and their rescued passengers were taken aboard first, by landing in an area smoothed by the *Astoria's* making of a 270-degree turn, then approaching a wire mesh sled towed behind the ship. Once hooked to the sled by a "J" hook on the keel of the float plane, it was attached to a crane hoist. The plane was then lifted aboard the cruiser, placed on the catapult, and readied for another mission. (U.S. Navy, courtesy Donald Comb, USS *Astoria*)

The rescuers and rescued pose for a picture on the deck of the USS *Astoria* following their return. They are (left to right) Lt. Charles Tanner, Ens. John Morris, Lt. (j.g.) Don Comb, and aircrewman ARM3 Cletis Phegley. (U.S. Navy, courtesy USS *Astoria*)

Commo. Arleigh ("31-Knot") Burke (left) and Vice Adm. Marc Mitscher, commander of Task Force 58, plan the last phases of the Okinawa support operations on the *Randolph*. Admiral Mitscher was relieved before the campaign was complete because of fatigue—an unprecedented move. (National Archives)

U.S. Carriers Damaged by Japanese Kamikaze Attacks

Feb. 16 through June 17, 1945*

Name & Type (CV, CVL, CVE)	Date	Extent of Damage, Casualties, Location
Bismark Sea—CVE-95	2/21/45	Kamikazied off Iwo Jima with heavy loss of life—318 died. Only carrier sunk during this period.
Lunga Point—CVE-94	2/21/45	Minor kamikaze damage off Iwo Jima—no loss of life.
Saratoga—CV-3	2/21/45	Severe damage by 6 kamikazes off Iwo Jima; returned to U.S. for repair. 123 killed, 192 wounded.
Randolph—CV-15	3/11/45	Moderate damage in night attack while anchored at Ulithi Atoll; 26 killed, 105 wounded. Repaired in 18 days at Ulithi.
Enterprise—CV-6	3/18/45	Slight to moderate damage by kamikazes off Kyushu remained operational; repaired at Ulithi Atoll.
Intrepid—CV-11	3/18/45	Kamikaze near-miss off Kyushu; damage negligible; ship remained on station; 3 killed, 30 wounded.
Yorktown—C10	3/18/45	Slight damage off Kyushu by kamikazes and dud bomb; ship remained operational; repaired at Ulithi Atoll.
Franklin—CV-13	3/19/45	Glide bombing attack off Shikoku with severe damage; 800 killed, more than 300 wounded. Did not sink, but returned to U.S. and was never returned to duty. Only carrier damaged solely by conventional bombing.
Wasp—CV-18	3/19/45	Major damage primarily to no. 3 elevator by kamikaze attack off Shikoku, but continued strikes to support April 1 invasion of Okinawa. 102 killed, 200 wounded; returned to U.S. March 28 for repairs.
Wake Island—CVE-65	4/3/45	Major hull damage by kamikaze off Okinawa; repaired at Guam.
Hancock—CV-19	4/7/45	Kamikaze damage off Okinawa required return to U.S. 110 killed, 90 wounded or missing.
Enterprise—CV-6	4/11/45	Slight kamikaze damage off Okinawa; repaired at Ulithi; returned to task group May 6.
Intrepid—CV-11	4/16/45	Kamikaze damage off Okinawa to no. 3 elevator required return to U.S; she recovered her own air group; 74 killed, 82 wounded.
Sangamon—CVE-26	5/4/45	Kamikaze attack off Okinawa damaged flight and hangar decks extensively; 11 killed, 25 missing, 21 wounded. Returned to U.S. but not repaired due to end of hostilities.
Bunker Hill—CV-17	5/11/45	Struck by 2 kamikazes in one minute off Okinawa; major damage required return to U.S.; 350 killed (including more than a dozen from Adm. Mitscher's staff and many pilots and personnel from her air group) Almost 300 were wounded and evacuated. Admiral Mitscher and staff depart for CV-6, the Enterprise.
Enterprise—CV-6	5/14/45	Kamikaze attack from Kyushu knocked her out of the war; 14 killed, 34 wounded. Mitscher departs for CV-15, the Randolph . . . his 3rd Flagship in 4 days.
Natoma Bay—CVE-62	6/7/45	Substantial kamikaze damage to flight deck, but remained operational. One killed, 4 wounded. On 20 June she departed for Guam for partial repairs. Last carrier damaged.

*The length of AG-12's tour in combat area. Note: The CE Bismark Sea was the only carrier sunk during this period.

(U.S. Navy Archives)

Fires on the forward end of the *Randolph's* flight deck were caused by an army P-38's crashing into planes and personnel while the *Randolph* was anchored in Leyte Gulf. The pilot was stunting over the anchored ships and fell out of a barrel roll, just missing an ammunition barge along the starboard side of the ship and the open forward elevator shaft (arrow). The force of the impact swept the plane, pilot, and flaming debris off the flight deck on the port side. (U.S. Navy, courtesy Tony Remkus)

A burial detail conducts services for some of the victims of the P-38's crash into the *Randolph*. Other victims of this second hit were not recovered for several days. (U.S. Navy, courtesy Tony Remkus)

The *Hornet* plowed through mountainous waves during a typhoon that slammed into Task Force 38 shortly after the *Randolph* departed for Guam with Admiral Mitscher aboard. Both port and starboard portions of the forward flight deck collapsed. (National Archives)

Bon Voyage! Air Group 12 departed the *Randolph* on 17 June 1945, with the ship's band saluting with "California, Here We Come." The air group arrived stateside six months to the day after departing NAS Alameda, California. (National Archives)

Leaving His Calling Cards

The *Richmond Times Dispatch* depicts the sentiments of many members of the task force. Mr. Fred Seibel added the "15" to his carrier cartoon as a favor to Roy Bruce. (Courtesy the *Richmond Times Dispatch*)

"They don't give Navy Crosses for dents! ARM your bomb!"

Dilbert's flight training was excellent, the best that money could buy, except for one thing: he kept forgetting to arm the bomb! (U.S. Navy art by Robert C. Osborn)

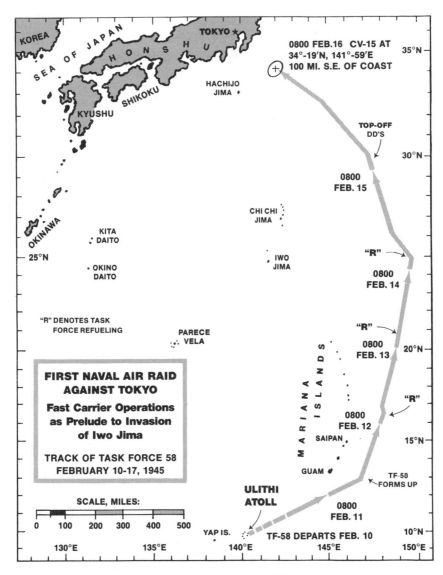

Task Force 58's course from Ulithi Atoll on 10 February 1945, northeastward past the Marianas, then north to a point one hundred miles southeast of Tokyo, arriving at 0600 on 16 February. (Roy W. Bruce)

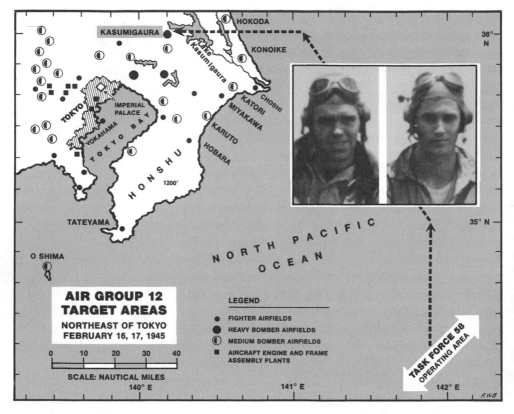

The circled targets north of Tokyo Bay were bombed and strafed on the
first naval air raids on 16, 17, and 25 February 1945 by Air Group 12.
Lake Kasumi-ga-Ura was the site of Ens. Charles H. Brown's ditching
after he was hit over the naval base. Inset (left to right): AMM3c John
Richards and Ensign Brown. (U.S. Navy, map by Roy W. Bruce)

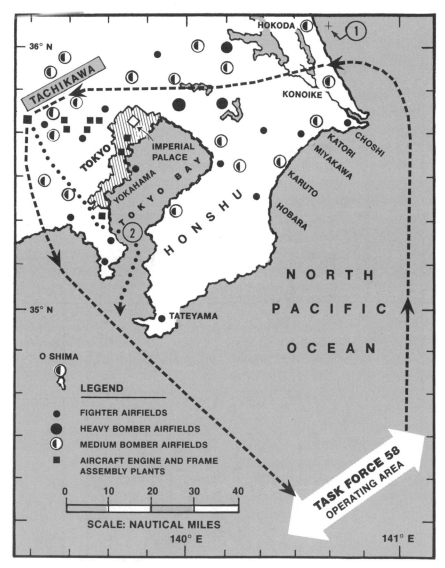

The circles designate the strike targets and alternates for 17 February. The course line was taken by the strike group to Tachikawa engine plant west of Tokyo. The circled "1" off the coastline near Hokoda marks the approximate location where Lieutenant Toliver made a successful water landing but could not be rescued. The circled "2" shows the flight path of Lieutenant Menard over Tokyo Bay and where his Hellcat was hit in the right wing by AA fire. He then headed south toward the North Pacific for rescue. (Roy W. Bruce)

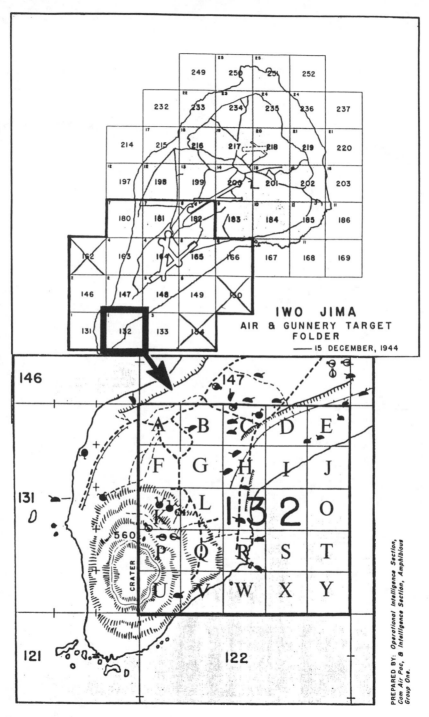

Grid maps carried by pilots on ground-support missions of Iwo Jima, 19–23 February 1945. (U.S. Navy)

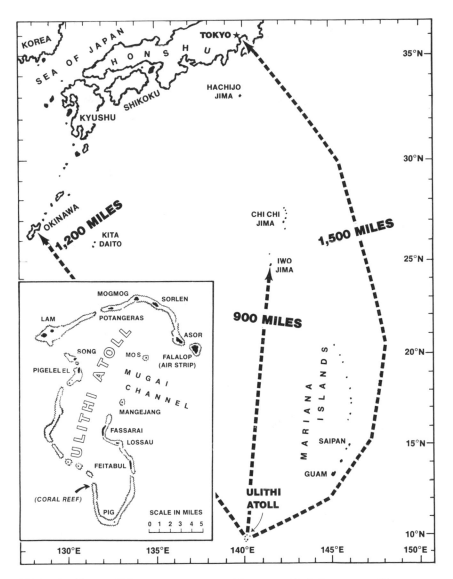

Ulithi Atoll, a well-kept-secret acquisition, provided the navy with an outstanding anchorage, centrally located fifteen hundred miles from Japan, nine hundred miles from Iwo Jima, and twelve hundred miles from Okinawa. (Roy W. Bruce)

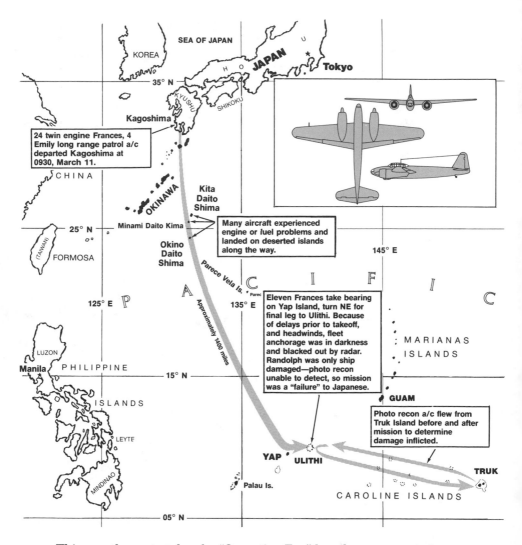

This was the route taken by "Operation Tan" kamikazes en route to Ulithi Atoll. The Frances (inset) that struck the *Randolph* was led by Emily flying boats most of the way to the target. Japanese reconnaissance flights from Truk Island the following day did not detect any carriers missing or damaged. (Map by Roy W. Bruce, Art by Maj. John M. Elliot, USMC [Ret.])

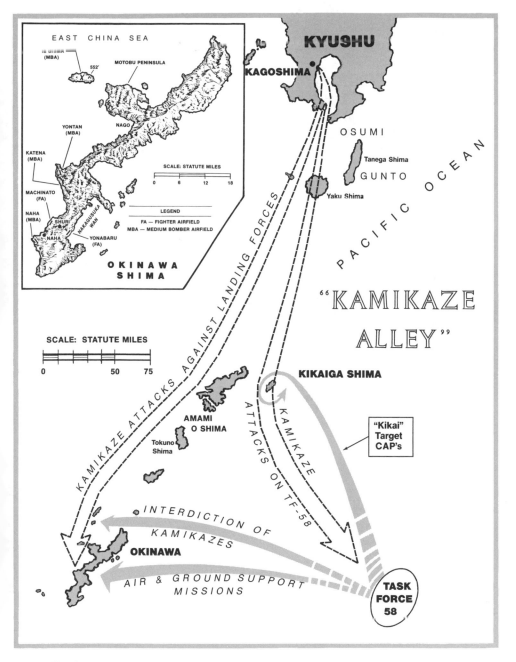

The ferry routes of Japanese aircraft from Kyushu generally followed along the islands Tanega Shima, Yaku Shima, Kikai(ga) Shima, Amami O'Shima, and Tokuna Shima en route to attack Okinawa amphibious forces and Task Force 58. (Roy W. Bruce)

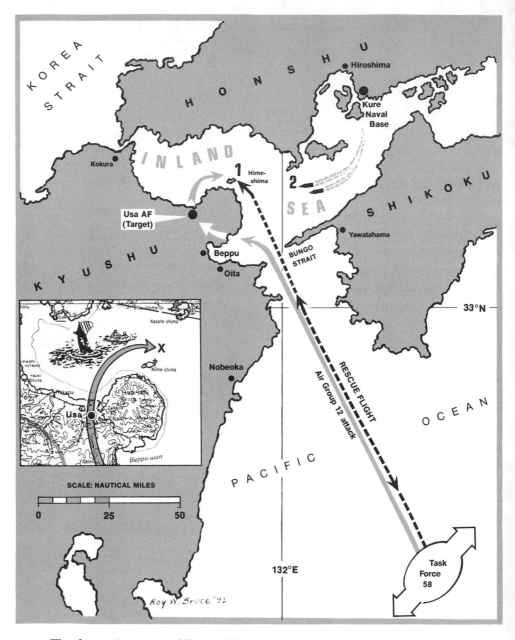

The dramatic rescue of Ensign Morris and Aircrewman Phegley was
accomplished in the hostile waters of the Inland Sea off the coast of Usa
Airfield, a suspected kamikaze base. The two airmen ditched several
miles due north of a small island, Hime Shima (number 1). The two
Japanese destroyers were on a general course (number 2) prior to attack
by Lieutenant Bardeen's division. The rescued airmen were returned to
the *Randolph* in time for the evening meal. (Roy W. Bruce)

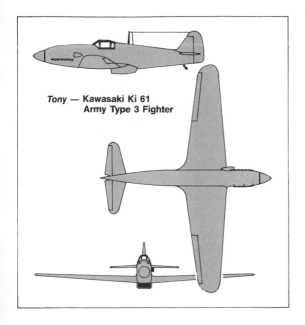

Tony — **Kawasaki Ki 61**
Army Type 3 Fighter

The Kawasaki Ki 61 Tony fighter was equal to the Hellcat in low-level flight but couldn't outrun the 5-inch rocket that Lieutenant Mcnard launched. The rocket sped ahead of the Japanese plane, splashed, and created a geyser of water that the Tony could not avoid. The Tony's flight characteristics were as follows: maximum speed 365 mph at 15,945 feet; rate of climb 5 minutes 31 seconds to 16,400 feet; service ceiling 37,730 feet; range 684 miles. (Art by Maj. John M. Elliot, USMC [Ret.])

Frank — **Nakajima Ki 84**
Army Type 4 Fighter

The Nakajima Ki 84, code-named Frank, was a sophisticated version of the German Focke-Wolf 190 and was faster than all Allied fighters at the time, with an estimated speed of 427 mph at 20,000 feet. Flown by a veteran Japanese pilot, it destroyed Ensign McConnell's F6F but was out fought by Lt. (j.g.) Dan A. Carmichael of VBF-12, also a seasoned veteran. (Art by Maj. John M. Elliott, USMC [Ret.], Photo U.S. Navy)

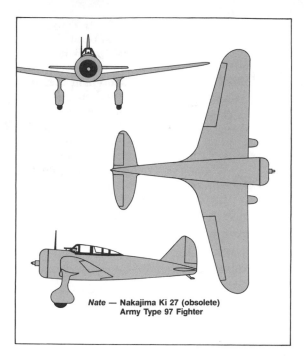

Nate — **Nakajima Ki 27 (obsolete)**
Army Type 97 Fighter

The Nakajima Ki-27b single-engine fighter, known as Nate. Flight characteristics were as follows: maximum speed 292 mph at 11,500 feet; rate of climb 5 minutes 3 seconds to 16,400 feet; range 1,060 statute miles. (Art by Maj. John M. Elliott, USMC [Ret.])

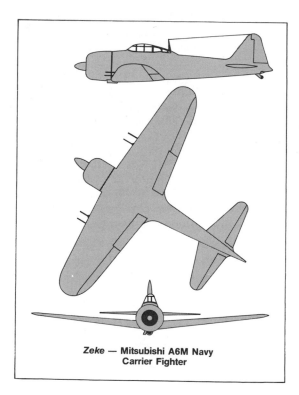

Zeke — **Mitsubishi A6M Navy**
Carrier Fighter

The Japanese navy's Mitsubishi A6M, known as Zero or Zeke, was the dominant aircraft during the first months of World War II in the Pacific theater. It had excellent maneuverability and range. After one was captured virtually intact in the Aleutians and flight-tested for its strengths and weaknesses, the Allies were able to overcome its advantages with new fighter tactics until the Hellcat and Corsair became operational. The Zeke's flight characteristics were as follows: maximum speed 335 mph at 14,900 feet; rate of climb 7 minutes 27 seconds to 19,685 feet; service ceiling 32,800 feet; range 1,675 nautical miles. (Art by Maj. John M. Elliott, USMC [Ret.])

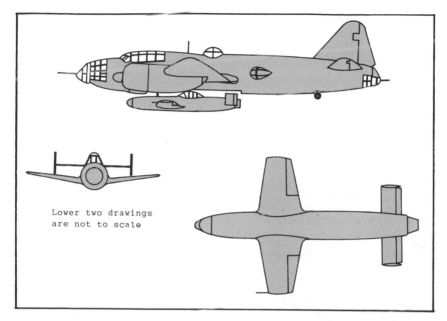

Lower two drawings
are not to scale

The American designated Baka ("fool" or "foolish") bomb was introduced late in the war. Officially known as the Japanese Oka (cherry blossom), it was basically a glider. The 500-pound explosive warhead was designed specifically as a man-piloted suicide weapon. When propelled by turbojet or solid-fueled rocket, it reached speeds of 276–403 mph, more in terminal dives. The medium bomber, Betty, was modified to carry this weapon to the target area by removing the bomb-bay doors to accept the 20-foot-long missile. (Art by Maj. John M. Elliott, USMC [Ret.])

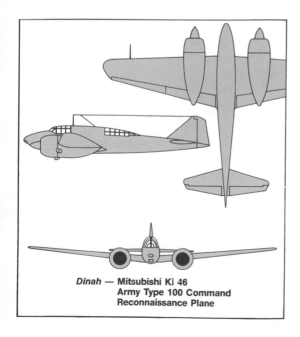

Dinah — Mitsubishi Ki 46
Army Type 100 Command
Reconnaissance Plane

This Japanese Dinah, a high-performance reconnaissance aircraft, is similar to the one shot down by Lieutenant Commander Michaelis during the rescue operation off the Japanese coast near Usa Airfield. (Art by Maj. John M. Elliot, USMC [Ret.])

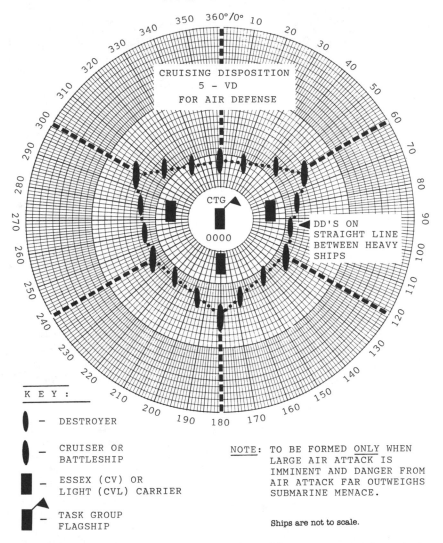

COMMANDER TASK GROUP FIFTY-EIGHT POINT ONE
OPERATION PLAN 1-45

CRUISING DISPOSITION
5 - VD
FOR AIR DEFENSE

CTG
0000

DD'S ON
STRAIGHT LINE
BETWEEN HEAVY
SHIPS

K E Y :

⬬ — DESTROYER

⬬ — CRUISER OR
BATTLESHIP

▮ — ESSEX (CV) OR
LIGHT (CVL) CARRIER

⬛ — TASK GROUP
FLAGSHIP

NOTE: TO BE FORMED <u>ONLY</u> WHEN
LARGE AIR ATTACK IS
IMMINENT AND DANGER FROM
AIR ATTACK FAR OUTWEIGHS
SUBMARINE MENACE.

Ships are not to scale.

Task group formation 5-VD offered the best ship arrangement to protect carriers against aerial attack (including kamikazes) and still provide antisubmarine protection for the following reasons: improved control of aircraft interceptions by the commander of the task group from the center of the formation (TG flagships generally had more information to disseminate); improved control of antiaircraft gunfire (a factor outweighing all others); and better all-around visibility for maneuvering the task group. The ships were separated enough to give the carriers maneuvering room in case of emergency yet allow them to maintain mutual antiaircraft support. (U.S. Navy, Task Force 58 Operations Report, redrawn by Roy W. Bruce)

5   Defanged, March 1945

Miserable weather in the Tokyo area dictated that the task force depart Japanese waters the night of 17 February and retire six hundred miles south to conduct support operations for the marines' amphibious landings on Iwo Jima. En route, our air group, led by Commander Crommelin, slammed Chichi Jima. It is one of the Bonin Island chain located about seventy-five miles northeast of Iwo Jima and one of the many volcanic islands curving northward from the Marianas to the Japanese mainland.

Many of these islands provided combinations of landing strips, seaplane bases, early-warning stations, and facilities for aircraft en route to harass our forces during any attack on Iwo Jima. More strikes against these strategic islands would be necessary in the future.

Savage antiaircraft fire was encountered from the island defenses, and it took a toll. One dive-bomber aircrewman was wounded. Ensign Morris of VB-12 recalled the flight when ARM3c A. D. Crook got hit in Ensign Fisher's plane: "I remember his conversation with Fisher went out over the radio instead of the intercom. His cries of pain during the flight back and in the landing pattern were unforgettable."

When Ensign Fisher's SB2C landed, aircrewman Crook was quickly taken below to sick bay, where Lt. (j.g.) Richard Williams, the ship's surgeon, operated on his severely lacerated leg. According to Doctor Williams, "Crook's leg was almost completely severed, and one inch of the bone was missing. We were able to save his leg, though, and when we transferred him to the navy hospital ship *Bountiful* upon our return to Ulithi, he was much better."

The accurate antiaircraft fire over Chichi Jima damaged about 35 percent of our aircraft in this strike. In addition, VT-12 lost two crews to the deadly fire: Ens. F. E. Hall and his crewmen, AOM3c Glen J. Frazier and ARM3c Marve W. Mershon; Ens. Rudolf F. Rohlfing and his crewmen, ARM2c Carrol C. Hall and AOM3c Joseph E. Notary.

The following day a welcome respite was dedicated to refueling ships and replacing aircraft and aircrew. In addition, it allowed time to prepare for intense air support for the marines on Iwo Jima on 20–23 February. This action was to be followed by more strikes on Japan on the twenty-fifth and twenty-sixth.

One of the routines for at-sea aircraft replacement required a pilot to be transferred from his carrier to a destroyer and then to a jeep carrier (CVE) with new aircraft.

Ens. Jack Schipper of VBF-12 was assigned to get a replacement aircraft. He remembered,

> I went over to the destroyer from the *Randolph* by breeches buoy. While there, I talked for about ten minutes to a man I thought a chief petty officer (wearing khakis, etc.).
>
> I then went by breeches buoy to the USS *Windham Bay*. Photographers came out of the woodwork to take pictures of the man I had been talking to who had followed me to the CVE.
>
> "Who is that?" I asked.
>
> "That's Ernie Pyle," was the reply.

Another one of the nuggets shared a similar experience. Ignoring the long-standing credo of "never volunteer for anything," Ensign Hazlehurst told of a chance meeting with the same celebrity:

> My squadron, VT-12, needed replacement aircraft for those shot down at Chichi Jima, so I volunteered and shortly thereafter was high-lined over to a destroyer with other pilots.
>
> The trip to the CVE in the rear area took about three or four hours, and I was getting a little queasy in the stomach. I joined several others for mess [dinner], and that helped. I wasn't used to being aboard a destroyer in rough seas.
>
> One of the guys at the table was dressed in khakis, a marine field cap with no insignia, and just didn't look like a gyrene. His face was wrinkled as though he'd spent most of his time outdoors looking into the sun, but he was friendly.

After conversing with some of the other pilots, he turned and asked me what I was doing in the war. So I told him all about our flight operations on the *Randolph* while he took notes in a small pad. By this time the destroyer had pulled alongside the CVE, so I said good-bye.

Ernie Pyle was killed not long after our conversation.

The refueling and replenishment may have been a breather from intense combat, but it was still busy for the ship and the air group. Dr. Williams kept a journal of activities in his "USS Randolph WW II Cruise Chronicle," where he recounted such a day:

2/20—Quiet day. Sent up lots of aircraft all armed to the teeth with bombs, rockets, fire bombs, guns and so forth. All return unharmed. Marines have taken one airfield on Iwo. Pilots and planes replaced from CVE—got seven new fighters, three bombers and two torpedo planes. Now have a full complement again. Gunnery practice. *Randolph* always seems to outdo others. Fueling operations at every opportunity. Sending CAPs and SNASPs every day. Strike at both HaHa Jima and Iwo Jima.

Following replenishment on 19 February, Task Force 58 camped in waters seventy-five miles west of Iwo Jima to provide four days of ground support for the marines. These missions differed from the strikes and sweeps over the Tokyo area in that here there was less threat of enemy air opposition.

Early emphasis was concentrated on ground support in areas surrounding two airstrips built by the Japanese in the central portion of the pork chop–shaped island. Later, we were tasked with methodically destroying gun emplacements dug in on the slopes of Mount Suribachi on the southern tip of the island. These gun emplacements reached almost to the lip of the dormant volcano and were laced together with a honeycomb of connecting tunnels.

At the crack of dawn, the *Randolph* launched sixteen VF, nine VB, and nine VT aircraft for the first of what would be a daily menu of ground-support missions through 24 February: Rendezvous, fly seventy-five miles to Pt. William ten miles west of Mt. Suribachi, and wait for assignment by Commander Air Support Control Unit (CASCU). Ordnance for these flights was a mix of napalm (fire bombs), 250- or 500-pound general-purpose bombs with instantaneous fuses, and 5-inch rockets for lobbing into the Mt. Suribachi gun emplacements raining gunfire on the marines below.

The targets assigned by CASCU were located by map grid numbers. On this flight an area northwest of airfield Number Two, virtually in the center of Iwo Jima, was assigned as a probable troop-staging point. After expending only half the ordnance in steep bombing runs, the flight was returned to orbit Pt. William until 0930, then ordered to repeat the process in an area northeast of the same airfield. This time the target was partially obscured, so flat glide-bombing runs were used because of low clouds over the assigned target. The flight returned to land aboard the *Randolph* at 1040.

By 21 February these ground-support missions had become somewhat routine, if combat flying could ever be described as such. A midmorning flight of nineteen VF and twelve VB arrived over the target area at 1100 and was directed to attack gun emplacements near the lip of Mt. Suribachi. Five runs were directed at the cavelike emplacements, expending a total of 104 rockets. The following was how the AAR described this mission: "This support group . . . was given a well done by both Glacier (CASCU) and target coordinator."

The only discernible flaw in these support missions was a failure of napalm fire bombs to detonate upon impact. These failures were duly reported to ship and air-group ordnance personnel, and appropriate corrective measures were started.

During the evening of 21 February the *Randolph* had to come to her own defense for the first time. After many months of gunnery drills, the gunners fired on enemy aircraft. And as if uttered as a sigh of relief, the *Randolph's* narrative summary stated, "The enemy withdrew without attacking."

However, the encounter was not without its damage. The "Randy's" gunners were among the best in the force, if not the best. There were rumors on the ship that the gunners had overridden safety cutouts that disabled the 5-inch–gun turrets so that the rifles could be depressed so low that they included aircraft on the flight deck within their blast range. Consider the dilemma of the pilots sitting in the cockpit while waiting to be launched. The 5-inch guns were tracking an attacking aircraft. As the ship heeled over while making a turn, the gun barrel was depressed farther and farther, perhaps tracking a low-flying kamikaze. Suddenly, you found yourself staring down the gun barrel, knowing someone in the gun turret had his finger on the trigger. Fortunately, no pilots were killed or injured, but many were shook up.

AMM3c Merrill E. Booth of VT-12 had his torpedo bomber damaged by the 5-incher's blast that evening:

> Our first encounter with the enemy as our ship was proceeding to some combat area, with the ship's crew not having made any contact with the enemy as of this point. As daylight began to fail, an enemy aircraft was picked up on radar, and immediately general quarters was sounded. The enemy kept coming closer and our [gun] turrets began to fire. As darkness fell, the enemy aircraft kept descending, and our guns kept on firing. I don't think we ever hit the aircraft, but the 5-inch guns sure did pop rivets and buckle the fuselage of our plane. Our crew chief told us too much damage had been done, and the aircraft would have to be pushed over the side. What a way for us to begin our tour of duty.

This evening was not so dull for the carrier *Saratoga*. She was stationed in the Iwo Jima sector to provide night-fighter cover for invasion forces. At dusk she was hit with a combination of conventional bombing and kamikaze attacks. Six times she was battered, suffering 123 killed, 192 wounded, and near-fatal damage.

Two enemy aircraft, although damaged and on fire, hit the ship's waterline; their bombs penetrated the hull before exploding. A third aircraft hit the forward edge of the flight deck with a bomb, and the fourth missed and crashed into the water. The fifth, a kamikaze, smashed into the port catapult area just as the sixth, and final aircraft of this group, crashed into flight-deck equipment and slid into the water.

The enemy then dropped flares to highlight the badly scarred veteran carrier for five more kamikazes boring through low clouds from out of the darkness. The *Saratoga*'s gunners downed four of them, but the fifth survived the intense antiaircraft fire and dropped a bomb that blew a jagged hole in the flight deck. Her airborne night-fighters had to find a new home that evening. The war was over for the gallant lady launched in the days of biplanes and wooden props.

Not far away, two escort carriers (CVEs of the landing forces) took more than their share of the kamikazes' wrath. The *Lunga Point* was grazed by a Jill (bomber) that had been hit by AA fire and exploded shortly before the residue skidded across the flight deck and into the water. The ship's crew doused the flames within minutes, and she was back in action after just a few minor repairs.

Not so for the CVE *Bismarck Sea*. Ten minutes later two more kamikazes plunged to their doom and achieved their goal. In ninety minutes the fire-wrecked escort carrier was gone. All efforts to save the ship failed when detonating ammunition ripped her apart, killing 318 and wounding hundreds. She was the last aircraft carrier sunk by suicide pilots, although many more were to be damaged and disabled.

The Japanese aircraft that struck these three carriers were from an organization known as the Mitate Unit No. 2 based at Katori, Japan. The unit consisted of thirty-two aircraft manned by former carrier pilots in training. They had refueled at Hachijo Jima (150 miles south of Tokyo), flying on to Iwo Jima and arriving late in the afternoon of the twenty-first.

This coordinated attack was among the first of many to follow. The volunteer Japanese pilots were some of the more experienced flyers and had been specifically trained in dive-bombing skills as well as night formation flying. The well-ordered attack included sufficient distance between aircraft so as to divide antiaircraft fire, even though they approached their target from the same general direction.

Lt. Jim Frith of VB-12, Bentonville, Virginia, was leading a support group inbound from Pt. William on 23 February: "We were circling in view of Mt. Suribachi when an announcement came over the radio stating that marines had raised the Stars and Stripes on Mt. Suribachi."

There were some flights in the combat arena where threat of enemy action was remote, but these missions were still important to the safety of the task force. These were antisubmarine patrols flown around the task force and its supply train (replenishment ships). Called search and antisubmarine patrols (SNASPs), they were flown by the bomber squadrons with crews trained in antisubmarine warfare.

The task force was at risk during these refueling and resupply operations. All ships were moving at reduced speed and were linked together with umbilical-like fuel and transfer lines that restricted evasive action to avoid submarine torpedo attack.

AMM3c Merrill E. Booth of VT-12 related what can go wrong on such a SNASP:

> Ensign J. L. Stirn, Bob Voelker, ARM3c, and myself had been assigned submarine patrol. Having taken off and reached our designated area, we began our search. Some two to three hours later Ensign Stirn called Bob and asked him to turn on the radar and see if he could find the fleet and give him a bearing back to the ship. (He has never admitted to us he was lost—only wanted to give Bob some practice with the radar.) Bob already had the radar on but could not find the fleet, so he advised Stirn to climb to a higher altitude in order to increase the range. Ensign Stirn objected due to the extra fuel it would take but finally relented. At twenty-six thousand feet Bob was able to find the fleet and give the pilot a good bearing. We did have enough fuel to make it back, but for a while none of us was sure. That was the last time Ensign Stirn got lost on an antisubmarine patrol.

The western Pacific Ocean is not unlike the Atlantic. Hurricanes, called typhoons in the Pacific, are as vicious as those in the Atlantic, if not more so. They occur at about the same time of the year as those in the Caribbean. Similarly, winter storms come off the continent into the Pacific Ocean as they do on the Atlantic seaboard. Under wartime conditions, no warning was available. It was inevitable that the task force would get caught in such a storm sooner or later.

The first serious encounter with a winter storm from the continent occurred on 24 February. Doctor Richard Williams described the incident in his "Chronicle":

> 2/24—Terrific storm lashes the task force. One DD is stove in and turns back sinking, one reported capsized. BBs and CLs do well but CVs take a beating, waves crash over the flight deck at one hundred feet and destroys seven planes, wrecks two 40-mm mounts on the bow, mangles the catwalks, washed one man overboard, overstrains our expansion joint. One *Randolph* plane lands on the *Yorktown*.

Despite the terrible weather, with winds nearing typhoon strength, CAPs had to be maintained over the task group. Soon after his division was launched from the *Randolph,* a VF-12 pilot reported that he was losing oil pressure and declared an emergency. He was directed to land on the nearest carrier in the group, the *Yorktown,* whose deck was ready to receive aircraft.

Events moved too swiftly for the ensign. He had charged his guns and switched to the 150-gallon belly tank as a standard procedure after becoming airborne. In the excitement he failed to jettison the nearly full belly tank and made his approach to land with the guns still charged ready to fire. When the plane caught the arresting-gear wire, the weight of the belly tank ripped it off, and it plunged forward through the propeller. The ensuing explosion turned the flight deck into an inferno. The situation was exacerbated when the pilot instinctively pulled back on the control stick upon landing, squeezing the gun trigger on the control. The machine gun sprayed the flight deck and ship's superstructure with .50-caliber bullets.

The *Yorktown*'s log described the incident in the usual unemotional language:

> 1321. Landed one VF plane from the USS *Randolph* with engine trouble. Belly tank came off and resulted in fire on the flight deck destroying the plane. The plane's guns discharged wounding several men (7).
>
> 1323. Sounded fire quarters.
>
> 1328. Fire out on flight deck.
>
> 1350. Secured from fire quarters.
>
> 1525. The following men were admitted to sick bay due to being wounded by accidental discharge of the guns of the USS *Randolph* plane.

The log then listed the seven men but did not state the seriousness of their wounds.

The pilot was burned around the head and wrists but not seriously because of the prompt action of the fire-fighting crews. Shortly after this accident, a message from the *Yorktown* appeared on VF-12's TBS screen, expressing the ship's extreme displeasure that one of VF-12's pilots had shot up seven men, three aircraft, and a radar antenna on the island superstructure.

The storm's ferocity also dealt the destroyers a rough time. ABM2c Glenn W. Putney of the *Randolph*'s flight-deck crew observed the smaller vessels' struggles: "I watched destroyers disappear from sight one minute and sit on the crest of a wave with bow and screws out of the water the next. I thought those guys deserved flight and sub pay [extra pay for hazardous duty]."

To watch is one thing; to get involved is something else. As Ens. Lee E. Furse of VF-12 related,

The ship was cruising one morning in extremely heavy seas—in fact, we were taking waves over the flight deck—when a single Zero passed over and made a strafing run at our ship. We went to general quarters and got the order to launch aircraft to protect the ship. The skipper's flight was the one to be launched, and I can remember the deck crew [hanging] on the ropes. I was in the Hellcat on the starboard catapult. This was great—the deck pointed high in the sky, then boom, down into the sea, with water flying over the plane. Then back up in the air, and Zap! the catapult hurled me into the sky.

We joined up, but the bogey was long gone. We circled long enough to be sure he was really gone. Then it came to me like a bolt of lightning: How were we going to get back aboard with the wild gyrations of the flight deck?

Thank the Lord for dear old Fred Kidd [landing signal officer]. I just followed his directions, and after one wave-off (deck on the rise) on the first attempt, I got safely aboard on the next pass, much to my relief.

By 25 February Task Force 58 was again knocking at Japan's front door. Again, few aircraft were encountered in the air. A cold front had moved across the islands, and snow blanketed much of the terrain. The weather continued to deteriorate so much that the afternoon sweeps and strikes were canceled as well as planned operations for the following day.

Moving closer to the Japanese mainland, the task force became more sensitive to submarine attacks as well as enemy aircraft. Ships were "blacked out" at night so that no lights showed externally. Working in and around aircraft on the flight deck required some light, particularly during night-fighter operations and during the early-morning hours in preparation for the first launches at dawn. Red lights were used for work during these hours. They provided enough light to work by, yet were not visible for any distance.

Failure to adhere strictly to darken-ship requirements could bring down much wrath. PhoM1c A. (Tony) Remkus of VF-12, Riviera, Arizona, testified to this strict policy. As the squadron's photographer's mate, it was his responsibility to service the aerial cameras on the F6Fs:

On one of the sorties, photo planes, numbers twenty-eight and thirty-one, were on the catapults in preparation for the Tokyo raid. It was about 0430. I finished installing the aerial cameras inside the belly of the fighter plane, using a flashlight with a red filter. The mechanic was revving the plane full throttle. The pilot was there when I came out of the belly, and I tried to tell him which switches to turn on for the different cameras. I always made a diagram for the pilot to follow for all cameras.

The pilot could not hear me with the plane's engine at full power. What the hell, I turned the flashlight on white lights so that he could read the diagram. Chaos followed.

Bells rang, loudspeakers screamed, someone grabbed the flashlight, turned it off, and threw it overboard!

The target areas assigned again were north of Tokyo. Lieutenant McWhorter was on the fighter sweep of airfields. Lt. Norman W. Sandler was his section leader:

Sandler was behind me. AA was very intense. I didn't know he was gone until Ensign "Stoney" Carlson called and said his plane came apart on pullout—whole tail section came off. Probably took a medium-size hit in the [rear] fuselage, enough to come off during pullout.

We had some problems coming back. YE [navigational radio aid aboard ship] was not the best, but it would get you back. Over land, the cloud cover was broken, but once over water the weather was closing in.

Weather conditions at the ship and in the target area continued to deteriorate, and predictions for the twenty-sixth were even worse. The planned afternoon strikes and those for the following day were canceled. At 1430 the task force began retiring at high speed.

Again, while en route south toward Iwo Jima for support operations, strikes were made against Hachijo Jima's seaplane base. Ens.

Roy W Bruce of VF-12 was a member of the sixteen-plane fighter sweep:

> Commander Crommelin was leading the flight in a radar-equipped Hellcat. The weather was grim during the one-hour flight to the island, with less than a one-thousand-foot ceiling and poor visibility. We approached within several miles, and Crommelin told us to orbit while he flew in over the volcanic island to survey the facilities to see if it was a worthwhile target. Because the air was so grey and murky, it was difficult to see just when he was actually over it, until the entire island seemed to have lit up like the Fourth of July.
>
> Arriving back to rejoin the group, he announced, "Well, fellows, I suppose we'd better give it a try." Although AA fire was heavy and concentrated, no planes were lost in this action. It was typical of Commander Crommelin to fly over a target alone, expose himself to enemy fire, and then survey the premises to make certain it was worth the risk. In this instance poor visibility—and because it was getting dark—made results difficult to determine.

That portion of the day given to sweeps and strikes in the Tokyo area was not completely lost. We managed to destroy eight planes in the air and thirty-five on the ground. According to the "History of Bombfighting Squadron TWELVE," the grand total for "three days, 16, 17, 25 February for Task Force 58 was 416 enemy airborne planes destroyed to the loss of thirty six of our own, a ratio of better than 11.5 to 1. These figures exclude all probables." (There were a bunch of them!) Air Group 12 accounted for fifty-four of those shot down.

VBF-12 suffered an operational loss on the twenty-sixth when Ens. Donald O. Tillery's Hellcat sustained hydraulic failure. While attempting an emergency landing on the *Yorktown,* he lost control on his approach and crashed into the water. The destroyer plane guard nearby was unable to rescue him.

The task force was again replenished on the twenty-seventh, and Task Group 58.4, of which the *Randolph* was a part, was detached and proceeded south to Ulithi Atoll. Routine CAPs and training flights were conducted en route, and the first naval air strikes against Japan came to an end when we anchored at Ulithi on 1 March.

The air-group commander's AAR on combat operations for the three days reflected some of the problems and successes of these first raids on the Japanese homeland:

In very few incidents were the Japanese pilots aggressive enough to make comparisons in aircraft performance. However, I believe that they have made notable progress in some of their tactics. In most cases, the enemy fighters climbed to a definite altitude advantage well away from the area in which they intended to do their fighting. This advantage coupled with cloud cover allowed them to attack only when conditions were ripe, that is, a straggler at the end of a strafing run, or a lagging wingman. They operated, for the most part, in very loose teams, and tried to strike a single target. Other enemy fighters acted independently and tried to maintain altitude advantage at any cost. This necessitated pushing their nose down and taking absurdly long range shots in order to recover in time to hold the altitude advantage. Once they lost their advantage, they were at a loss as to what to do. They dove for the deck, taking minor evasive action, and offered easy targets for pursuing planes. A team of fighters maintained in a good position of mutual support were very seldom attacked. The first two days of combat, I noticed a bad tendency among my own pilots to give chase to any enemy aircraft, regardless of the situation. It was not uncommon to see eight, and even twelve, F6Fs strung out in a line chasing one enemy plane. Had there been any enemy support above, the tail end of the chase could have been clipped off one at a time. I believe this tendency was remedied on the 25th by assuring that only one division (the division making the "tally-ho") gave chase. . . .

Our only objection to the use of the "G" suit is that it may allow too much "G" [force] to be applied to the aircraft, thus stressing it when not absolutely necessary.

On another subject he wrote:

Only about thirty percent of the napalm filled belly tanks or wing tanks, ignited. The prescribed anemometer type fuse vane was used with a single igniter. Napalm with two igniters were prepared for use on the afternoon of 21 February but the flights were canceled. I believe that this type of bomb would be extremely effective against personnel on any type of terrain and I recommend that every effort be made to assure successful ignition in the future.

The ship and air group reviewed the lessons learned during the combat period and, where needed, developed remedies. To perfect them the *Randolph* departed Ulithi Atoll and began a series of training exercises aimed at modifying old and improving new operating procedures and tactics. Practice sessions were conducted on 9 and 10 March. These exercises and training flights were to pay dividends later at Okinawa and Kyushu. Unfortunately, the cost of training was high. On the tenth Ens. H. M. Allen of VT-12, flying a TBM, crashed into the sea during a glide-bombing run on a target sled towed by the *Randolph*. Allen and his crewmen, AOM2c C. P. DeMoss and ARM3c D. E. Downing, were killed in the accident.

Ensign Hazlehurst of VT-12 was among those on the flight deck watching the torpedo pilots practice their glide-bombing skills: "Allen and I shared the TBM he was flying that day. When I saw he couldn't pull out of the dive because the elevators separated from the tail, I realized it would have been me had it been my turn to fly. I have retained an element of guilt ever since." The problem was traced to a defective elevator trim tab.

By late evening of the tenth the *Randolph* was again anchored in Ulithi Atoll. An incident the following evening would dramatically alter the course of events for both ship and air group.

Ulithi Atoll was acquired at no cost in September 1944 when a regiment of U.S. soldiers went ashore in rubber boats but encountered no resistance. The Japanese had departed. The atoll consists of thirty small islets connected by a submerged ring of coral, sheltering a deep ten-by-twenty–mile lagoon, ideal for a fleet anchorage. Within two months a security system of sensors and nets, buildings, and an airstrip were ready for fleet support. One of the most closely held secrets of the Pacific Campaign, Ulithi began maintaining and supplying ships of the Pacific as fast as supplies from Hawaii and California could be trafficked into the facility. The extensive anchorage could hold Task Force 58 and all the associated supply ships comfortably.

Located some nine hundred miles from Iwo Jima, it also provided an ideal staging point for the invasion of Okinawa. The fifteen hundred miles to Japan placed it fairly well out of reach of mainland enemy aircraft, except for that evening of 11 March.

This was the first entry in the *Randolph*'s log on the 2000–2400 watch:

2007—A twin-engine Japanese bomber (Frances) hit the flight deck aft, starboard side, exploding between flight and gallery decks at frames 205–210, destroying planes in vicinity of flight and hangar decks, the CO_2 Room, Aviation Repair Shop, and the fantail. Personnel in the near vicinity were killed or injured, fire broke out on the hangar deck aft; 40-mm and 20-mm ammunition was detonated.

The hangar deck of most carriers was the movie theater while in port. A movie screen was hung at the forward end of the hangar deck, and the steel curtains along the sides were usually raised for ventilation. The first showing of the movie that evening had just been completed; lights on the hangar deck were turned on, and moviegoers were beginning to move aft when the kamikaze hit. Twenty-six men were killed, 3 were listed as missing, and 105 were injured.

As Lieutenant McWhorter recalled:

I was working in the squadron offices. All of a sudden, I was lifted about two feet off my chair. Then, a tremendous explosion. I was about two hundred feet from the impact of the Frances. I ran out on the flight deck, and there was nothing but flames. Flames were blowing forward on the flight deck. I went forward ahead of them, and shrapnel had been thrown up the flight deck. Aircraft fuel was leaking from punctures in fuel tanks.

The hangar-deck area was worse—many bodies. All flight personnel reported to the wardroom to go through a man-overboard drill as a way to check for the loss of personnel.

ARM3c Harold McMahon of VT-12, the only air-group casualty, recalled that evening:

Perhaps we'd all seen too many war movies because everyone hit the steel deck. The fragments must have been projected very low, resulting in many leg and foot injuries. My left foot was suddenly knocked sideways—breaking several toes and severing the main dorsal tendon connecting my big toe. Those with severe injuries were treated first, so my foot was later sewed with wire before I was transferred to the hospital ship *Hope* the next day. I still walk with a slight limp, but compensate for it OK.

ABM2c Glen W. Putney recalled:

The night at Ulithi when the Jap Betty struck our fantail, the movie had just ended, and I had been standing at the rear of the crowd. I had just stepped into a stairwell that had a water fountain to get a drink when the plane hit. Thirty seconds later and at least one quarter of those on the hangar deck would have been killed or injured.

Shortly after general quarters sounded, an announcement followed that all air-group pilots were to report to the wardroom—immediately! Commander Crommelin waited for everyone to settle in, while scanning the entire group to make certain he had everyone's attention. Finally, in very deliberate, measured words he began, "Gentlemen, we may have another Pearl Harbor!" It was as if someone had suddenly sucked all the air out of the wardroom. At that time it was unknown if the attack on the *Randolph* was the first of a desperate last effort by the Japanese to sink the Allied fleet anchored in Ulithi. He continued, "If you can be of help to the ship's company, fine. If not, then stay out of their way." Fortunately, this was one instance in which Commander Crommelin overstated the problem. The *Randolph* was the only ship hit that night. It could have been worse.

The following description is taken from the *Randolph*'s war-cruise book *Gangway:*

11 March, there was a boatswain's mate gang in the Fifth Division Gear Locker. Warren, MacDonald, Swinhart and others were whooping it up with their joe pot when all hell broke loose practically on top of them. Not more than twenty five feet away the Jap hit, with his plane, gasoline, and bombs all exploding together. The boatswain's mates were tough and lucky, and all got away unhurt. Others did not. Chief Gunner's Mate Laws of the five-inch singles, competent, respected, and beloved, met the concussion and flame face on at the top of the ladder to Chief's Quarters

and was instantly killed. Three men from the Fifth and one in L Division, handling stores at the after crane, were also killed.

In the fire from sprayed gasoline, all the ammunition in fantail shields cooked off, making it impossible to work there and very dangerous even at some distance. Twenty thousand rounds of 20-mm went off in Air Group 12 clipping room. The fires in the aviation issue room heated through to the ready ammunition for the after five-inch singles, raising them to a dangerous point. Fifth F and Second Division men risked their lives to jettison it, throwing overboard two hundred projectiles and powder cases while the hot ammunition burned their hands and the paint smoked on the bulkheads. Lieutenants (junior grade) Rollins and Brazzell, Chief MacDonald, and thirteen Gunnery Department men received citations for this work and for fighting the fires.

Cdr. Ellery Clark, the damage-control officer, Annapolis, Maryland, pointed out that the ship was more fortunate than some of the other carriers that were hit by kamikazes:

. . . the carrier arrived at Ulithi on 1 March, seemingly a backwater. Not so! At anchor on the 11th shortly after 2000 an undetected Japanese Frances kamikaze struck the ship aft, tearing a hole in the flight deck and creating an inferno of flames, heat, debris, and death. Most fortunate, many of our complement were forward on the hangar deck, where the first showing of the movie, well-named "A Song to Remember," had just finished. I was there at the moment and just about to walk to the fantail to talk with various marines and chief petty officers. Suddenly, a voice, which I identified as God, spoke and said, "Go immediately to Damage Control Central." I did. Moments later the Frances struck.

Well-trained damage-control parties and other personnel were prompt, efficient, and brave. By good fortune the structural damage was limited to relatively noncrucial superstructure areas, unlike the damage to hulls and personnel of other American carriers in this war. The sad loss of "Randy's" complement was small in number. Ship's bombs, aviation and engineering fuel were spared, also engineering power and navigational systems. The hull-repair ship *Jason* performed a fast and fine job of temporary repair to enable "Randy" again to be ready for action in only eighteen days.

While the damage-control officer and his crew were stopping the hemorrhages of the ship's wounds, the ship's surgeon had his personnel repairs to perform. Doctor Williams described his part in the tragedy in his "Chronicle":

3/11/45—On the occasion of the kamikaze hit on the *Randolph* the ship's surgeon had again been ashore for a beer party and recently returned to the ship and hit the sack. When general quarters sounded there was immediate sprinkler system water coming down from overhead and I assumed of course, that we were sinking. There was immediately smoke, as well as the water from overhead, and the horrible noises of general quarters and the thumping of feet going to their battle stations. I could not find both of my shoes but found one sneaker and I proceeded aft on the first deck to the hatch leading down to the third deck sick bay fully assured that the ship was sinking. By the time I got to the sick bay, there were already a number of casualties. I operated for approximately thirty six hours non-stop and it was not until 3/13 that all surgery had been performed and casualties transferred to appropriate hospital ships.

Vice Adm. Takijiro Onishi, commander of the First Japanese Air Fleet at Clark Field, Luzon, in the Philippines, started kamikaze attacks by Japanese pilots during the Philippine campaign. The first attacks occurred on 13 and 14 October 1944 against Allied ships during the Battle for Leyte Gulf. This suicide squadron was called the Kamikaze Special Attack Corps. The word kamikaze had its origin in the years 1273 and 1279 during the attempted invasions of Japan by Korea's Emperor Kublai Khan. Typhoons scattered and sank the invader's ships and were called kamikaze or "divine wind." The World War II version of that term meant a one-way trip to heaven.

Those first strikes damaged six escort carriers. From 13 to 30 October these new suicide attack forces carried out assaults on the aircraft carriers *Franklin, Hancock, Intrepid,* the medium carrier *Belleau Wood,* and six escort carriers, sinking one, the *St. Lô.* The navy's reaction was to double the number of fighter aircraft, as reflected in the reorganization of Air Group 12.

The Japanese planned the events leading to this blow to the *Randolph* much earlier as Operation "Tan." The main objective was to attack Allied ships at anchor in Ulithi Atoll. When Japanese intelligence found that a large number of Task Force 58 ships were at Ulithi, the operation was put into effect to be carried out on 10 March. However, a mix-up in decoding intelligence transmissions from Truk forced a delay of the mission, and the attack was postponed until the next day.

The operation involved twenty-four Frances bombers from the Azusa Special Attack Unit. Emily flying boats and other land-based bombers were to assist the flight, providing weather reconnaissance, advance patrols, and guides to lead the twenty-four bombers to Ulithi.

Bad luck, poor maintenance, and other troubles began to plague the flight. One of the Emily guides disappeared, six of the bombers had to turn back because of engine trouble, and the flight, already thirty minutes behind schedule, was forced to climb above clouds, losing critical visual navigation checkpoints.

When they descended through the overcast some eight hours later, supposedly on top of Ulithi, they were near Yap, 120 miles west of the atoll because of a navigational error and unexpected head winds. And instead of the original twenty-four bombers, only two reached Ulithi well after dark. They started their suicide attacks at 2005.

Of the twenty-four Frances bombers comprising the special unit that departed southern Kyushu, eleven developed engine trouble and landed on islands along the route to Ulithi. Two ditched at sea. Of the eleven remaining planes, only six were accounted for in the Ulithi area. One struck the *Randolph,* and the other plowed into the lighted baseball diamond at Mog Mog, the adjacent recreation islet. Four of the group crash-landed on Yap.

It is indeed rare to have such details of a large and coordinated kamikaze operation. The flight leader of the Azusa Unit, Ryosai Nagamine, was one of the eleven landing on an atoll en route. He survived on rats for two months before being rescued by a submarine. Only a couple dozen kamikaze pilots are known to have survived their one-way suicide flights. Only one pilot is known to have survived a direct hit on a U.S. warship. Consequently, only surveillance flights following an attack such as this one could provide evidence as to successes. The six-hundred-mile surveillance flight from Truk to Ulithi the next day reported no carriers missing from this attack.

Damage to the ship at any earlier time would have been cause to send it back to Hawaii or stateside for repairs. The decision to make repairs at Ulithi was made at the highest level of command. Admiral Spruance toured the damaged area with Captain Baker, and the decision was all but firm that the *Randolph* would have to go stateside for repairs. The problem was that the violent explosion aft had destroyed the number one and two flight-deck arresting-wire engine. For flight operations, this was unacceptable and would result in the loss of one more CV during the crucial Okinawa invasion. D-Day was scheduled for 1 April.

Lt. Cdr. Sam Humphreys, the *Randolph*'s catapult officer who was also responsible for the arresting gear, convinced Captain Baker that his gang, with assistance from the repair ship USS *Jason,* could move number six (forward) arresting-gear engine aft to the destroyed number one arresting-gear space. The result of this exchange would mean that the ship would lose only the forward two of the twelve arresting-gear wires, a condition that was operationally acceptable. (Each engine controlled two arresting wires.)

Cdr. Charles Minter, assistant air officer, was convinced that Lieutenant Commander Humphreys's intervention was crucial to the decision to make repairs at Ulithi: "That decision to remain in the forward area [for repairs] allowed us to complete the war in an operational status. I doubt that anyone could estimate how long we would have been in the [navy] yard had we gone back to the States, and the loss of the *Randolph* at that particular time would have been crucial. Slingin' Sam saved the day."

Also influencing the decision to remain at Ulithi was the determination of Captain Baker, the availability of the repair ship, and the *Randolph*'s habit of not following customary procedures. Eighteen days later she was ready for flight operations.

The decision was fortunate for TF-58. It would lose two more CVs before D-Day, the *Wasp* and *Franklin* on 19 March. Five CVs were hit by kamikazes or bombed on 18 and 19 March.

The kamikaze attacks were not carried out solely by aircraft but were also perpetrated by surface craft, small plywood power boats equipped with bow-mounted depth charges to be driven into Allied vessels, especially those supporting amphibious landings. The tally for kamikaze airborne attacks through 9 January 1945 was 43 vessels damaged, 4 of which sunk, and 738 men and officers killed and 1,400 wounded.

Anticipating continuing pressure from these suicide air attacks on the task forces during the invasion of Okinawa, the navy ringed the island with picket vessels in the direction of the expected attacks, to provide early warning of approaching enemy aircraft. Okinawa was well within range of the Japanese airfields on southern Kyushu.

Realizing that the damaged *Randolph* would be out of action for an appreciable time, Commander Crommelin took stock of the situation, as indicated in the Air Group 12 Narrative History:

> . . . due to damage sustained which would prevent her departure with the rest of the Task Force, Commander Crommelin, never a good spectator when action was in the offing, requested and was assigned temporary duty with Commander Task Group 58.1. So when, on 14 March, Task Force 58 sortied once more he went with them as strike coordinator.
>
> . . . he left his "Thunderbirds" promising to lead them again when the Randy rejoined the Task Force. But that was not to be.

Cdr. Ralph Embree, skipper of the bombing squadron, became acting air-group commander and immediately checked out in the Hellcat. Lt. Joseph F. Guyon, executive officer and an American Indian, assumed command of VB-12.

Two days after the *Randolph* was struck by the suicide bomber, Task Force 58 received reinforcements. The *Intrepid* (CV 11) and the *Franklin* (CV 13) arrived at Ulithi after having undergone repairs from damages received off Leyte in late 1944. As part of Admiral Halsey's Task Force 38, both had been victims of kamikaze attacks. The next day they upped anchor with Admiral Mitscher's Task Force 58 for strikes at the soul of the Japanese Empire, the Inland Sea. There, the divine wind would retaliate with the force of a typhoon.

The mission for the task force was to neutralize the airfields and supply ports of Kyushu, then proceed north to smash Inland Sea facilities between Shikoku and the western portion of Honshu. These scheduled strikes were two weeks in advance of the planned invasion of Okinawa. The southernmost island, Kyushu, was the first target: specifically, Kagoshima and nearby Izumi. Kagoshima was the staging point for the launching of the surprise attack on Ulithi on 11 March. The *Randolph* would not be able to repay the Japanese visit to Ulithi.

Following the sweeps north, the task force would return south for hits on the half dozen islands connecting southern Kyushu with Okinawa, among them Kikaiga Shima, the primary airstrip that would be funneling kamikaze aircraft toward Allied forces in the Okinawa area. Soon this island would be the thorn in the side of Task Force 58 and become known simply as "Kikai."

Meanwhile, the *Randolph* had buried her dead, transferred her wounded to nearby hospital ships, and begun the cleanup necessary for repairs to begin. On the fifteenth her log read: ". . . 1012—Commenced catapulting aircraft. Part of the officers and men of VF 12 left the ship for temporary duty Falalop Island. 1145— Completed catapulting aircraft a total of 25 VF's, 6 VB's and 10 VT's. . . ." Although anchored, the *Randolph*'s catapults were capable of launching aircraft, and she sent part of the air group to Topaz Base (Falalop) Ulithi for temporary duty. The crew of the repair ship *Jason* could then begin the first of many twenty-four–hour workdays.

For pilots, aircrewmen, mechanics, and four or five supervising chief petty officers, life on Falalop was certainly different from that aboard ship. To describe it as casual would be an understatement. The uniform of the day was, simply stated, as little clothing as possible: shorts, shirts with sleeves rolled to the elbow, G.I. combat boots occasionally with socks, and lastly a short-billed marine field cap without rank or rate markings. Laundering clothes was totally unnecessary. Almost all hands attended the evening movies, and it always rained. Whatever was worn got a good soaking and rinse as no one ever left the movie because of a downpour.

Those who did not attend the movie could be found at the bar promptly at the 1600 opening. By 1800 the local marine VT squadron and Thunderbird pilots had consumed enough green beer to debate the relative merits of "you damn swabbie" or "you worthless gyrene." The debates usually ended as they tried outshouting one another in songs that usually deteriorated both in musical quality and subject matter. General MacArthur was mentioned, as were various admirals, though not in a particularly flattering manner.

These episodes usually began when the Thunderbirds asked what the marine pilots were doing when "we" were attacking Tokyo. The obvious point being made was that the marines were here flying antisub patrols in the middle of nowhere while the navy was on the front line where the action was. The remarks, of course, were influenced by a genuine rivalry and a liberal quantity of 3.2 beer.

Housing, if it could be called that, consisted of large G.I. tents erected on two-foot-high platforms. There were no steps up to this home. The reason was to discourage the four-foot-long monitor lizards, common to the island, from cohabiting with naval personnel. They had short powerful legs and a tail that could knock a man down with one swipe. No encounters were reported.

Near the tents and mess hall (a shack) was perched a Lister Bag of water for drinking and presumably for cooking. Regardless, no matter what sort of meal was being prepared, everything tasted like desalinated water, so beer was the preferred liquid. After a tour of "beach" duty, shipboard homemade bread and coffee sounded awfully good to us.

No one remained in the hot, gloomy tents during the day. Paradoxically located under palm trees, they were covered with coral dust from the nearby airstrip. They were periodically dusted by air-group, marine, and transport aircraft taxiing to and from the three-thousand-foot airstrip that stretched across the island from water's edge to water's edge. The transport aircraft were constantly arriving to disgorge cargo for this staging port. Rumor had it that Lt. Tyrone Power, movie heartthrob of the forties, drove one in now and then, but the Thunderbirds didn't wait around to get his autograph.

We were either flying CAPs over the fleet anchorage, practicing bombing and strafing missions on Yap Island, or prowling the beaches for cat's-eyes, exotic shells, or coral for folks back home. Our trips to Yap were anything but practice for the Japs. Abandoned to a lonely existence on the bomb-cratered island, they became very adept at moving and concealing their AA guns every day, and they fired them only when fairly certain of a hit. It was virtually impossible to locate these installations on this dense bushy island.

Presumably, Ens. Delbert Martin of VF-12 (affectionately known as "Snuffy") was hit by one of these installations, then failed to pull out of a low-level strafing run over the island. "Snuffy" had knocked down VF-12's first Japanese plane over Tokyo and was the unofficial mascot of the fighter squadron. This deadly AA hit several other planes before the air group rejoined the *Randolph* at the end of March.

Lieutenant McWhorter, who was one pilot involved, recalled:

During this strike, while strafing a Jap AA-gun position, my plane was hit in the starboard wing in the area of the gun charger lines (as I found out later)—and ignited the hydraulic fluid. As I was pulling out of the strafing run at about fifty feet above the middle of the Jap-held island, I looked down on my right wing (about four to five feet from the cockpit), and there was a blast furnace blazing away, with a stream of flame back past the tail. My first impulse was to get out, and I actually opened the canopy and unstrapped in preparation to bailout.

Fortunately, considering where I was, common sense prevailed over the panic of the moment. Because the wing had not yet burned off as I was expecting, I headed for the water and started gaining altitude. The flames finally stopped (all of the hydraulic fluid had burned out), but I had no way of knowing how much damage the main wing spar had incurred. So I flew back very carefully, ready to bail out if the wing decided to part company with the rest of the plane. It turned out upon later inspection that almost all of the fire was aft of the main spar and did little damage to it.

Meanwhile, Commander Crommelin was doing what he did best, leading strikes against worthwhile targets. All four task-group aircraft hit airfields and port facilities, possible staging areas, on Kyushu on 18 March, challenging the Japanese to react. They did, violently. Dozens of bogeys were knocked down within the task force, and one kamikaze barely missed the *Intrepid,* plunging into the water close by. Minutes later she was grazed by another that showered the entire starboard side of the ship with flaming debris. It was so scattered that the huge pillar of smoke and flame belied the actual damage. Within an hour she was launching her aircraft.

It was a day when reports of bogeys close to the task force were constantly interrupting the launching sequences. CAPs swept the cloudy skies, ideal weather for kamikazes.

The *Yorktown* was victimized in this action. Bogeys were being knocked down with disarming regularity, and at 1308 one intruder was shot down within the task group. Just a minute later her guns knocked down a single-engine aircraft making a dive-bombing run on the starboard side. She was lucky: the bomb had been released but passed over the flight deck to explode close abeam near the number two elevator. Still they came. Another plane, on fire, crashed three hundred yards abeam. Seven minutes later a fourth suicide bomber was hit by AA fire but was still able to drop a bomb that exploded very close on the starboard side. It was so close that the concussion tripped (unlocked) the fore and aft gyro compasses, leaving the ship without good directional control. A minute later the fifth plane in this attack entered its final dive, on fire, and crashed a quarter mile off the starboard side. The ship's log described the onslaught: "1500. This ship commenced firing and scored hits on enemy single engine dive bomber making an attack on this ship starboard bow. . . . Ship hit by bomb on starboard beam. Plane broke up on pullout and pilot parachuted."

The bomb went through the starboard side of the signal bridge, exploding in the vicinity of the second deck. The resulting fire was extinguished in less than an hour, as the log indicates that at 1556 the flight labeled "Number 5" was launched. The *Yorktown* was back in business. Her gunners and damage-control teams functioned as planned, saving the ship to fight on. The *Enterprise* also suffered some damage during these attacks, but by the following morning both ships were repaired sufficiently to continue the raids. This time the target was Kure on the Japanese island of Honshu, home of the Imperial Japanese Navy.

The armament for the *Franklin*'s aircraft was primarily the Tiny Tim rocket carried beneath the belly of the F4U Corsair. This aircraft's gull-wing design gave it the distinction of being the only single-engine aircraft with sufficient clearance to carry the monstrous weapon underneath the fuselage. The nickname belied its size: 11.75 inches in diameter, 12 feet long, nearly 1,000 pounds total weight. Resembling an aerial torpedo, it was a semi–armor piercing rocket-propelled 500-pound bomb.

The first strikes were already on their assigned targets as the second strike was being launched from Task Group 58.2. The *Franklin* was the flagship of this group, with the *Hancock* and the light carriers *Bataan* and *San Jacinto*. A short radio message from the *Hancock* to the *Franklin* was all the warning received before a Jap plane was upon them. The *Franklin*'s log recorded what was to be one of the most disastrous conflagrations at sea that a ship would survive: "0708. Ship under attack by enemy aircraft. Took two bomb hits, first bomb hit flight deck frame 68, exploded hangar deck frame 82; second bomb hit flight deck frame 133, exploded frame 142." The two bombs penetrated the hangar decks, one exploding in the third-deck area. The gassed and armed aircraft, many with Tiny Tim missiles, began exploding. The resulting fires and explosions killed many of the fire fighters and damage-control personnel. Pilots and flight-deck personnel were lost to gaping holes in the after end of the flight deck as the exploding armaments devastated the entire hangar deck.

As fires and explosions continued throughout, the ship appeared to be but one huge fire. The death toll began to rise among those trapped below. The hospital ward, doctors, corpsmen, and patients died after a gallant fight against the fire. The ship was now beginning to list to starboard as a result of water taken aboard to fight the fires. She had lost steering control, and rescue attempts by the cruiser *Santa Fe* became dangerous. She was heading generally toward Japan and now was less than sixty miles off the coast, the closest any major surface vessel had been in this war.

Lt. George H. Wenglein of VB-5 was awaiting takeoff amidships behind four or five other SB2Cs when the two bombs pierced the *Franklin*'s flight deck. He didn't see the Japanese plane or the bombs, but there was no doubt in his mind that the ship was in serious trouble. Lt. Wenglein described the next three hours:

> Almost immediately, pandemonium erupted on the flight deck from smoke and fire below, which quickly enveloped all aircraft [with engines turning over] awaiting takeoff.
>
> I shut down my engine and tried to locate my aircrewman but couldn't find him in the smoke and confusion all around the flight deck. I heard later he'd stumbled into a prop. In a minute or so the announcement came over the bull horn for the air group to abandon ship. The smoke and fire was awful, and it was obvious that the *Franklin* was already listing to starboard from the tremendous weight of water collecting in spaces from fighting the

fire, which by now had enveloped the entire ship as far as we could see—and that wasn't far.

Those of us who found ourselves on the port side began leaping off from the catwalk into the water sixty-five feet below. We literally bailed out. The impact was horrible—I broke a leg, which wasn't treated for hours. Fortunately, all us pilots and crewmen had Mae Wests on, so drowning wasn't a threat—as long as you kept your head up and out of the water. The water was filled with debris blown off of the ship, which had drifted away from the survivors. Most of the debris was teak planking from the flight deck—not large enough for more than one guy at a time, but we took turns hanging onto it. That was the only time you could relax during the three hours in that frigid water.

Wenglein remembered one event that he can still laugh about:

I heard one of the guys [without a Mae West] holler, "Somebody help me, I can't swim." Well, I don't remember exactly what happened—no one was in a position to go to his assistance—but all of a sudden he goes barreling by me at about thirty miles an hour. He sure learned fast!

While in the water, we had constant fighter protection in case the Japs came back for more. We'd been in the water for more than an hour because most of our ships were involved in trying to control the inferno aboard the *Franklin*. Thus the cold water was numbing us by the time our destroyers began picking up survivors. They threw lines over the side for us to grab as they slithered by—barely moving—they didn't dare stop under the circumstances. One was DD 676, the *Marshall*—I'll never forget that number! It was then about 1100, and we remained on the can for a day or so before being high-lined over to the battle cruiser USS *Alaska*. Two more transfers, and we rode the tanker *Tuluga* into Ulithi Atoll.

Lt. Wenglein spent four to six weeks in the naval hospital in Honolulu prior to being flown back to the States.

The wounded and air-group personnel were removed from the stricken ship as by this time she lay dead in the water. The cruiser *Pittsburgh* took her under tow, starting a long and slow journey toward Ulithi. As she subdued most of her fires, she began to get her engines back on line, and by the following morning she was under way on her own power. Escorted by the heavy cruisers *Guam* and *Alaska* and two destroyers, she had been harassed all night by the enemy, which was seeking to complete her destruction. The following afternoon at about 1400 a Japanese plane bore in for an attack but was so surprised by the few remaining AA batteries still operating that it swerved just a little, enough to cause the pilot to miss his sick target by just a few hundred feet.

The toll was grim: 743 had died in the holocaust. The carrier had had little more than one day of combat to prove just how ready she was to fight. For a ship that had traveled so far after having been repaired from previous wounds, it was a disappointment to say the least. But the valor of her captain and crew in saving the ship was a tribute to the fighting men of the navy. Only 704 were left aboard to take her home.

The holocaust aboard the *Franklin* had special significance for the *Randolph* and Air Group 12. Certainly the crew of the *Randolph* could understand, having suffered some of the same devastation less than a week before. And for some members of Air Group 12, the disaster was more closely felt because those pilots who had come to the Thunderbirds in December were former members of Air Group 5, the air group that was aboard the *Franklin*.

The *Franklin* was certainly the worst hit but not the only casualty of 19 March. The *Wasp* also suffered a hit by a bomb-carrying kamikaze that penetrated the flight deck, blew a sixteen-by-twenty-four-foot hole in the hangar deck, totally destroyed the galley and laundry, ruptured fire mains, demolished two aircraft on the hangar deck, and misaligned the number three elevator. Casualties were 102 dead or missing and approximately 200 wounded. The damage to the elevator was the most serious. Although the fires were brought under control and air operations were commenced within an incredible one hour after the hit, the damage to the number three elevator shaft severely restricted air operations.

Two of the four first-line carriers damaged in Mitscher's second sortie against the Japanese main islands were knocked out of the skirmish, the *Franklin* for good. The *Wasp,* though she continued to operate off the east coast of Okinawa to soften up opposition for the pending invasion, was ordered to return to the West Coast on 28 March for repairs to her aft elevator shaft, repairs so technically complex they could not be accomplished at Ulithi. Meanwhile, the *Enterprise, Intrepid,* and *Yorktown,* with less serious wounds, limped into the atoll along with other units of the task force.

The *Jason's* twenty-four-hour work schedule had miraculously restored the *Randolph* to operational status in eighteen days. Soon, she could help fill the CV gap in TF 58 created by kamikaze attacks. More carriers were on their way.

First, however, her complement of aircraft had to be replenished, having been hard hit by combat and operational losses and the kamikaze hit on 11 March. The nearest place for resupply was NAS Agana, Guam. Fourteen Thunderbird pilots boarded an R4D transport on the airstrip at Falalop for Guam to ferry replacements, six torpedo bombers and eight fighters, back to Ulithi.

6 Back to Hostilities, 1–18 April

Ens. Richard W. Harris of ComAirPac Staff (SubComForward-Guam), Austin, Texas, was stationed at Oroti Peninsula on Guam. When he found out about the *Randolph* pilots' coming to pick up new aircraft, he tried to find them because he had a friend in Air Group 12. He missed the group but managed to flag a ride on the twin-engine PV-1 Harpoon that was to lead the F6Fs and TBMs on the four-hundred-mile trip to Ulithi. He was impressed by the air-group pilots' performance:

> About three-fourths of the way down to Ulithi, we ran into some thunderstorms. The six torpedo planes were off our left wing, and the eight fighters were off our right side. As the weather began to close in, our pilot told the group to close up, and did they ever! I could hardly see the PV's wing tips, but those fighters were so close I could see two of them and one of the torpedo planes.
>
> We were in the clouds about ten to fifteen minutes, and when we came out of the bad weather, there were all of Air Group 12's Avengers and Hellcats still tucked in real tight. We didn't lose a one. (They must have had some previous experience.)

Ensign Harris did get to see his friend in the air group. Little did he know that one of the pilots in the flight had been hunting for him on Guam with greetings from that friend.

The *Randolph,* repaired and replenished, upped anchor. She got under way for refresher training to include gunnery exercises and carrier landings and to recover aircraft temporarily land-based on Falalop. The date was significant. It was D-Day for our forces going ashore at Okinawa; it was Easter Sunday; and it was April Fool's Day.

Following what amounted to a mini–shakedown cruise, the ship returned to Ulithi for additional supplies, forming up with other units of the task force departing for Okinawa. At dawn on 5 April she, the *Enterprise,* and nine destroyers plowed through Mugai Channel and headed northwest.

Task Force 58 had been hard hit during the mid-March activities and needed all the repaired carriers available for support of the Okinawa invasion. The *Randolph* was now part of Task Group 58.2, with Rear Adm. Forrest Bogan and staff on board. After departing Ulithi until late on 29 May the ship and air group participated in supporting operations on Okinawa. This fifty-one-day period of combat would be one of the longest sustained at-sea operations on record, punctuated only by refueling and resupplying every fourth or fifth day.

The menu of combat flights included sweeps against suspected kamikaze airfields on Kyushu and on the Ryukyu Island chain between Okinawa and Kyushu, CAPs over the task force, and target combat air patrols (TCAPs) over Okinawa. The CAPs over the outlying ring of picket ships (RAPCAPs) were often as dangerous and deadly as flights over island targets with experienced antiaircraft defenses.

On 6 April the Japanese launched a three-phase attack that appeared to be one final desperate kamikaze effort to halt the invasion on Okinawa. In the first phase more than 355 older aircraft left airfields on Kyushu to attack Task Force 58 and the Fifth Fleet ships involved with amphibious landings. Approximately two hundred planes eluded task force CAPs and penetrated the Okinawa air defenses. Some plunged into radar picket destroyers, destroyer transports, and ammunition ships.

One Japanese attacker was shot down by a CAP about ten miles from the task force. The pilot was observed to have bailed out of his crippled plane. The destroyer *Taussig* was on the scene and was proceeding to recover the pilot when a Japanese plane attacked, forcing evasive action and delay en route. Later, after a near bomb miss, she continued on toward the Japanese pilot. He was recovered, administered first aid for burns on the face and wrists, and transferred, along with his gear, to the *Hornet.* He was later reported to have died of his (minor) injuries.

The pilot, Sata Omaiti, an NCO in the Imperial Japanese Navy, told his captors that the fleet would be hit again on 11 April. Forewarned, Admiral Mitscher ordered the dearming and degassing of all aircraft not needed for increased CAPs over the fleet and picket ships. The attack did not materialize until 12 April.

Japanese claims for the 6 and 7 April operation labeled Kikusui included the sinking of an aircraft carrier, two battleships, and thirteen other miscellaneous ships. Actual damage summaries indicated two destroyers, a destroyer-minesweeper, and an LST sunk; the *Hancock,* light carrier *San Jacinto,* battleship *Maryland,* eleven destroyers, three destroyer escorts, and seven miscellaneous vessels damaged; and two ammunition carriers obliterated. These totals came at the expense of 252 Japanese planes and pilots.

The desperation of the Japanese was also reflected in the second phase of their attempt to halt the Okinawa campaign. The same day, 6 April, the largest battleship in the world, the 70,000-ton *Yamato;* one cruiser, the *Yahagi;* and eight destroyers sortied from the Inland Sea en route to Okinawa. The mission was to beach the *Yamato* on Okinawan shores and blast away until all ammunition was exhausted. Then, in what was to be the third phase, her two thousand crew members would join army-reserve ground troops hidden in caves and, in coordination with kamikaze pilots and Baka suicide bombs, halt the Okinawa invasion. The ships were fueled with the last 2,500 tons of oil left in the Japanese navy.

Once this armada was discovered, Admiral Spruance, the strategic commander of Task Force 58, planned to have his surface group intercept the *Yamato* far enough south of Kyushu so as not to be overly concerned with land-based enemy air cover. Admiral Mitscher had different plans, and Spruance acquiesced by not countermanding Mitscher's plans. Mitscher's forces proceeded north and, once his search planes located the *Yamato,* launched a strike group of 180 fighters, 75 dive-bombers, and 131 torpedo bombers at 1000 on 7 April. The group sank the *Yamato, Yahagi,* and two destroyers and damaged two others so badly that they were destroyed by the remaining four destroyers during the retreat northward.

Air Group 12 tried to participate but like a clumsy kid stubbed its toe and fell. The weather tripped up the bombing squadron. Lt. (j.g.) Charles R. Hauth of VB-12, Pittsburgh, Pennsylvania, told why:

On 7 April 1945 our task group was refueling off Okinawa. A cold front separated us from the rest of the task force. Nevertheless, it was decided that Bombing 12 would launch a major strike against the Japanese battleship *Yamato*.

I was flying lead on the second section behind the skipper, Lieutenant Joe Guyon. While making a steep turn to the left, trying to find a opening in the clouds, all twelve SB2Cs flew into a solid bank of clouds. I lost contact with the first section, and my wingmen lost sight of me. Before I could switch to instruments, the artificial horizon tumbled, and flying by the seat of my pants, I ended up in a graveyard spiral.

I went onto needle, ball, and airspeed and got squared away so that I started my pullout at approximately 3,500 feet. At about three thousand feet I broke out of the clouds—still in a steep dive—blacked out, and approached a power stall, but was able to recover to level flight at about fifty feet off the water.

My crewman, McGinnis, tried to bail out but fortunately was unable to get the hatch open. No one from Air Group 12 got to the target, but one by one everyone returned safely to the *Randolph*.

Planes from the rest of the task force did get to the target and sank the *Yamato* without any help from VB-12.

That ride of Ted's [McGinnis] in the rear pit had to be sheer terror. It had to last twenty to thirty seconds, and to know that the end could be approaching and to be completely foiled in trying to save yourself is impossible to imagine. In this case, however, his failure to save himself probably saved his life. I've often wondered what might have happened if he had been successful in his effort to parachute to safety.

The ride taken by ARM3c Ted McGinnis, Uniondale, Pennsylvania, was indeed one of sheer terror. He provided his version of the ride:

When the word came to man planes, everybody hustled to the flight deck. I remember seeing one of the pilots, Lieutenant Whiting, I think, looking ghoulish with flash cream coloring his face a greenish blue. Startling at first, then sobering when you thought why he was wearing it. You think maybe you should have used it, too.

After the excitement of the launch, my pilot, Mr. Hauth, now a "j.g." and a section leader, joined up on the division leader and his two wingmen. Our section's two wingmen snuggled in on us. I was, naturally, facing aft, with my twin thirties locked on the scarf ring and pointing up about forty-five degrees so that my canopy could be nearly closed with just the muzzles sticking out. When we were nearing the target, I planned to open the canopy and drop the turtle-back, thus opening up my field of fire, which was limited somewhat by the huge tail assembly on the Helldiver. If a gunner wasn't careful he could do a lot of damage to his own plane. Those twins could put out about twenty rounds a second.

We were settled into formation and climbing smoothly as we went into the overcast. At first it wasn't too thick but rapidly became darker. The wingmen came in closer. It seemed to me that their wings were overlapping, they were so close. Turbulence caused a few bounces, and the wingmen drifted out and faded away.

It was uncomfortable with all the aircraft so close—a midair collision was possible. We flew on, and I looked over my right shoulder at the altimeter reading eight thousand feet and climbing. After what felt like an easy pushover, we picked up airspeed and then heavy positive Gs forced me down in my seat. I wondered what in hell was going on? Which way was up? Then zero Gs! I floated up against my straps. Then negative Gs—things moved around the cockpit in a most confusing manner. The ammo in my cans cascaded out and began to twist and tangle as side forces banged me about. I knew that we were out of control and that I had to get out. I tried to crank the canopy open—which would free the gun muzzles so I could move them aft off the scarf ring. I couldn't get out of the seat unless the guns were moved. At the same time, with my other hand, I was unfastening my chest armor, which was attached to the seat but fastened together in front of my chest. We now were going from negative Gs to positive Gs. There were too many things to do and no time—no time. I looked over my shoulder at the altimeter, and it was passing two thousand feet and unwinding fast. No matter how hard I tried, I just couldn't move everything out of the way and realized that I was going to ride it into the water. I grabbed the handles of the gun mount and waited for the impact.

Suddenly, we came out of the snow-white blanket that was surrounding us. We were inverted, nose down, and the water was very close. Mr. Hauth rolled and commenced a hard pullout, harder than any I had ever felt. I think my chin was pulled down on my chest armor. I started to black out, but the pressure eased, and we were skimming over the water so low and fast that it seemed slick. We climbed slowly, and as we settled down I called Mr. Hauth and said, "If you're going to try that again, just let me out!" He answered, "No chance, we're headed home!"

We straggled back to the ship and set up in the landing pattern. After landing, I saw that there were no rockets on the wings, and I could swear that there were popped rivets. My logbook shows, however, that six days later we took the same plane on an Okinawa [ground support] strike, so it couldn't have been too stressed, just me. For the next three days, when I thought about it, especially the giving-it-up-and-riding-it-in part, I was sick to my stomach.

The same day, 7 April, Task Force 58 experienced one of the few penetrations by enemy aircraft while in support of the Okinawa campaign, having successfully defended the major attack of the previous day. A kamikaze got through the air defenses and hit the *Hancock* with a bomb on the flight deck. The plane turned and struck the aft part of the flight deck, causing severe fires among the parked aircraft. The fires were controlled within a few minutes. So efficient was her damage-control party that she was able to recover her own aircraft returning from an Okinawa support mission. The severe structural damage that was sustained required stateside expertise to repair. She was the seventh major carrier kamikazied within a month, three of which would be out of action for four to six months.

The kamikaze raids on 6 and 7 April were two of ten major attacks against Allied ships during the Okinawa campaign. One- or two-plane attacks were experienced almost daily, and ships were required to go to general quarters. It seemed we remained in this alert condition for hours.

On 8 April, the *Randolph*'s first day on the job at Okinawa, the task force struck back at the source of its kamikaze tormentors.

The Ryukyu Islands to the north were considered prime targets, specifically Wan Airfield on Kikai(ga) Shima, from which many kamikaze planes were thought to be launched. Deadly antiaircraft defenses at Wan Airfield and the poor weather conditions provided a mix that created a strange story exemplifying some of the workings of the Japanese Air Force and the kamikaze flights. The episode started as described in this entry in a VF-12 AAR:

> Ensign Jay M. Finley is reported as missing. He was last seen with the formation prior to its final strafing attack on Wan Airfield, when his division passed through a cloud layer above the target. Subsequent events leading to his loss were not observed. Successive flights over the same area were instructed to be alert for any remnants of the F6F, but all such searches have been negative.

Ensign Finley, Diamond Springs, California, related what happened:

> It was about 1500, 8 April 1945, and I was sitting on the number two catapult; we were going to Kikai Shima. Flight Leader McWhorter told us it would be no problem getting there, even though the cloud ceiling was only two hundred feet.
> Our mission, like the others of that day to Kikai Shima, was to fly target combat air patrol over the island to keep the kamikazes from landing at Wan Airfield. At the end of our TCAP time, we were to make strafing runs on the airfield. On our last run, we were to be a diversion for a photo plane.
> Lieutenant McWhorter got us to Kikai Shima with no problems. The ceiling was only about five hundred feet over the ocean and thirty-five hundred feet over the island. We flew our TCAP for about two or three hours. To make our strafing runs, we had to go over the airfield and out to sea, dropping down to about four hundred feet to get under the cloud cover.
> On the last run as a diversion for the photo plane, Lieutenant McWhorter led us up over the island in an echelon. As he pulled up to make his run, he went up into the clouds. I followed and waited a short time. When I came out of the clouds, I was number four man, not number two as I had started. As I pulled out of the firing run at about five hundred feet, I felt a jolt in the rear of the plane. The right rudder pedal went to the fire wall, and I had

no control of the plane. At about 350 knots I rolled the canopy back and tried to put my head out to see what was going on. At about that time the plane came apart and started to tumble. I got out at about four hundred feet. I don't remember pulling the rip cord, but I must have because I saw the chute trail, although I don't remember it blossoming. The next thing I knew, I was in the water.

You have heard the story before. You don't know which end is up. I must have been ten to fifteen feet deep in the water, looking around, and dog-paddling up to the surface. I am glad my head was up and feet down because if it had been the other way around I would have been going straight for the bottom. When you get to the surface, the first thing you do is inflate the life raft. Well, that was easier said than done.

I went around all of the corners twice, looking for the valve. After finally getting the raft inflated, the next thing to do is save the chute. This proved to be an impossible task, so I cut it loose and let it go. Now I was ready to get in the raft, but you have to remember that when you are in the water you inflate your Mae West. Have you ever tried to get into a life raft with an inflated Mae West on? What a job!

I had landed about one to two miles off the island near the airfield. Lieutenant McWhorter, his section, and his wingman came back looking for me and flew right over me, but I did not try to attract their attention. It seemed as though nobody on the island was paying any attention to me; maybe everyone was shooting at the photo plane; maybe because my chute didn't open they thought I was dead. At any rate, if I had tried to attract my flight's attention, I would also have attracted some attention from the island. The flight only had enough gas to get home, and even if they had seen me, they couldn't stay around to help. So I put the blue side of the poncho over me and watched them fly back to the ship. As soon as they left, I started to paddle away from the island.

After about ten minutes I heard some planes coming out of the clouds. Along came fourteen Jap planes, flying at about five hundred feet right over me. I am glad I didn't have my .38-caliber pistol with me because I probably would have been trying to shoot them down. They must have been waiting out in the clouds until our flight left. When they flew over me, they were so low I could see the pilots in the cockpits. Fortunately, they didn't see me. For the next half hour I paddled away from the island. However, not being able to see that I was getting anywhere, I pulled the poncho over me, said to heck with it, and went to sleep.

When I woke up it was night. The first thing I saw was what looked like a searchlight, and I thought, "Oh boy, they are out looking for me." After a minute or two, I noticed the light was not moving, only going around; it was a light at the airfield, so I went back to sleep.

The life raft that comes with you when you bail out is like an elongated inner tube with a rubber sheet across the bottom. When you sit in it, your butt is against one end and your feet, with your knees bent, are at the other. To lay down, you curl up and hope you get everything inside and pull the poncho over you so everything is nice, except for the three to five inches of water you are sitting in, supplied by waves splashing over you.

And speaking of waves—the next morning when I opened my eyes and lifted the edge of the poncho, I looked straight out horizontally and saw water. I looked a little higher and saw water, and then I looked a little higher and saw more water. What a scare! I was in the bottom of a trough, and the waves were about twenty feet high. I had been going up and down those waves and had not even felt them. What a roller-coaster ride, and I don't like roller coasters! One nice thing about that morning was that there was no land in sight in any direction. As you can guess, I didn't want to be a guest of the Japs. I would rather be skipper of my own ship at sea.

Over the next five days, about three or four times I was flipped over by the waves. It was a very funny feeling—the poncho on the bottom, me in the middle, and the raft over the top of my head, upside down. And you have to remember that during all this time, you are either sitting or lying in three to five inches of water in the bottom of the raft and always cold. Southern Kyushu, which was about 150 miles north of me, had snow on the ground.

About the middle of the third day I lifted the poncho to look around, and in all directions there was nothing but water. So I pulled the poncho down and started to doze. In a short time I felt a bump-bump-bump on the bottom of the raft. It was as if you were in shallow water and the waves were letting you down on the rocks; however, I had just looked out a few minutes before, and there was no land in any direction.

I decided I had better look out and see what was going on. Pulling up the edge of the poncho, I started to put my head out. About twelve inches from my face there was a head as big as mine attached to a long thin neck. That was all I saw. I retreated and pulled the poncho down, scared to death. I figured I had better find out what it was that was out there, but I held my face way back and lifted the poncho. I didn't see anything in front of me or to the sides, but when I looked behind me and behind the sea anchor [a rubber bucket on a rope], there was a very big turtle going up and down like a porpoise. He was as big as my life raft. When I saw him right behind the sea anchor, I thought he might take a bite out of it, and I didn't want that. As I pulled in the sea anchor, the turtle followed. There he was right beside the raft. If he had taken a bite out of the raft, I figured I would be walking (and it was a long way home!). I picked up the sea anchor and gave him a good bop on the nose, and away he went. I guess all he was looking for was a friend.

When you get out of the plane, the life-raft pack comes with you. In that pack there are three pints of water. In the backpack you wear with the chute harness there is also some water, a desalting kit, citric-acid tablets, vitamin tablets, a map, and other useful items. I tried the citric-acid tablets, and they were great, but made the mistake of chewing the vitamin tablets. They tasted just like fish oil, which is probably the reason they didn't go down too well. I had enough water, only using one and half pints in the five days I was in the raft. I guess I was getting ready for a long stay.

During these five days it was raining, cold, and there was no sunshine. I could hear planes, but I could not see them. I didn't know whose they were. On the fifth day, in the afternoon, the clouds broke, and the sun started to shine. Did that feel good! Now, the best of all, I saw two PBMs [twin-engine seaplanes] coming my way at about four thousand feet. I got out my signaling mirror, read the directions, and started to try and attract their attention. They flew right over me and kept going. I thought I needed the practice, so I kept trying. I guess I was just lucky: I had attracted the attention of the tail gunner in the last plane. They both turned around and came back. One came down low, and the other stayed up high. The low one was making passes at about thirty feet off the water, dropping a line of smoke flares. By the time he would get back, the smoke flares were out. On each pass I was standing up in the raft, signaling with my arms for them to land.

What they were doing was radioing the base through the plane at four thousand feet as to what to do. They were not rescue planes but rather had been on a fourteen-hour mission around the most northern part of Japan and were on their way back to their base at Okinawa. I found out later that the base had told them to use their own judgment. You know what that means. If you do good, OK, but if you mess up, it's your neck. As you guessed, they decided to land and get me.

They made another trip around and dropped smoke flares, came back, and started to land. As they came down, they hit one of those large ocean swells that come along every once in a while. It flipped them about thirty to forty feet in the air. When they came down and hit the water, their wings went up and down like two rubber bands.

They taxied back to me, didn't stop the engines, and as they went by at about five knots they threw me a rope but missed. They took a trip around again, threw the rope, and missed again. On the third time around, missed again; but this time I jumped out of the raft and grabbed the end of the rope. There I was looking like a surfboard on the water, sometimes under. The rope was slipping through my hands, and I wondered if the next slip was the end of the rope. Just then I felt two hands grab me and lift me into the plane. What a relief!

Everyone on the plane was wondering if they were going to be able to get off the water. When they hit the water, one crewman standing in the nose galley broke through the deck and went through to the hull. The pilot's seat broke away, and he landed the plane with his feet on the rudder pedals and holding onto the yoke, nothing else. In addition, the starboard engine had dropped six inches out of the engine nacelle, and it was just hanging there.

When they pulled me aboard, the first thing they wanted to do was to put me in a bunk. However, I had never been on a PBM, so I wanted to look around the plane. I heard the crew talking about how they were going to get off. I told them I didn't care, they could taxi all the way home. What had caused part of the problem was that they had a full bomb load in the engine nacelle, which they had not unloaded before they landed. After much checking and discussion by the pilots and crew, it was decided they would give it a try. So they powered up the engines with half power on the starboard engine and full power on the port engine, thereby successfully taking off by going in a circle.

They landed at Kerama Retto, just west of Okinawa, and transferred me to their supply-ship sick bay. Through all of this I had not received even a bruise; however, the next morning when I woke up I was so stiff I couldn't even sit up.

I stayed on the ship about two or three days. During my stay a news reporter by the name of Joe Hainline set up an interview with me. This interview was broadcast over NBC to the United States the same day they announced the death of Ernie Pyle. I was transferred to the air strip at Naha Airfield on Okinawa to await a TBM from the *Randolph* to take me back to the ship.

At the debriefing on the ship, they asked if I still wanted to fly. I said, "Sure, why not?" So back on the schedule I went.

Finley apparently had drifted northward for about half his stay and southward the second half, as he was rescued very close to the area where he had crashed. Although the tail of his aircraft was evidently shot off, the Hellcat still seemed at times to fly with less than a full complement of parts. Affectionately termed the "Grumman Iron Works," it often was forgiving of our mistakes, but better yet, it kept getting us home.

Finley's rescuer was crew number eight of the gull-winged PBM Mariner squadron, VPB-18, based on the seaplane tender USS *St. George,* AV 12, at Kerama Retto. Lt. Dino Marati landed the huge plane safely—if not gently. Flight Engineer Carl Stanway, Deerfield Beach, Florida, recalled their grinning passenger:

He was exuberant upon rescue. His attitude was, "I don't care what happens now—I'm among friends." He couldn't believe we had coffee aboard, not wanting more than his share and depriving any of us. Unfortunately, we didn't get to know Finley well—he was whisked away to sick bay aboard our supply ship.

As fate would have it, the damaged PBM used to rescue Finley would never fly again. It was hoisted onto the *St. George*'s deck for repair—only to be totally consumed in a kamikaze attack on 5 May. Apparently, it was the focal point of the attack.

The ship suffered multiple casualties, including one pilot, and structural damage. Though its mission was primarily long-range patrol/bombing, VPB-18 rescued twenty pilots during its combat tour.

Wan Airfield antiaircraft defenses had become tough on Thunderbird aircraft. Ens. George C. Collins of VBF-12, Lakewood, Colorado, attested to the Hellcat's durability:

> Our division was flying number three in a bombing and strafing raid. I was the last pilot flying wing on Bud Christie. We pushed over at about ten thousand feet, and within seconds my faithful Hellcat took flak in the left wing root. There was a two-foot hole, with fire coming alongside the cockpit. My thoughts were to be blown free, so I opened the canopy. My left arm was immediately sprained by the rush of air, and my goggles were pinned to the back panel.
>
> Recovering from the initial shock, I put my F6F into a full skid, hoping to extinguish the fire—which was successful! I pulled out at fifteen hundred feet in a valley between two mountain ranges . . . using jigs and jags I managed to reach the open sea. I looked out, and Bud Christie, thank God, was on my wing.
>
> Returning to the *Randolph* with all systems out except the engine, I managed, after two wave-offs without flaps, a safe landing at 105 knots [normal landing speed was 75–80 knots].
>
> I got chewed out by the landing signal officer, but I was happy to be aboard. The underside of the plane was full of holes; it was necessary to dump the plane over the side.

Not all damaged planes had to be junked. The Hellcat, in addition to being tough, was repairable and quite often was repaired quickly and returned to service. Ens. Allen Splittgerber of VBF-12, Wayne, Nebraska, commented:

> While I was in combat with Air Group 12 I got hit twice, once on the wing tip, but was able to land. The second time I had my head down and low, and the canopy was shot off, but I landed OK. Both

times I was hit and got back, the mechanics fixed the planes up, and they flew again the same day. I was lucky both times that the Japs didn't get me instead.

Some mishaps occurred not because of enemy action but because of miscues on the part of our own people. Takeoffs from the flight deck were either deck launches—in which the aircraft became airborne through its own power plant—or by catapult. The latter involved attaching a bridle to hooks on the lower side of the wing behind the propeller. The bridle was attached to a hook riding in a slot in the flight deck. When the catapult was activated, the plane was yanked along the flight deck and literally whipped into the air like a slingshot. Once in a while, as with most man-made things, something went wrong.

Lt. Matthew S. "Bob" Byrnes of VBF-12, Kalamazoo, Michigan, could attest to that:

> On a catapult launch, a steel cable got hung up on the hook under my right wing. It kept swinging back and punching holes in the fuselage right behind the cockpit. I tried everything I could think of to shake it off, but no luck. The whole fleet had to turn back into the wind so I could land. It's the only incident like this I ever heard of.

Our first ground-support mission really wasn't assigned, neither was it anything to write home about. We weren't supposed to write about any of our missions. The assigned flight began as a TCAP, but lousy weather dictated otherwise. VF-12's AAR of 8 April gave the following description:

> When TCAP arrived at Kikai the ceiling had lowered to three hundred feet. The flight then proceeded to Amami O'Shima and Tokuno Shima where same conditions prevailed. Not wishing to return without using their armament . . . called in on station at Okinawa Shima. Inasmuch as they were not equipped with target grids, the Support Air Director directed to return to base, which they did, unwillingly jettisoning their armament enroute.

Fortunately, that mission was an exception to the rule, as indicated by an April AAR about a mission involving four Hellcats and elght Avengers led by Lt. Cdr. Tex Ellison, the commanding officer of VT-12. Every ground-support mission was accompanied by at least one division of Hellcats, just in case, that "case" being enemy fighters.

According to Lieutenant Commander Ellison:

> We were directed by the target coordinator to proceed northwest to Mobotu Peninsula, where marines were encountering considerable artillery fire from the nearby island of Ie Shima. To consolidate their positions, it became necessary for us to neutralize this fire. We were instructed to bomb the heaviest area of enemy concentration, located on a hillside, indicated by grid squares on our maps. There, in well-protected caves, were large numbers of weapons ranging from light automatic machine guns to medium-sized artillery pieces. We made our approach from the southwest, and glide-bombing tactics were used. Our bombs were dropped at fifteen hundred feet. None of our planes were hit, although the hillside twinkled, according to other pilots, like lights on a Christmas tree from small-caliber gun flashes. We used ten-second delay fuses to permit bombs to penetrate deep into positions before detonating.

In many cases, these caves were actually burial sites used by Okinawan natives but taken over by the Japanese forces in their defense scheme.

Since 6 April when Sata Omaiti had boasted about another attack on 11 April, task-force commanders had been preparing defenses. The attack came one day later than Omaiti had forecast and was directed primarily against the landing forces at Okinawa. Admiral Mitscher had postponed support at Okinawa and added more CAPs to the flight schedule. Some eighty-five Japanese army and navy aircraft were sent in to stop the invasion and livened up activities for Air Group 12. VBF-12's AAR of 12 April related: "Lieutenant Bolduc's division was catapulted from Satan Base (Randolph) as a reinforcement CAP over Okinawa, the enemy having appeared there in considerable numbers. . . ."

Lt. Alfred Bolduc of VBF-12, Winter Garden, Florida, continued his description of the action:

> Our flight-schedule assignment was ready-plane standby on the flight deck. The time was about 0730. I settled down in the cockpit

with a good book. My plane was on the port catapult, and Joe Mangieri was on the starboard catapult. My whole concern was to last out the three hours of boredom by reading. The weather was clear, and because the ship was headed downwind it was rolling slightly. It was just a beautiful day that could only be experienced at sea.

I had read about a page and a half when someone jumped up on my starboard wing and handed me a piece of folded paper. On it was written, "Call Whiskey Base on channel 8." By the time I had read the message, there was pandemonium around the catapult. The catapult officer was frantically motioning me to start my engine. We cranked up the engines and were launched in about two minutes flat. We rendezvoused while checking out guns, etc., and I called Whiskey Base about four times. No answer. I called the ship to check it out, and a crisp message came back to "vector 270, ninety miles, climb to twenty five thousand feet." Okinawa!

We arrived over Okinawa at twenty-five thousand feet about ten miles north of the Yontan airfield. So many transmissions were being made on the radio that it was impossible to call anyone or to understand what was going on. After a few minutes a break in the radio traffic gave me an opportunity to call Whiskey Base. He came back, "Circle 'til I need you. I'm too busy."

During our approach to the island and while waiting to call Whiskey Base, the scene below us was unbelievable. Antiaircraft bursts carpeted the entire area up to about eighteen thousand feet. Ships were burning. Two destroyers were on fire and beaching on the western shore. Several planes were seen crashing. The radio was reporting all kinds of activity, including a midair collision and several bailouts.

After making a couple of wide circles, a twin engine plane passed about a half mile in front of us on a southerly heading. I recognized it as a Dinah. No mistaking the distinctive tail silhouette. It was moving very fast. No doubt a reconnaissance or photo plane. We immediately swung in about one-half mile behind it and went to full power. After a minute or two it was apparent we weren't gaining. We upped to maximum power. No gain. I dropped my belly tank and put on water injection. Now we were gaining at a pretty good rate. Shortly, we were within about two thousand feet. Because the guns are bore-sighted for fifteen hundred feet, I just hoped they'd reach at this distance. This is where the Mark 23 sight paid off. I turned the throttle handle until the sight was set for maximum range and put the pipper above the right engine and let go a two-second burst. Almost immediately, smoke started coming out of that engine, and the Dinah started losing speed. I rapidly closed in and from about three hundred feet observed the rearmost hatch flip open, and a gun barrel poked out in our direction. I could have sworn it was at least a 75-mm, but in reality knew it was a .30-caliber. Before he could get off a round I riddled the entire fuselage very thoroughly, and the Dinah immediately started to spiral down. I pulled up, and Jim Funsten fell in behind and administered a coup de grace.

We resumed circling, and it soon became apparent that something was amiss with my engine. It began cutting out whenever I made throttle adjustments. We let down towards the northern end of the island and returned to the *Randolph* just about on time for the next scheduled landing.

While all of Air Group 12's pilots had qualified to make night carrier landings before embarking on the *Randolph,* they were primarily intended for emergencies. Routine night flying was left to the VF(N), which took charge at dusk to fly CAPs and harass the airfields at Kikai to interrupt the kamikaze resupply. Like Air Group 12's predecessor, Group Able, the night-fighter group began its training in Florida, with specialized radar-intercept training at Rhode Island bases. The fighter squadrons stressed teamwork within and with other flight divisions. The night-fighter pilot's training involved single-plane tactics, intensive instrument flying (utilizing cockpit instruments only), interception and tracking of aircraft targets at night, and use of gun sights incorporated into the aircraft's radar system.

Night-fighter pilots, once training was completed, moved on to squadrons. Ens. Robert F. Monaghan, Chicago, Illinois, one of the original VF(N)-12 members, completed his training in mid-1944:

Thereafter, in September or October, the squadron was moved to Alameda, California, and thence to Barbers Point, Oahu, Hawaii. The flight from California to Oahu was done on Thanksgiving Day, with cheese sandwiches and pineapple juice celebrating the occasion while [we were] strapped in bucket seats on an old bomber at twelve thousand feet—hardly an auspicious celebration. . . .

Intense training in gunnery, dive-bombing, rocket firing at night, and controlled intercepting of enemy aircraft and surface vessels at Barbers Point concluded with the checkout for night carrier landings on the USS *Saratoga*. The arrival of the USS *Randolph* at Pearl Harbor caused the detachment of six night-fighter pilots to that ship. They were Lieutenant Donald M. Hypes (officer-in-charge), Lieutenant (junior grade) Leadean Levis, Ensign LaMar O. Woods, Ensign David G. Howard, Jr., Ensign Francis Sullivan, and myself. The four specially night-adapted F6F Hellcats were flown aboard the *Randolph* while she was under way with other vessels en route to the Pacific Fleet. The record will show that the four night-fighters made one pass each, the landings being done in record time. Captain Baker called down to the ready room with a "welcome aboard" and congratulated the four on the landings with a "well done, night-fighters." At this point, it is only fair to say that the landings made by those four night-fighters in question, of which I was one, had an added incentive. Carried in the belly of each aircraft was a parachute bag with fifths of assorted alcoholic beverages carefully wrapped in skivvies, T-shirts, pants, socks, etc. There is no doubt in my mind that the safety of that cargo contributed to the excellent performance of the night-fighter pilots on that occasion.

Once in the combat arena, the night-fighter's flight routine was the antithesis of that of the other fighter squadrons. The tasks were basically the same, but the manner in which they were achieved was radically different. Ensign Monaghan explained:

After being briefed, night-fighters would on many occasions be on standby if they were not on patrol. This meant that you sat around the ready room, wearing red goggles to preserve night adaptation. It was of maximum importance that the ability to see at night be maintained at all times. Wearing those glasses contributed to the gloom in the ready room. Card-playing was possible by outlining the hearts and diamonds with black or dark green ink, otherwise you couldn't tell the red cards at all. If you didn't play cards, you played "acey-deucey"—where the different colors of the board being white or black were easily discernible. Other times, the pilots just jawed with each other. Sometimes tactics were discussed, call procedures, and various aspects of the problems of getting on and off carriers at night. We also talked of family, school, and girls.

The night-fighters participated in combat air patrols, taking off between five and five thirty in the evening and proceeding to assigned stations and patrolling the area under instructions from CIC [Combat Information Center]. At this stage, the patrols were, in the main, uneventful, unless an attack was coming in. If the four aircraft were to do two flights, then at the end of four hours, the planes would be taken aboard another aircraft carrier in the task group that was spotted forward, an arrangement of aircraft that permitted both the landing area and the catapults to be available. Upon landing, the aircraft would be taken down on the middle elevator to the hanger deck, brought up on the forward elevator after being serviced, and placed on the catapult. [In daylight the aircraft were moved forward and parked on the flight deck.] It would then be fired off, and the patrol would continue until the following morning, when we would return to our own ship after the early-morning day-fighter sweeps had been launched.

To some of the night-fighter pilots, flying at night was a very beautiful thing. Upon takeoff and gaining altitude, you quickly became used to the sound of the engine and the utter silence that accompanies night air-patrol missions, as this was done by a single aircraft in his assigned area. The solitude was not a burden; in fact, most night-fighter pilots on this type of patrol considered it a relief from all the hectic activities going on below. The sky would be dark, black at times, so that the soft green glow of the instruments would be all that gave illumination. On moonlit nights the clouds would be grey, soft, fleecy, giving an impression of peace. The sky would be a dome of solitude speckled with tiny points of light in a vast, brilliant panorama of quiet. This condition would be breached only by an occasional communication from "Smitty" in CIC, the night-fighter director.

Things would change, however, when enemy planes came into the range of the ship's radar, and the pilot would be vectored to intercept. The problem here was one of being directed behind and under the aircraft to be intercepted. As you got closer and closer, supposedly you could do it on gun sight alone. It was a terribly tricky maneuver and quite technical in its application. It was very difficult to ascertain exactly how close you were to the enemy aircraft in the last stages of closing for attack. Most of the pilots would look up and out of the cockpit when they were close to see if they could find the dark outline of the enemy aircraft ahead and above. Upon seeing him, the pilot climbed, to be directly aft of the enemy aircraft, and fired everything he had. On night-fighter aircraft, the armament consisted of two 20-mm cannons and four .50-caliber machine guns. During this period, thought was occasionally given to the fact that the target might be a Betty with a tail gunner looking down your throat instead of a Frances with no tail gunner.

Lieutenant Hypes had the first night-fighter kill the evening of 14 April, shooting down a Paul, and Ensign Monaghan shot down a Frances later in the evening. These successes capped a day of kills by both fighter squadrons: VF-12, Lieutenant Vita, a Zeke; VBF-12, Ensign Colin, two Tonys and a Myrt; VF(N)-12, Ensign Howard, one Betty and one Myrt.

On the fourteenth Ens. E. Jindra of VF-12 launched as part of a CAP during the concentrated attack on the fleet. His takeoff was faulty, and he skidded and went over the side. He had to remain in the water until after the attack, when a destroyer picked him up.

ARM3c Robert Staszak, Sun City West, Arizona, of VT-12 observed another accident:

> While under a kamikaze attack aboard ship I was drafted to act as a plane captain to bring up fighter planes from the hanger deck and turn them over to the flight-deck officer.
>
> The first plane roared down the deck, and after traveling only twenty feet, its port wheel brake locked, causing the plane to do a ninety-degree left turn, flipping over the side of the ship and into the water upside down. The plane sank within seconds, trapping the pilot inside.
>
> I never did learn the identity of that pilot. My role in the events leading to his demise has remained hauntingly with me.

The events of 14 through 17 April pressed the ship's gunners also, as the *Randolph*'s cruise book indicated:

> Rarely did a day pass without general quarters or torpedo defense

being sounded because of the approach of enemy aircraft. Several days will be long remembered. One was 14 April when, at 1915, two enemy aircraft were reported. One of these closed to about six miles and showed a red light which remained burning until a string of almost a dozen closely-bunched flares were dropped; against these lights the ships must have stood out clearly. The first plane started in, not more than 150 feet off the water. *Randolph* turned, twisted, zig-zagged to get out of the way. Below decks we sweated and prayed as the guns began pounding and the empty ammunition casings rattled on the decks over our heads. Then came the welcome announcement that the plane had been shot down. We sighed with relief. It seemed the Jap plane had crossed five hundred yards ahead of our ship. As it passed over a destroyer on our starboard quarter it was hit, burst into flames and crashed into the dark sea.

Another plane was shot down a short time later.

The flares mentioned in this report were also a startling sight for one of the night-fighters. Ensign Monaghan, who had already shot down one Frances, was vectored to another. The VF-12 AAR detailed the action:

Monaghan closed to within one mile of another plane on a third vector, when his contact was broken off upon approach to the Task Group screen. Just as he turned the bogey was taken under AA fire and subsequently knocked down. . . .

The approach of the Frances was apparently in conjunction with an abortive attack against one of the Task Groups which was being undertaken simultaneously. During his successful interception, while flying at an altitude of twenty-five hundred feet, Monaghan was startled by a flare which burst into light directly above him at three thousand feet. Each flare was composed of eight to ten balls of intense white light, each suspended from its own parachute, and all strung together horizontally. Several of these sets were dropped. Each flare lasted for about ten minutes and was replaced immediately, when it had burned out or submerged, by a fresh release which began to glow at the same altitude (three thousand feet). A total of three groups of flares were dropped. The plane performing this operation flew a straight and level course at six to seven thousand feet, and dropped window simultaneously [aluminum strips that produce false echo on the radar]. This illumination was estimated to be at a distance of fifteen miles from the group under attack.

The *Randolph*'s action report also described the events of 17 April that seemed to involve everyone:

About 0520 a Jap plane was sighted off the starboard quarter, closing fast. Trying to crash our stern, he missed and flew along the port side of the ship, close aboard and about fifty feet above the water, his guns blazing. Under fire from our batteries he crashed into the water one hundred feet off the ship's port bow.

About nine o'clock that morning more bogeys were sighted. Two dived at us from about six thousand feet. As the leading plane came out of a cloud he was hit by one of our five-inch shells. The plane exploded and the pilot bailed out, floating down to the water in view of all those on the flight deck. The second plane continued its run to a point closer to the ship where one our 40-mm shells knocked its right wing off, causing it to spin into the water. . . . During this morning's attack in which still other Japs dived on ships in the group our gunners accounted for three enemy aircraft. We had learned to play for keeps.

About this time Ensign Finley began to have a few repercussions from his five-day ride in the life raft. He continued his account of what occurred:

Everything went well for about a week or so, but one evening I looked at the schedule for the next day. My fight was on the same day of the week I was shot down. The takeoff time was the same; there were the same four pilots in the same positions, and [we were] going to the same island for the same purpose. I sat down and talked to Lieutenant McWhorter, my flight leader, and said, "I am not going." His reaction was that if I didn't go, I probably would be scared to fly again. I mentioned to him, "What if I got scared and left the flight right in the middle?" He said he didn't think I would, so I said, "OK, let's go."

The next day at about 1500, I was again sitting on the number two catapult with my engines turning up and ready to go. The flight was canceled. It was the first flight that I had ever had canceled since we had been on the ship.

I am not superstitious, but that was too much for me. About three days later, I was on my way back to the States.

Up until this eventful 14 April, Air Group 12's participation in the Okinawa campaign had been mostly in support of ground action on Okinawa and interdiction raids on the islands to the north. With the exception of occasional raids against Kyushu, the routine was to patrol the Ryukyu Islands for enemy aircraft on the ground, harass the airfields, and maintain CAPs over our picket destroyers and TCAPs near Kikai Shima, with emphasis on Wan Airfield. Later these patrols were extended as far north as Yaku Shima, almost within sight of Kyushu. The primary purpose was to stop the Japanese from infiltrating aircraft into these islands where attacks could be launched against the fleet and landing forces at Okinawa. Successful attacks such as the devastating blow to the *Franklin* on 19 March apparently encouraged the Special Attack Air Forces to continue the suicidal attacks. Their attempts to repeat a success like that dealt the *Franklin* continued until the middle of August. However, no CVs or CVLs were struck after the middle of May. The *Natoma Bay*, a CVE, was the last carrier kamikaze victim, hit on 6 June off Okinawa. Fortunately, she suffered no casualties.

The *Intrepid* again paid for the raids on 16 April. She was attacked by five kamikazes. She took the two ahead and two astern under fire. The fifth was downed near the battleship nearby. The two attacking from astern caused problems. One was set afire by 40-mm and 20-mm batteries and crashed within fifty feet of the starboard side. The second, although hit, continued its approach and crash-dived with a bomb near the number three elevator. Ignited aviation fuel from Air Group 10's damaged aircraft on the flight and hangar decks became life threatening. The toll was remarkably light—ten killed or missing, two dozen badly burned, and sixty-six slightly wounded—considering the damage caused by the lone kamikaze.

However, the intense heat generated warped one of the elevator's drive shafts beyond the repair capabilities of Ulithi. The *Intrepid* was returned to the West Coast for three months. After repairs she rejoined the Task Force for a short stint just before peace was declared.

The toll of hits on the fast attack carriers had reduced their numbers such that after the 17 April raids on the fleet, Task Group

58.2, of which the *Randolph* was a part, was eliminated. The losses following the *Franklin's* were the *Wasp, Hancock, Enterprise,* and *Intrepid,* all to be out temporarily for two to three months. The task force was temporarily operating with five fewer attack carriers until the *Enterprise* and *Yorktown* were repaired at Ulithi.

In spite of the many raids and sweeps among the airfields and landing strips on the enemy islands to the north, many potential kamikaze aircraft remained, and the enemy was determined to stop the Okinawa invasion operation. The aggressive Thunderbirds continued to push hard at the enemy, exemplifying the philosophy and personality of the air group's founder, Commander Crommelin, even though he was no longer leading them. That the actions of strike leaders of other air groups were sometimes frustrating to us was reflected in VBF-12's AAR#24 of 15 April:

A large fighter group of twenty aircraft was to participate in a sweep on southern Kyushu. The pilots were briefed about fifteen minutes before launch. The sweep leader was from a different ship. CV-15's twenty fighters rendezvoused with the sweep leader's eight fighters, and the group proceeded north. On approaching Konoya A/F, the senior aviator of CV-15's twenty planes called the sweep leader to say he would continue on to A/F 313 and rendezvous afterward. The leader rogered. The fields were only five miles apart.

The twenty fighters made their rocket run and before rendezvous was completed, were ordered to join up with the sweep leader and return to base. One lone Tojo was observed and shot down. However, on the apron by the hangars were some twenty S/E [single-engine] planes. The revetted bomber areas to the south of the field were not investigated. There was no enemy airborne opposition. Although there is AA at A/F 313, none was observed on the only run made. It seems unfortunate that an opportunity was missed to take care of whatever was at A/F 313 that day.

This same day, 17 April, could have been called "bogey day" for the ship and air group. "Memories," the history of Air Group 12, recorded the action:

It started at dawn with a Zeke getting inside the destroyer screen. It was taken under fire by all batteries as it closed in a fast glide from astern, evidently attempting a crash dive on the flight deck. Fortunately, the pilot missed the ship, passed along the port side just above the gun mounts with his guns spitting and plunged into the water off the bow. . . . At about nine o'clock many bogeys were reported northward at a distance of thirty five miles, and shortly thereafter all hell broke loose. Several Jap planes broke through the combat air patrol and approached the task group at high altitude. Suddenly every ship began to fire. AA bursts dotted the sky. Two planes dived at the *Randolph* from about six thousand feet. They were in column and, as they passed through the cloud cover at about three thousand feet proceeding at high speed, were taken under fire. The leading plane exploded, the pilot bailing out. The second plane continued its run to a point very close to the ship where its right wing was shot off and the plane spun in. A medium sized bomb continued travel from the first plane, hitting the water and exploding about one hundred yards off the *Randolph*'s starboard beam. It is believed that 5-inch gunfire accounted for the first and 40-mm for the second. A few minutes later another dive-bomber came streaking down for a suicide try at a light cruiser on the port beam, narrowly missing her stern. At 0930 two other diving attacks were made by planes on other ships in the formation, but heavy AA fire accounted for both of them and they crashed into the water. Additional bogies were reported, but none closed the formation, and at about 1100 the [radar] screen was clear. Thus ended the first big daylight attack, and the subsequent rest at the refueling area the next day was doubly appreciated by all hands.

On a ground-support mission the same day, Lt. Curtis Hamilton, VT-12's executive officer, assumed the role of flight leader when Tex Ellison's radio failed. The VT-12 AAR of 17 April described this flight as a standard support mission, with several exceptions:

An unusual degree of accuracy was attained (1) by very good target spotting by target coordinator, and (2) by starting the glide and dropping the bomb at low altitudes. Each defensive position was "pinpointed" to the extent that bombs were dropped on specific gun installations, rather than general area bombing.

Glide attacks were started at 3500 feet, just below the cloud base. Delayed fuse settings allowed planes to go in close and retire without danger of bomb blast.

Another aspect of ground-support missions: Seldom were pilots able to see, or verify, their attempts at precision bombing. This mission was an exception, according to CASCU. From the same AAR:

Target coordinator was quite enthusiastic about the attack and when it was completed wanted to know the name and hometown address of the leader. He stated over the radio that the strike was excellently conducted, and added . . . the men in the trenches stood up and cheered every time an enemy gun position was blasted. These particular guns had been giving the infantry plenty of trouble and the men were jubilant to see them eliminated.

The terrain over which these Okinawa ground-support missions were conducted was probably as different from the black dust of Iwo Jima as could be. As one of Ens. Roy Bruce's flight team remarked, "It's like middle-Ohio farm country with plenty of trees for the Japs to conceal their gun positions, and they are very good at that."

The island is a narrow, irregularly shaped, sprawling piece of land about seventy miles long with high ridges running along the center for three-quarters of its length from northeast to southwest. The southern quarter levels out noticeably, and there is where most of the native Okinawans lived and where the Japanese built most of the airstrips. We started using them as soon as they were captured.

The following day, 18 April, as the task group pulled back to resupply, Dr. Williams's "Chronicle" reflected both the good and the ominous:

4/18—The night was quiet. There are only six CVs left out of eighteen. We hear the *Hancock* took her bomb (7 April) in Officers' Country and lost twenty nine officers. We spent the day in retired position while Task Group 58.3 refueled. We hear that there are many bogies up north all day. There is to be a big push on Okinawa and we are to support it closely. Loading planes tonight with 1,000-bombs and napalm fire (belly) tanks. Army Colonel wired us today that the support we gave yesterday was the best he'd ever seen. (Each of) our planes dropped four 500-pound bombs on gun emplacements over southern Okinawa.

The grim side for us was the loss of another pilot not to the enemy but to an operational accident. Ens. W. L. Mason of VF-12 was lost when his plane veered over the port side upon landing.

By this time Ensign Brown and Airman Richards, shot down in February north of Tokyo, had been transferred to permanent camps. They continued their account of their ordeal as prisoners, Brown noting a sad day for both the task forces and the prisoners of war:

Brown: The interrogators were all U.S. educated. Most of them had been in business on the West Coast, in the Seattle and Los Angeles areas, and spoke excellent English. They kept us informed about the progress of the war and, as it turned out, accurately. By way of the grapevine we were told that President Roosevelt had died. No one had any idea who the vice president was!

Each morning while at Ofuna, all prisoners were required to leave their cells and fall in formation for calisthenics. They began by facing the direction of the Imperial Palace and bowing to the emperor. The first time, I didn't bow with the rest until the man behind me said, "Dammit, bow and spit." I bowed and observed each prisoner bow and spit. It was a wonder the guards didn't notice the straight dotted lines made in the dust.

One of the rules enforced by the guards was that if one of us disobeyed or committed any infraction of their rules, all prisoners in that unit were severely punished. Not being able to speak Japanese made it rather difficult to learn the rules.

After I was let out of solitary confinement, I was permitted to join the other prisoners in an outdoor compound to spend several hours a day. Although we were not allowed to converse with each other, I soon learned that the other prisoners' preoccupation with killing flies and placing them in a can was not purely a health measure. For each one hundred flies a prisoner was allotted one cigarette. Each cigarette was usually cut in thirds and one-third smoked in a bamboo holder three times a day. The guard on duty would go from cell to cell, lighting each cigarette. I joined the others in the fly-killing operation and had no difficulty in killing one hundred flies per day. When it was time to exchange your can of dead flies for the cigarettes, the guard on duty would pick one of the prisoners at random and sit down on a bench while the prisoner counted each one of the flies. The first time I observed a counting, the prisoner had apparently only stunned one of the flies, since the count was ninety-nine. The Japanese had a great dislike for dishonesty. The short count was evidence of dishonesty, and each prisoner in the unit was punished with a clubbing by the guard. Thereafter, each can had at least 110 flies. Although I was a nonsmoker up to that time, I quickly acquired the habit, which I didn't kick for thirty-two years!

Richards: They took us to Omari, then they made us stand out there a couple of hours, I think, standing at attention. Poor McCann's leg was real bad. One of the guys from the USS *Tang* was there, and we both pushed against McCann to try to help hold him up because he couldn't stand. Then they finally took me and McCann—they said we were the only two shot down over Japan itself. They took us out of that group and about fifteen guys out [of] the cell—I don't know how many were in there. We were standing out there three or fours days, trying to sleep laying down at night. The only thing that touched the ground was your butt, because you had your head over on some guy's stomach and your feet over another guy. Then they gave us sour rice.

We went back over to the barracks. Of course, we didn't know anybody when we got there. But they didn't fool with blindfolds anymore, and it was a real enjoyment because you got to talk to people and sit around the cell.

Brown: That was the problem up at Ofuna, you couldn't. They wouldn't let us talk to each other.

Richards: About two weeks later they started taking us out on work parties. All we would do was to clean off whole blocks that had been burnt to the ground and then plant gardens. We would come back, and still there was no medical attention for anybody. They kept saying we weren't entitled to medical attention.

Brown: The camp at Omari was a regular POW camp, but still the fliers and submarine men were "captives" and kept locked in their barracks. We were not permitted to associate with the other prisoners. Many were captured at Singapore and in the Philippines. There was no further interrogation at Omari. Greg Boyington was in the same barracks and on an occasion "chewed me out" for not eating what little there was. But after one full week of nothing but cucumbers and hot tea, my dysentery and beriberi had reached the point where I was losing interest. I was sent out on one work detail, clearing away burned houses to make room for garden spots, but was too weak to be effective and was not sent out again.

On 20 April, four Hellcats escorted a flight of twelve Helldivers and eleven Avengers to the southern tip of Okinawa to orbit until directed by CASCU. This mission was to support the advance of the Twenty-fourth Army Corps in the south-central part of the island, particularly a heavily wooded area.

VB-12's AAR gave this description: "Attacks were begun from 5,000 feet, from east to west and bombs were released, one at a time, at 1500 feet." The low release altitude allowed a pilot less than thirty seconds to locate the target in his gun sight and release the bomb before pulling out of the dive. This procedure depended on the target coordinator's locating only a general target area within the grid map the pilot carried. In this instance, there was no specific objective, an exception to the rule that usually pinpointed the target.

In his summary of this mission in the VT-12 AAR, Lieutenant Commander Ellison had some recommendations for future support missions:

(1) better radio discipline,
(2) fewer planes in the target area at one time and,
(3) supplement bombs with rockets on torpedo planes. . . .

Item number three would certainly have been helpful if applied to a ground-support mission on 22 April.

Equipping dive-bombers with four rockets had been standard operating procedure for some time, as indicated on this mission involving the usual four fighters, ten dive-bombers, and twelve torpedo bombers. The group was directed by CASCU to attack a group of caves at the base of a ridge on the Nagagusuku Wan, a large semi-sheltered bay on the southeastern coast. Fierce fighting had erupted near an airstrip under construction.

Two cave entrances assigned to the dive-bombers were hit with 500-pound bombs, rockets, and 20-mm cannon. One entrance was sealed shut. If this cave had been a burial site before being used as a gun position by the Japanese, the fate of war intervened to restore it to its original purpose.

Continued operations in the Okinawa area were relatively quiet until 22 April, a day flight-deck crews would not call normal. Ens. Lowell W. Rund, flying an F6F, dropped his auxiliary gas tank while landing. Apparently, he had some sort of emergency but failed to jettison the full (150 gallons) belly tank. It broke lose and was sliced open as it hurtled forward through the propeller. Fortunately, the alert fire crews quickly doused the flames while Rund was pulled from the cockpit. He suffered third-degree burns on his neck and first- and second-degree burns on his face and shoulders.

The problems of the day were still not over for the flight-deck crews. An SB2C piloted by Ens. R. R. Andreason crashed ahead of the ship right after takeoff, and he and his crewman were rescued in good condition by the *Tingey*. Then an SB2C piloted by Ens. T. J. Miller failed to engage the wire upon landing and crashed into the barrier. Fortunately, no one was injured.

Shortly thereafter the *Randolph* received word that Commander Crommelin had been missing in action since 28 March, as a result of a midair collision over Okinawa.

The rest of the day was not very normal, according to the "History of Bombfighting Squadron TWELVE":

All hands mourned the loss of a great leader and friend. During his assignment with Task Group 58.1, he displayed that same ability to coordinate and lead large strike groups as he had so brilliantly shown at Tokyo. On 19 March, he led a large strike against the Kure Naval Base and on 18, 23, 24, 25, and 28 March, he led strikes over Kyushu and the Nansei Shoto Islands. In addition to possessing so fully those qualities which enable him to be so fine a tactician—a type the navy needs so much at this stage of the war—he was a man whom pilots revered and would follow enthusiastically. He liked a pilot who as he said, "thought aggressively."

At an air group picnic at Mog Mog when the Grog Grog [green beer] had flowed freely, the ensigns decided to throw their lieutenants and superiors into the ocean. Commander Crommelin was heard to say almost as if in disappointment, "They used to do this to me, but now that I am a commander, they probably won't." However, he was soon surrounded and hauled off unceremoniously to be dunked in the Pacific, a performance in which he joined with enthusiasm.

If Air Group TWELVE is remembered at all, it will be remembered as "Crommelin's Thunderbirds," the title being derived from the air group insignia, an Indian Thunderbird. ("History of Bombing Fighting Squadron TWELVE")

How ironic that this fearless and innovative leader, consumed with one ambition, destroying the enemy who had partially blinded him, met his death not at the hands of this enemy but in a midair collision with another F6F making a photographic run over the southern tip of Okinawa. The F6F collided with Commander Crommelin, both planes crashing in the sea off Chimen Peninsula.

7 Okinawa, 22 April–4 May

More TCAPs were now in place to deal with the increase in offensive and kamikaze aircraft coming south through the Ryukyu Island chain, but not in sufficient numbers, as witnessed on 22 April when VBF-12 aircraft were stationed over Wan Airfield at Kikai Shima. Actions the night before signaled that something was brewing for the next day: Ens. D. G. Howard of VF(N)-12 shot down two Bettys snooping near the task force. The VF AAR reported his activities. He had intercepted the first Betty at eight thousand feet, but concerned that there were many other friendly aircraft in the area, he challenged: "Twin-engine plane with a night-fighter on your tail, if you are a friendly, flash your signal lights." Speculation has it that there were numerous flashing aircraft lights around the fleet. Thirty minutes later he disposed of the second Betty, again in the vicinity of the task force.

Commenting on his activities, Ensign Howard indicated that there was really nothing to it. "All you have to do is follow the fighter director's instructions and pull the trigger." Simple as that! He did not mention, however, that visibility was very poor, with a murky haze to five thousand feet and clouds from twenty-five hundred to four thousand feet, both of which his second contact used to advantage. The task-force commander, Admiral Mitscher, dispatched a few words of congratulations to him about his accomplishments.

The VBF-12 AAR on the activities of 22 April also addressed the situation that had been developing at Kikai:

The actions of the Kikai TCAP herein reported are typical of the many daily missions of similar TCAPs from dawn to dusk, and through some nights by VF(N). Where no airborne opposition is met, the TCAP drops its bombs, fires its rockets, and strafed certain wooded areas south and east of Wan Field where photo intelligence reveals hidden revetted areas in woods and even a possible underground hangar—the latter not unlikely. Results other than fires cannot be observed. Operational planes are rarely seen on the field. AA is heavy and accurate but not always encountered. The main function of the TCAP is of course, to deny the enemy the use of the field, and to fulfill that function the TCAP remains on station. Some TCAPs are relieved on station (for continuity), but the majority go according to an almost consistent schedule.

Strikes have been sent to Kikai to bomb the field and revetted areas. The field, however, is a landing area, not a strip, and is some forty five hundred by fifteen hundred feet. To keep the field unoperational [sic] would take constant daily strikes, and the Task Force 58 is at present devoting its striking power on Okinawa. The field is daily reported operational.

That the Japs use the field and know our schedule of CAP was known to Air Group 12 early in the game. A pilot from VF-12 (Ensign Finley) was hit by AA on 8 April and landed in the water very near the airfield. He was picked up on 12 April and returned to the ship on 19 April. He stated that 15 minutes after his flight left the island, six jap planes landed and fourteen took off. His flight reported no Jap planes visible. At a later date, one VBF pilot observed a plane on a taxi strip while making a bombing run. After pullout and rendezvous, he returned to rocket and strafe but the plane was gone. On 22 April an eight plane TCAP at Kikai observed seventy planes arrive in three groups: Group one, 18–20 fighter types; group two 25 Vals; group three 22–26 Nates. Our planes took on the first group leaving fewer planes and a very disrupted fighter escort for the Vals and Nates. The approach was of course reported, and F4Us intercepting the Vals shot them down by getting on their tails and cracking flaps to thirty degrees so as not [to] overshoot. The Vals had no rear seat gunners—hence destruction in no time. Nates never present a problem to any of our fighter types.

Kikai and Amami are obviously the only reference points between Tanega and Okinawa for Jap aircraft coming south from Kyushu, and they have been coming and have been destroyed. Our losses compared to the loss to the Japs of aircraft and pilots are, it is hoped, considered worth the price. Is it better to leave Kikai-Wan Field operational and destroy more and more Jap aircraft which perhaps would come in much smaller numbers if the field and its facilities were completely denied them?

If the purpose of bombing, rocketing, and strafing is to destroy aircraft on Kikai, a much more effective armament plan would be napalm.

The napalm problem mentioned in the air-group commander's report occurred early in the use of this deadly weapon. Napalm's effectiveness was less than what was expected because of a poor fuzing system that often did not work. This weapon, which had been only partially successful on Iwo Jima, was now enhanced with a new igniting system. A VF-12 AAR explained:

Napalm bombs, with which this squadron had experienced so much difficulty at Iwo Jima, worked to perfection on Okinawa. A method of installing the igniter was developed aboard (this ship) which assisted in this success. . . . Pilots are enthusiastic about the performance of napalm, so arranged, on two scores; the increased safety of the weapon due to the arming feature, and the increased damage results from the napalm. It is believed that fighters equipped with napalm wing bombs would be far more effective and damaging to the enemy than under the present armament of rockets and general purpose bombs . . . it is felt that [with] the perfections contributed by Air Group 12 personnel the "Napalm problem" would be a thing of the past.

Lt. A. A. Bureau, Ordnance Officer, the developer of the ringtail aircraft torpedo, is largely responsible for the perfection of the ignition and improved fuzing [of] the napalm wing-tank bomb.

The Air Group 12 shoot-out mentioned in the VBF AAR of 22 April involved eight planes in two divisions as a TCAP over Kikai Shima and eight VF-12 planes in two divisions over Okinawa. The seventy-odd Japanese aircraft were first intercepted at Kikai. Our pilots were at an altitude disadvantage. Out of the first group of eight Japanese escorting fighters, six were no sooner destroyed than sixteen to eighteen more appeared at twenty thousand feet. This time the Japanese had a definite altitude advantage, but even more serious was the determination of the enemy pilots to make head-on suicidal runs into our aircraft. This maneuver of self-destruction was a desperate effort to get the Nate and Val bombers closer to Okinawa and the Allied landing-force ships. Fortunately for the two VBF-12 divisions, the Japanese fighters not shot down retreated northward, leaving the Nates and Vals to the mercy of our fighters and marine Corsairs covering Okinawa. Another disadvantage at Kikai was that one Hellcat had engine trouble and had to be escorted back to base. The remaining six Hellcats accounted for the destruction of eight enemy fighters.

Lt. Robert M. "Bob" Witmer of VBF-12, Radnor, Pennsylvania, a division flight leader, was at Kikai:

> We were northeast of Kikai Island on TCAP with my division, trailing Rube Denoff's division. My wingman tallyhoed a bogey, rogered by Rube, and we climbed to intercept what turned out to be twenty-five plus Oscars and Zekes. In splashing two, I became separated from my division (or vice versa) and climbed to fifteen thousand feet, trying to find some friendlies.
>
> Just under a thin cloud layer about eight Oscars and Zeros in a column were diving for the water. I figured to get on the end, and pick them off one at a time till we ran out of airspace. Got one, and was closing to firing range on the next, and checked my mirror—too late! One of them was on my tail, already firing. Shot off the port horizontal stabilizer, and I spun to about three thousand feet and finally recovered.
>
> After being lost for a while, Earl Manhold and I found each other. With the help of a couple of marine Corsairs, we located Yontan Airstrip on Okinawa, where I made a controlled crash landing.

When the Nates and Vals arrived in the Okinawa area, another melee ensued, but this time the advantage was with the F6Fs and F4Us. The major difficulty was the higher performance of both the Hellcats and Corsairs: they kept overrunning the slower Japanese aircraft. The VF-12 pilots destroyed four of the enemy, and other squadrons downed the remainder. None of the enemy aircraft penetrated the CAPs to get to the landing forces at Okinawa.

The VF-12 Narrative Report for 22 April provided some more details of one of the division's encounter with two of the Nates. Lt. (j.g.) John "Tubby" Franks, Allentown, Pennsylvania, and his team of three—Ensigns Steve Maloney, Tom Northcutt, and Bill "Skull" Smart—were orbiting at about seven thousand feet east of Okinawa. Second-section leader Northcutt spotted two aircraft at his nine-o'clock position and peeled off to attack. Franks and Maloney were not far behind when Northcutt and Smart dove with guns blazing on one of the obsolete fixed–landing gear bombers. Northcutt missed.

"I didn't realize he was so slow," he recalled, "but was aware I would overshoot despite yanking all power off. My mistake was in pulling up ahead of this guy, almost a fatal mistake, because he unloaded on me before I fire-walled my Hellcat and got out of there."

Franks remembered it well: "Northcutt hollered for Smart to get that S.O.B. off his tail, which Smart did, smartly." Franks knocked down the other Nate in a textbook gunnery run. Northcutt, still shaken by the close call, observed from a short distance away as the Nate disintegrated in a ball of fire.

Three-hour ground-support missions at Okinawa were becoming milk runs with just enough variations to keep both pilots and controllers alert for tricks by the Japanese defenders. On 28 April the usual mix of Air Group 12 aircraft was orbiting in the vicinity of Yonabaru, where a cave had been restored to its original use on 22 April, and was awaiting assignment. CASCU advised the group to ignore the white phosphorus shells normally used to mark targets. The enemy was also using them to confuse pilots. The Japanese were very adept at adopting any device we might use to make close air support more effective. The ground support was executed, white phosphorus was totally ignored, and except for a few dings in our aircraft from small-arms fire, the mission was successful, with all aircraft returning safely to the *Randolph*.

The role of our aircrewmen during these ground-support flights was relegated to that of observers because there was practically no chance of enemy air opposition over southern Okinawa. Nor were there many opportunities for SB2C and TBM gunners to use their .30-caliber machine guns: they were facing aft, and whatever target the pilot picked out zoomed by too quickly for gunners to aim and fire.

It didn't take long for Ens. William Hazlehurst of VT-12, Towson, Maryland, to realize how boring these flights must be for his crew. During the last dive of an uneventful flight over Okinawa he strung out his recovery prior to rendezvous, putting his turkey (TBM) into a steep turn so that his top turret gunner, ARM3c Lester Brinson, a sailor barely out of high school, could rake the dense brush below: "It was a great feeling to finally open up with my guns. However, I have grave doubts that I hit anything intentionally."

By the end of the month our AARs looked like carbon copies of one another except for the slight deviations of geographic locations. On 29 April the usual mix of aircraft rendezvoused over the west side of a ridge near Machinato fighter airfield and the town of Shuri. These ridges were honeycombed with gun positions in caves. In the attacks our dive-bombers dropped bombs on the first two runs, fired a pair of rockets on the next two, and followed with strafing on the fifth. By spacing out these runs, each pilot could observe the bomb or rocket hit of the pilot ahead. Using that hit as a marker, the next pilot could make any necessary adjustments, as coached by CASCU. To help identify a specific target, Commander Embree, as leader of this particular flight, strafed the target several times prior to the attacks. He was a perfectionist long before being chosen as skipper of the bombing squadron by Commander Crommelin. His bombing exploits against the Vichy French fleet during the invasion of North Africa in 1942 are well documented. His continual striving for perfection, in which he emulated Crommelin, would soon take his life.

The next big shoot-out was not until 4 May. Until then, there was some lively activity in and around Wan Airfield at Kikai Shima. It was in this area that the durability of the Hellcat continued to prove the worth of its selection and gained more and more of our respect. Ens. Thomas J. Northcutt of VF-12, Fort Lauderdale, Florida, attested to its toughness:

We left the carrier early in the afternoon, a flight of four F6Fs with Lieutenant (junior grade) John "Tubby" Franks in the lead; Ensign Cobb, his wingman; myself, leading the second section; and Ensign Smart, my wingman. The planes were loaded to the limit with six 5-inch rockets, a 500-pound bomb, ammo for the .50-caliber machine guns, and a full 150-gallon belly tank.

The ceiling was two hundred feet, and our target was Kikai Shima, approximately 125 miles northeast from the carrier and the launching site for a number of kamikaze raids. When we reached the island, we were still flying at two hundred feet, with an indicated airspeed of 220 knots (not exactly a difficult target for the AA). Shortly after making landfall, my plane was hit by an antiaircraft shell somewhere behind the cockpit armor plate— which caused the rear end of the plane to go up and the nose straight down. This, of course, was only for an instant because we were flying so low.

After overcoming the initial shock, my reaction was to get the plane out over the water. Anything was better than going down on the island, where rumor had it the Japs were starving and had become cannibals. The plane was still flying reasonably well, although the hydraulic lines had been ruptured, so the cowl flaps came open, radio was gone; and I later learned from Franks by hand signals that the rear end of the plane was in horrible shape: tailhook and tail wheel were gone.

Since I still had all the rockets, bombs, and ammo, and the plane was still flying, I made the foolish decision to bomb the strip—which was our reason for being there in the first place. After unloading everything on a single pass, I noticed my bomb did not explode and realized I had not armed it. All I could think of was the Dilbert cartoon at Pensacola showing Dilbert diving his SBD on a Japanese carrier and the bomb not going off. The navy lesson being, after twenty-seven thousand dollars being spent in training Dilbert, the ultimate moment arrives to do your thing and it was all for naught. He forgot to arm the bomb.

Following the aforementioned brilliant heroics, I turned southwest for Okinawa, the closest place to land not Japanese held.

Lieutenant (junior grade) Franks flew on my wing the 130 miles to Yontan airfield on Okinawa, while the other two returned to the carrier. Yontan airfield was a dirt strip still being fought over, with the Japanese on the left side and the marines on the right. The rifle fire seemed quite intense to me at the time, but the possibility of landing without wheels was getting my immediate attention. The landing was somewhat abrupt without landing gear, but I was very happy to be on the ground.

I noticed a marine running toward me from the ditch on the right side of the field. He climbed up on the wing to help, and we instantly recognized each other. He exclaimed, "Northcutt!" and I cried, "Cromer!" We had gone to high school together in Cincinnati, Ohio.

He was a real scavenger, totally ignoring the rifle fire, and asked if he could have the gun camera. I told him he could have the entire plane, but please bring me the clock from the instrument panel.

Before running for the right-side ditch, I made a very brief inspection of the plane and was astounded to see how badly it was damaged. The fuselage looked like a sieve from behind the cockpit all the way to the tail. The control cables, completely visible, were in shreds. It was apparent to me then how lucky I had been that the plane held together through the bombing run and long flight back to Okinawa.

Within the hour a TBF flew in and picked me up on the run, taking me back to a jeep carrier for the night. The next day I was returned to the *Randolph.*

Note: The clock still works and resides in an old English secretary desk in our living room.

The VF-12 AAR covering this incident stated that the AA damage was from a 40-mm hit: "It is a credit to the durability of the Hellcat that his plane clung together for the trip; 150 shrapnel holes were counted in the vicinity of the hit. Upon landing the F6F was scrapped and assigned as a source for repair parts."

A damaged F6F got the pilot home a few nights later when the officer-in-charge of VF(N)-12 also had trouble over Kikai. While flying a night patrol over Kikai Shima on 29 April, Lt. D. M. Hypes and his wingman, Ens. F. Sullivan, spotted lights and activity on Wan Airfield. Both pilots picked out lights that were still burning after the majority had been switched off and dove on them. The VF-12 AAR continued:

During their dive both night-fighters were met with moderate, medium and light automatic weapons. On his pullout Lieutenant Hypes' Hellcat received a hit from medium AA which demolished its port elevator and a large portion of its port stabilizer. For a few seconds following this point, Hypes experienced what he thought were his last moments. He lost his oxygen mask due to the force of the shell's impact, and his vision was blurred. It was pitch black at this time. He was unable to observe the horizon or to read his instruments. He literally did not know which end was up. After violent pushing, pulling and kicking he recovered control of his plane at about two hundred feet. He was able to climb to about six thousand feet whence he started immediately for base, with Sullivan alongside in a modified wing position.

The *Randolph* and CTF 58 were advised of Hypes' condition. He was at first directed to bail out near the Task Force Screen, then instructed to land in the vicinity and finally told to return to the heart of his Task Group and prepare for a water landing. On the return trip Hypes had to maintain an air speed of at least 140 knots. When his speed fell below 140 knots, the F6F went out of control following crazy and unpredictable courses. By the time he had reached home base, the moon had risen, and afforded him [a] clear view of the Task group formation. All ships switched on their truck lights and Hypes turned into the space between the *Randolph* and the *Bunker Hill* and made a good full-power water landing about two hundred yards abeam of the *Randolph*. Before leaving the cockpit he removed a float light, 38-caliber tracer ammunition, a safety light, and a whistle. A group destroyer picked him up ten minutes after his landing and returned him aboard the following morning.

The kamikaze threat, ever present, continued to consume much of the energy of our CAPs over the task force, over Okinawa, and over the picket destroyers ringing the task force. How many suicide flights were launched and how many completed their mission is a matter of speculation. There are reports now available that some planes returned to their bases because they were "unable to find a target." Others sometimes hesitated before making their suicide dives, and this hesitation proved costly, according to Lt. A. B. "Chick" Smith of VBF-12, La Jolla, California:

My morning TCAP assignment (29 April) was over destroyers northeast of Okinawa. Kamikazes were the principal threat. On arrival over the destroyers I checked in with our controller, and we (Ensigns Phil Anderson, Bruce Hayes, and "M" "W" Smith) were given a station to the north at fifteen thousand feet. The weather was pretty good: some clouds, and a bit hazy.

It started out like a typical dull CAP—orbits and more orbits. After about an hour that changed. Other divisions in the area started getting vectors, and we began to see antiaircraft fire from the surface ships, but nothing for my division. Then we did get a vector, but it produced nothing. I believe the controller had the altitude wrong. Anyway my wingman, Phil Anderson, and I were ordered back to our station. We had been detached as a section to attempt the intercept. As we were approaching the destroyers, flying at about thirteen thousand feet, I saw a Jap plane off to my right flying about a thousand feet above us and some two to three thousand yards from us. I "tallyhoed" to our controller, who responded that they didn't have him. My flight went to full power, and we were closing on the target but still below him. I didn't want to lose speed while climbing. We closed enough to identify the plane as a Japanese fighter. As we closed to about a thousand feet, the Zero turned and started a shallow dive, fortunately in our direction. I informed my controller, who then told me that they had him. He passed ahead of us and increased his dive angle. We did the same, and we seemed to be closing.

At about ten thousand feet he increased his dive angle. I told the control ship that I didn't think we would catch him. The fighter director's response was, "We have you and we are holding fire." We were closing, and at about five thousand feet I started firing, out of range I thought, but my tracers seemed to be close. Suddenly, some smoke started coming from the Japanese plane, and it veered right. The destroyer was in a tight turn. The Zero crashed into the water and blew up. I pulled out and went into a circle over the destroyer. Their fighter director gave me a "well done." I wasn't sure it was deserved but modestly accepted it.

My section was directed to take station at fifteen thousand feet again, and I started the slow climb, feeling pretty good about the dive intercept. As my section passed about twelve thousand feet my fighter director gave me a "heads up above." I reported no contact, "no joy." A few seconds later I "tallyhoed" a Zero above us about two thousand feet, but he appeared to be going away from our surface forces. I reported this to the fighter director and also told him I didn't think I could get to him before he started a dive.

I kept climbing, but thinking it was useless since he had too much altitude and could run away from me in a dive. But he didn't dive, just stayed in a lazy turn! Unbelievably, I kept gaining on him while cutting inside his lazy arc. Looking up at him, I saw him go through some light clouds. I thought I would lose him, but as I came up to his altitude he came out of the cloud and still had not started a dive. So, now at his altitude, I continued to close, feeling that I could soon fly wing on him. At close range I opened fire. His plane started burning, and he jumped. I could not see if his parachute opened or if he had one. Of course, I was satisfied that he had not attacked our ships, but in my mind, I started thinking of him as the "reluctant kamikaze."

I made my reports to the fighter director, got together with my division, and returned to *Randolph,* where I made the usual report to the ACI officers. Sometime after that I started thinking about my "reluctant kamikaze." Why had he not attacked? Why had he appeared to be turning away? Why had he not countered my closing on him? The more I asked those questions, the more puzzled I became, until a new thought came into my mind as I lay in my bunk. That thought was that it wasn't a Zero that I shot down, it was an F6F! The more I thought about it, the more possible that seemed. Was it possible that the lazy plane above me was simply an F6F separated from its flight? We all knew how often that happened. The more I thought about it, the more convinced I became that the plane was one of ours. It was a long night.

The next morning I went to Lieutenant Truman Morsman, our administrative/intelligence officer, who had debriefed me, and told him I wanted to see my gun-camera film as soon as possible. I gave no reason, but I do know that a rush development was done. How soon exactly I can't recall, but I do recall my relief when Truman told me the film confirmed two "kills." Later, when I looked at the film, there was no question that both planes were Japanese. There was some question in my mind that the first kamikaze had been destroyed by my fire. His plane was trailing smoke, but did that really cause his crash or did he simply lose control and crash? That really didn't matter to me. What mattered was that my "reluctant kamikaze" was indeed Japanese.

After the kamikaze attack on the *Randolph* at Ulithi followed a week later by the devastation on the *Franklin,* a command decision was made to use the officers' wardroom as a briefing room and pilots' general-quarters station. Many pilots had been killed in the *Franklin's* ready rooms. On all *Essex*-class carriers like the *Randolph* and *Franklin,* ready rooms were located just below the flight deck. The one and one-half inch armored hangar deck over the wardroom provided more protection during air attacks.

The wardroom was fitted with a large flight-data board on the forward bulkhead. There was some clutter, mostly pilots' flight gear, plotting boards, helmets, and .38-caliber service pistols, which were usually stacked along the bulkheads for ready access for scheduled flights.

Designed for safety's sake, this arrangement gave rise to a dangerous incident, as Ens. Chuck L. Galbreath of VB-12, Gainesville, Texas, recalled:

It was in late April on a calm and peaceful evening off Okinawa in the wardroom. All our personal flight gear including Mae Wests, helmets, plotting boards, and .38-caliber pistols were hung on the bulkhead just outside the wardroom.

Suddenly the room was a cave filled with thunder as two stewards streaked through the room, the first fleeing a second with a gun in hand. Six shots rang out from the "borrowed" .38 and ricocheted off the bulkheads and ceiling as in a shoot-em-up western movie. Five others and myself dove for shelter under a nearby table. Don't tell me six grown men can't get under one table at the same time!

After the shooting had stopped, we cautiously emerged from our shelter. No one was hurt, but on the top of our table was one spent projectile. War can be hell, even in the wardroom.

The incident was duly noted in the ship's log:

Name [withheld], Stewards Mate; Offenses: (1) stealing government property (revolver); (2) assault with intent to murder;

(3) assaulting superior officer with deadly weapon; (4) destroying government property (revolver); (5) unauthorized possession of explosives (TNT demolition charge); Disposition: general court martial.

This fellow was mad!

TCAPs over Kikai Shima also continued to be dangerous both from infiltrating enemy aircraft and Wan Airfield's antiaircraft defenses. The purpose of the patrols, as always, was to interdict enemy aircraft trying to attack invasion forces at Okinawa. Those invasion forces were making headway but still needed air support, as reflected in the VF-12 AAR of 30 April:

From the point of view of damage inflicted to enemy personnel, this support mission is considered the most successful launched from the USS *Randolph*. Enemy troop concentrations were pointed out on the slopes and ridge of a hill in TA 8072 [coordinates for target spotting and identification]. Fighting Squadron Twelve in company with VB-12, made six live runs against these situations. Foxholes, slit trenches, cave mouths, and mortar positions were pinpointed targets.

Panels and red smoke marking friendly front lines were visible about two hundred yards to the north. As the planes attacked, holding down the enemy, our troops were seen to rush forward in their advance.

The enemy was monitoring VHF [radio] and caused some confusion by firing phosphorous rockets into our lines when our ground observer used the same means to pinpoint enemy targets. This difficulty was again overcome by close cooperation between aircraft and ground forces. Several dummy runs were necessary to discover the exact point of attack.

Besides causing an unknown number of enemy casualties and holding others down during friendly advances, the mouths of three caves were closed by rockets and bombs.

Upon their retirement the ground observer gave the support group a well done and inquired whether there was any Jap blood on the wings.

On the night of 2 May the early morning TCAP flown by the night-fighters over Kikai lost two pilots to unknown causes. The flight was a dawn air patrol, and the weather was, simply put, miserable. The cloud base started at five hundred feet and extended to ten thousand feet without a break. It was so bad that flights scheduled later in the morning were canceled.

Lt. J. J. Wood, and his wingman, Ens. L. O. Woods, left Kikai and went to nearby Amami O'Shima, and nothing was ever heard from them. A third member of the night-fighter group, Ensign Monaghan, who had remained over Kikai, detected some activity on Wan Airfield at about 0530. Upon investigation, he found two Tony aircraft in the process of taking off. The first one got away into the clouds, but Monaghan managed to shoot down the second one. Obviously, the problem of Kikai persisted.

The loss of a pilot or aircrewman is always tragic, more so in the close-knit, six-pilot night-fighter unit. Ensign Monaghan reflected on the losses:

> The loss of every night-fighter was felt keenly, especially the original ones as we had been together a long time. It was a void that could not be filled by the replacements. It was a somber moment when you had to pack up your friend's effects for shipping back to his home. Don Hypes, the skipper, and myself wrote letters to the families, with the usual platitudes. How effective they were to explain what happened is impossible to judge. The men were there one minute, and all of a sudden they were gone, without a word—just gone. The discussions between the night-fighters as to what or how the loss occurred were brief and never talked about thereafter.
>
> Don Hypes was returned to the U.S., and Ben Mitchell and D. T. Lempke came into the night-fighter unit. The loss of the two Woods boys was a blow that was felt very heavily by the men that remained. LaMar Woods had been one of the original group. It was hard for us to understand what had happened. Three weeks later, two more of the original night-fighters went down, Lea Levis and Davey Howard.
>
> Levis was known as a very quiet man who loved to play poker in the ready room. He would play every chance he had. What very few people were aware of was that whatever Lucky Lea won, he sent home to his mother.
>
> Davey Howard's loss was particularly painful to me since Davey and I came from Vero Beach, Florida, together. He was an electri-

cal engineer from MIT, a good athlete and an accomplished hunter with the bow and arrow. To pass the time, he crocheted doilies in the ready room's red gloom, using string. After David's death, these items were packed carefully by me and sent to his mother and father with his other effects.

Sometime during one of the many briefings or debriefings of Ensign Howard, Lt. Bud Hewlett, Amherst, Massachusetts, VF-12's air-combat-information officer, recalled, "I asked him if he ever crocheted in public. His reply was, 'Sure, it's a wonderful way to meet nice old ladies.'" This statement was certainly a grim reminder by a very gentle person that he was still a human being even though his missions at night were among the most dangerous. He could often be seen sitting on the edge of the flight deck late in the afternoon, watching air operations and crocheting his doilies.

Monaghan, one of the last two remaining members of the original night-fighter group, continued with a macabre ending for the other last member of the night-fighter unit: "Another tragedy occurred when one of the pilots 'lost it.' He could no longer perform his duties as required, and he was returned for medical reasons to the United States. The stress was too much."

The loss of night-fighters apparently accentuated the problems at Kikai and was coming under more and more scrutiny by the operational planners.

A new tack was taken at Wan Airfield on 3 May as reported in the VBF-12 AAR for that date:

> In VBF report No. 29, the situation at Kikai was described at some length and comment made that no further report on routine TCAP's at Kikai would be made unless the situation changed. Since 22 April, the date of that report, daily and usual TCAP's have been scheduled and launched, VF carrying the same armament: one 500-pound general purpose bomb and rockets to be dumped anywhere in wooded areas where hidden revetments were supposed to be.
>
> On this day not only was VF armament changed to napalm bombs, but strikes of VB and VT from this and other ships hit Kikai, and Air Group 12 photo planes obtained excellent vertical and oblique photographs. The photographs reveal the landing area temporarily cratered, but more important to VF TCAP's, they

reveal at least twenty five camouflaged revetments and many AA positions, the exact location of which was not previously known. There are also to be seen four operational planes. The results of napalm and depth charge bombs are a little disappointing in the wooded areas, but appear to be more effective than previous arming. The reasons for the change in tactics are a subject of surmise.

It is to be noted that due to Lieutenant A. A. Bureau's excellent work in the matter of fuzing napalm bombs, they all now go off.

Air Group 12 was greeted on 4 May with plenty of action. This penultimate shoot-out for the fighter squadrons again occurred at Kikai Shima. One literal translation of Kikai Shima would be "Opportunity Island." This translation certainly would be appropriate for one group of VBF pilots.

The usual TCAP for Kikai was beefed up to three divisions loaded with two 500-pound general-purpose bombs for Wan Airfield and its associated buildings. The weather was perfect, with an unlimited ceiling and visibility. Lieutenant Bolduc of VBF-12 described his part in the action:

After a normal flight to Kikai and the routine welcome by the AA and dropping of the 500-pounders, my division bid adieu to the other two and started climbing to our designated position over the island at twenty-five thousand feet. At this point the hop was no longer routine. I decided to climb directly into the sun and as high as the F6s could get. We managed to get up to thirty-six thousand feet about fifteen miles northeast of Kikai. After about one orbit at this altitude we heard the cry for help from our fellow pilots. We immediately started down, picking up speed and looking for the other two divisions. I called for a position, and a very clear and calm voice said, "About ten miles southeast of Kikai." Someone else said, "Hurry!"

I spotted a big ball of planes below and directly ahead at about sixteen to eighteen thousand feet. I was indicating 350 knots plus. My division had spread out about one hundred feet apart. I went through the top of the ball of planes horizontally from east to west in the same direction all the planes were moving. I came up behind a Jap plane and nailed it. Immediately, I did a chandelle into the sun, gaining about four thousand feet. I dove back into the top of the pile, fortunately behind another Jap. Two down. Another chandelle, all this time at full power and never slowing down except at the top of the chandelles. Three down. Another chandelle. Four down. Another chandelle. I am all by myself. I then spotted a lone Jap plane headed due north for home. Since I had the altitude advantage, I decided to give it a try. I closed up to about a mile behind and could see black smoke start to pour out of his exhausts. So I fire-walled the F6 with everything it had, including water injection. This gave me a fifty-knot advantage, and as I got close behind he made a sharp turn. I discovered that the Hellcat could turn inside of a Zero at high speed. Splash number five.

I then headed south and saw the rest of our planes rendezvousing just east of Kikai. They were chasing a Jap. He was flying in a large circle. I cut across the circle and was right behind him when tracers streamed past me from behind. I had cut in front of another F6 so quickly that he didn't have enough time to quit firing. I dove out of that position with great haste. This was evidently the last of the enemy planes.

I started looking for my wingman, Joe Mangieri. I finally contacted him. He gave his position at five hundred feet about three miles south of the area of the dogfight, about ten miles southeast of Kikai. He also stated that he was a "sick chick." He couldn't put on more than half power without the engine cutting out. Otherwise it ran just fine. We flew back the hundred miles to the *Randolph* and were the first on board.

The next thing I know I was up on the bridge, talking to Admiral Bogan [the task-group commander] about the flight. At debriefing, I learned that Joe's engine had a cylinder shot off by a .30-caliber bullet. Joe, who had just swallowed a jigger of navy "tension reliever," smilingly said he didn't think the guy could hit him and was surprised when his engine started cutting out. This flight was the largest engagement with enemy planes during my tour, and our training really paid off. The fifteen enemy planes were sent out to divert or shoot down our Kikai patrol but instead lost their entire flight.

Lieutenant Bolduc was credited with four kills, and other members of the three divisions were credited with an additional six kills. The fracas had started when Lt. W. R. Jemison of VBF-12, the lead-division leader, returned to Wan Airfield to photograph damage inflicted by the group's bombs. As he was rejoining his division, six enemy fighters attacked him from above and out of the sun. He was hit in both wings, and all his guns were rendered inoperative except one. He was able to join with his division and, using the Thach weave defensive tactic, was able to survive the superior numbers and altitude advantage of the Japanese planes until help arrived.

All the action was out of sight of the ship, but Dr. Williams, the ship's surgeon, described what this day was like aboard ship. From his "Chronicle":

> 5/4—Jap came in after us again in the early hours. Four Zeke's and one large flying boat shot down by night-fighters of the *Essex* under the *Randolph's* direction.
>
> —We get congratulatory message from Admiral Mitscher. We hear that the Italian campaign has ended in unconditional surrender. Hitler is probably dead and Berlin has fallen. Resistance over there is just a frantic flailing and deaths [*sic*] throes. The British have landed at Rangoon and the Yanks on Borneo. Later today the Jap sends many planes down from Kyushu. We defuel and debomb all planes except fighters and put them below and send large fighter sweeps. They meet the Japs and shoot down thirteen, one pilot getting five by himself. One of ours makes a forced landing on Okinawa, another on the water is picked up by a float plane from CL [light cruiser]. About five land here badly shot up but no personnel injuries.

This day had been an exceptional one for both Air Group 12 and other air groups. Captain Baker read the following message to us from the task-force commander, Admiral Mitscher, addressed to Task Force 58:

> Today we in this Force have reached and well passed one thousand enemy aircraft shot out of the air by aircraft and ship's gunfire since 1 April. The enemy cannot take it at such a numerous rate much longer. Be alert and keep them splashing.

Terse and factual, this message was high praise in the navy where "excellent" performance was expected "in the line of duty." The total score of planes shot down on 4 May by pilots of the force was ninety-six.

Dr. Williams's journal continued with descriptions of additional activities of the day:

We hear that one tin can was hit by five kamikazes and reported "in danger of sinking." The world's greatest understatement. Another is sunk. We get thanks from DD *Sherman* in our screen for permitting them a good night's sleep. Today we saw land for the first time in over a month, the high blue mountain of Tokuna Shima. This is Jap held and lies between Okinawa and Amami— We were close in and this fact belies the Jap's impotence. We get information on Baka today. A new Jap suicide rocket plane, twenty feet long, sixteen foot wing, single place, conventional controls, 1,000-pound warhead, four rocket motors with venturi tubes. She is carried under a Betty's belly and released close in. However, she carries altimeter, speed and climb indicators, and oxygen gear. No landing gear, and so forth, so she is 100 percent suicide.

The squadrons' aircraft had now accumulated over thirty days of intense and near continual use, much of it at high power. This usage began to tell on this eventful 4 May as two F6Fs made water landings near Kikai as a result of failures in engine-oil pressure. Both pilots ditched successfully and were rescued by radar-picket destroyers. From the VF AAR: "The failure of the oil systems in these Hellcats is probably a result of their extended use—perhaps overuse—without sufficient overhaul in the Okinawa support. This is a situation difficult to remedy, but a constant bugbear during current operations."

Regardless, the enlisted ranks of mechanics, ordnancemen, and radiomen continued to keep the planes flying and shooting both at Kikai and nearby islands and for the main and current objective, Okinawa support. As hard as they worked at keeping their planes in top shape, problems like the F6F oil-pressure failures, other engine problems, and radio-equipment failures did happen. When these difficulties occurred, they were invariably compounded by other factors.

For example, two divisions of fighters had been briefed for a deliberate and methodical bombing of targets on Amami O'Shima. At the last moment the strike leader was replaced by a pilot not briefed for the flight. Two photo planes were added without the knowledge of the briefing officer. The second division leader's aircraft had a "bum" engine, and his substitute was not briefed for this specialized flight.

Some planes had radio trouble and some were improperly armed. As a result, the strike was inadequately led and accomplished only a small part of what had been planned or could have been done. Complete narrative of details would reveal a comedy of errors.

Fortunately this complete snafu is rare and at times cannot be avoided. (AAR; Squadron identity mercifully withheld.)

Antiaircraft fire was not too much of a problem at Okinawa, but once in a while could give a little scare. According to aircrewman ARM3c Robert Staszak of VT-12:

> We were the skipper's [Lt. Cdr. Tex Ellison] starboard wingman. On a strike against Okinawa we flew over a Japanese antiaircraft gun emplacement while in formation. We were at an altitude that was pretty close to the maximum range of their guns, as you could see the rounds coming up as if in slow motion. I recall seeing one 40-mm round coming up at a speed slower than a hummingbird. I was able to track it and watched it as it struck a cockpit canopy support on the skipper's plane. Fortunately, it was a glancing blow that caved in the support, allowing the round to continue upward and then explode about ten yards above the plane. It was a close call!

There was no letup for the Thunderbirds as all elements flew close-air-support missions. The army slowly took real estate and few prisoners. We all hoped our effort was helping the guys on the ground because our aircraft were coming back with more and more holes from antiaircraft shrapnel. Sooner or later it wouldn't be just a hole in the plane to repair.

On 5 May our aircraft rendezvoused near the southeastern tip of Okinawa and were directed to destroy an AA gun, which was preventing observation planes from effectively spotting enemy artillery emplacements. From the VB-12 AAR: "Many fox holes, trenches, and small gun positions were discernible on the crest and on the northwest slope of the ridge. They [were] well covered with bomb and rocket hits . . . one bomb dropped [by] Ensign Tom Miller hit a ready ammunition [cache,] which exploded violently."

Commander Support Air finally decided that the AA gun in question must have been a mobile unit, after our flight had hit all the possible sites.

Perhaps familiarity does breed contempt. Perhaps some of our dives weren't as steep as they should have been or were along the same flight path. Whatever the reason, Item VI, sheet two of the AAR began to get more attention. This item was labeled "Loss or damage, combat or operational, of own aircraft." It was filled out by flight leaders and was a dreaded item when one was trying to explain some damages occurring to aircraft.

On 8 and 9 May VB-12 flight leaders Lieutenants Joe Guyon and Jim Frith, respectively commanding and executive officers of the squadron, got plenty of practice on Item VI. Five SB2Cs were holed on 8 May. All shrapnel punctures in the wings and ailerons were from below, indicating that all aircraft were directly over AA fire when hit. Close calls.

Item VI on the following day's report wasn't quite so bad but certainly raised some questions and perhaps a few eyebrows. Two of the four SB2Cs holed on the mission had been hit by our own .30-caliber guns. Fortunately, all aircraft landed safely. One SB2C reported a buckled port wing—meaning too steep a dive for the low-altitude entry often required by the weather conditions.

Enthusiasm and determination can get pilots in trouble as well as mechanical problems. The flight tactics drilled in during our training provided a measure of safety without causing us to compromise the effectiveness of the aircraft's weapons systems. Any violation of those principles invariably spelled trouble. AMM3c Merrill E. Booth of VT-12 described what could—and did—happen:

> We were trying to bomb cave openings on the side of a hill on Okinawa. On this day we either flew too close to the aircraft in front of us or the bomb fuze was not set correctly. The bomb went off just as we came over the target. I saw whole trees going over us, with dirt and debris going everywhere. We did not take a fatal blow but knew some damage had been done. On return to our ship we found bomb-bay doors pushed in by the force of the explosion. In addition, dirt and small gravel [were] embedded in the leading edge of our wing, along with blood. There was even blood on the outside of the windshield.

Occasionally, support aircraft did not get very close to their assignment. A *Randolph* log entry for the 0800–1200 watch on 5 May reflected an ignoble end for one of the torpedo squadron's pilot and crew:

> 1004—A TBM, Bureau No. 23632, piloted by Lieutenant C. Hamilton, crashed into water three hundred yards off starboard bow while attempting to take off. Pilot and both crew men were seen to be out of the plane in life raft. . . .
> 1015—USS *Erben* (DD-631) picked up crew of crashed plane.

Lieutenant Hamilton and his crewmen, ACRT(T) G. D. Bothell and AMM2c E. H. White, were returned promptly to the *Randolph* at 1250. Ironically, on 23 May there was a repeat performance for Hamilton and his crew. Again his engine failed, and he landed in the water. And again the *Erben* was in position to rescue the downed airmen. More ice cream for her crew. (Twenty-five gallons of ice cream was the going rate for picking up downed airmen. The cans didn't possess the equipment or space to make the treat.)

Harassment of the islands to the north of Okinawa continued on a daily basis, as well as the ground-support operations. However, these seemingly mundane trips could, on occasion, deviate from regularity. From the VF-12 AAR of 9 May:

> Eight Hellcats were launched in an almost routine patrol and rocket/bomb attack on military targets on Kikai Shima and Amami O'Shima. The objective of this attack on Kikai was a group of covered revetments about a mile east of Wan Airfield along the main taxiway skirting the western shore of the island. There were no direct hits on the revetments, but all six bombs dropped hit in the area just north of the objective. . . .
>
> Proceeding to Amami, the group attacked small shipping in the coves just southwest of Koniya town. Many small craft were gathered here, a number of which were well and skillfully camouflaged. Lieutenant Rex D. Thompson scored direct hits with two rockets on an LST (type vessel), which started to burn. Other pilots strafed a lugger, setting it afire, and damaged an LCI. Several of the vessels were arranged with branches and foliage to resemble fingers of land jutting out into the bay.
>
> Bomb release was at about thirteen hundred feet following dive bombing tactics. Only two rockets were known to be direct hits, six others did not detonate, and an additional eight were jettisoned

by two planes which withdrew to Yontan Airfield, Okinawa, from the Kikai attack. Ensign Robert A. Moore retired from the target area. . . .

This "almost routine" patrol didn't end here for Ensign Robert A. Moore and his section leader, Ens. Roy Bruce. Ensign Moore, Fort Worth, Texas, picked up the description of the action:

The reason I left the target area was an AA burst, which clunked into the engine just forward of the cockpit. Almost immediately it began coughing up oil all over the canopy, blanking out my forward visibility. The engine seemed to be running OK, for the moment at least. I began making preparations to bail out after I got well away from the island, remembering Finley's experience near this very same island.

The engine didn't fail me, and a few minutes of flying away from Kikai calmed me down. I then realized Roy Bruce was there off my right wing, pointing at the stream of oil spewing from the cowl flaps.

Ensign Bruce added,

By mutual consent, Moore and I agreed that to continue on out to the task force and risk a carrier landing with a damaged engine was not a very bright idea, especially when Yontan Airfield on Okinawa was about the same distance. So we headed southwest, with Moore still nursing his Hellcat on towards friendly territory.

The half-hour diversion flight to Okinawa was uneventful. We then entered the traffic pattern and alerted the tower of a possible emergency landing. We also requested that a message of our arrival be relayed to the task force. Our transmission was met with stony silence. We discovered the reason why shortly after landing. It seems the tower had been knocked out of commission during an earlier kamikaze attack by Japanese infantrymen aboard a half dozen Bettys, which crash-landed on the runways. Soldiers leaped out of their damaged aircraft, spraying everyone in sight with gunfire, tossing grenades into aircraft revetments, then the control tower, before they were all killed.

Moore and I advised the repair crew on the base regarding his engine problem. At least two of the cylinders had been blown away by the AA fire, and a replacement engine was found. Repair would take two or three days, so we went about locating a place to bed down for the night, a couple of cots in a large tent not too far from the runway. Keeping track of our gear was no problem—we had none, except for the khaki flight suits we had on. We went about touring the area on foot, with the ground fighting not too far away, if gunfire was any indication.

That evening we had settled in for our first night's sleep on terra firma since March when many of AG-12's pilots flew CAPs off the coral strip at Falalop, while the *Randolph* was being repaired. We were used to hearing aircraft overhead. However, following one section of Corsairs into the pattern was an unfamiliar engine sound. The Japs were right behind the F4U night-fighters coming in to land and proceeded to drop several bombs on the runway. That got our attention, and [we were] on the move right behind the other guys in the tent. We dove into a nearby ditch until things quieted down for the rest of the evening.

We couldn't complain about the food in the various messes we visited because chow aboard the "Randy" had fallen below normal navy quality. The *Randolph* had been at sea for more than a month, and the daily menu consisted of dehydrated mashed potatoes and rice, fortunately laced with good navy coffee and bread baked aboard ship. Here on Okinawa spaghetti was the blue plate special, more often than not—for breakfast, yet.

One interesting episode occurred while on a walking tour of the island when we came across an Okinawan native house surrounded by a stone wall. It was slightly damaged, but our curiosity was aroused, so we strolled through one gate to the stone house, picking up small oriental plates and tiny sake dishes, then out the other gate. What we saw made the hair perk up on our necks. A posted sign read, "AREA IS MINED—KEEP OUT." That ended our tour of the Okinawa countryside, except for noticing native graveyards and hillside tombs on the way back to Yontan airfield.

The area around the tombs was scorched black by our troops using flame throwers. They had been firebombed and sealed forever by our troops, entombing Jap soldiers using them as fortifications. To Bob Moore and I, it was an indication of just how brutal the fighting must have been once the Japanese decided to resist the invasion of Okinawa.

By this time our flight suits had become very odorous. We also noticed that the seams and folds of our grungy garments were black and moving with fleas, millions of them. After shaking most of them off our flight suits, we ignored them.

We looked in on the mechs, and being told the repairs would take another day, that meant one more night with the troops. Almost the same scenario: Get settled in for the night, planes come over and drop bombs. This time we noticed that very few bothered to get up, cursed the intruders, then [went] back to sleep—live and learn.

By the third day, 11 May, both of us were anxious to return to the *Randolph*. The replacement engine had been installed, checked out, and we headed east towards our task group, making certain the IFF [Identification Friend or Foe] was switched on to prevent a possible interception by our combat air patrols. Fortunately, the *Randolph* was headed into the wind, and we made a normal landing. Hardly had the props stopped turning when two deckhands rushed up on the wings of our planes and began spraying generous quantities of DDT powder on each of us in the cockpit. Obviously, they had been forewarned of the little critters we brought back with us.

Moments later we learned that the *Bunker Hill* had been struck by two kamikazes just two thousand yards abeam of our ship an hour or so earlier. The results were disastrous.

It took three or four days for our flea bites to heal.

 **8** **Ending,
May–June 1945**

Beginning 11 May, Air Group 12 and the *Randolph* participated in three of the wildest days since the first strikes on Tokyo in February. The first day began as many before it had, with fighters maintaining CAPs over Okinawa and radar-picket destroyers. In addition, there were ground-support assignments for the VB and VT squadrons.

Most of the time CAPs were vectored to intercept bogeys by the carrier fighter directors. The radar equipment on the carriers was sensitive enough to direct the CAP close to the enemy so that pilots could usually make visual contact with the target. The equipment on the destroyers was not so sophisticated, but their fighter directors did a commendable job.

This morning the radar-picket destroyer and the pilot put together a bizarre interception. Lieutenant Bolduc of VBF-12 was the flight leader:

> This flight was my division's first radar-picket combat air patrol (RAPCAP). We arrived over the radar-picket destroyer, called Rustic Base, as scheduled and were stationed about two to three miles northeast at fifteen hundred feet. The weather was fairly decent, with good visibility and cloud banks of various thicknesses scattered through the area. The picket destroyers were in an open area, with good visibility of one to four miles in all directions. We had just settled in for a boring two hours of circling when the radio crackled, "Vector zero two zero, angels two, buster." That woke us up.
>
> Off we went on the assigned heading. Just about the time we got squared away on course we entered a cloud bank. So here we

were, four F6s in tight formation, not being able to see fifty feet. This situation continued for a minute or so, and then I heard static on the radio. The intensity of that static rapidly built up until it was quite loud and then just as suddenly started to diminish. I thought, "He passed us." We made a steep right turn, reversing direction, successfully keeping all four planes in formation. After another minute or so we popped out of the clouds. Ensign Jim Funsten, section leader, immediately spotted an enemy plane about one-half mile off our starboard beam at five hundred feet below. He shouted, "Tallyho" and did a wingover to a position behind and slightly above the enemy plane. He opened fire with deadly accuracy, and the plane started down in what appeared to be a shallow glide, smoking slightly. This all happened within ten seconds after we popped out of the clouds. The Zeke appeared just to barely touch the surface of the water when it blew into smithereens. No doubt his bomb was armed. After the original vector there was no communication with the picket destroyer until after the Zeke hit the water. The rest of the hop was routine.

The other division that was over Rustic Base at the same time as Lieutenant Bolduc's was under the lead of Lieutenant Witmer of VBF-12 and destroyed two Tonys. Both these aircraft were carrying bombs. One of these kills was nearly missed because the radio channel used by the fighter directors were so badly jammed with transmissions that the controller's directions were often missed, and these misses had deadly consequences.

Some kamikazes got through the CAPs and antiaircraft defenses of the *Randolph* and *Bunker Hill,* to rain havoc on the ships. The task group's antiaircraft systems were pushed to the limit. The USS *Bunker Hill,* with TF-58 commander Admiral Mitscher aboard, was hit by two kamikazes in less than two minutes. From the *Bunker Hill*'s log:

1005. Ship was hit by an enemy suicide bomber on flight deck just aft of No. 3 elevator.

1006. The ship was hit by second suicide plane inboard of No. 2 elevator; general alarm sounded, but operation doubtful; bridge-ship service telephones out.

These matter-of-fact log entries do not begin to describe the horror and heroism that the *Bunker Hill* witnessed for the next several hours. Fire-fighting and damage-control teams were overcome by fire and smoke and were still grasping their fire hoses and axes when they were found later. In at least one instance, pilots awaiting their next flight evacuated the ready room only to suffocate in the adjoining passageway.

The casualties: more than 350 dead and 264 wounded, many so seriously that they would be added to the final death toll. Next to the *Franklin's* inferno, this was the worst damage suffered by a surviving *Essex*-class carrier, and CV 17 left the task force for stateside repairs. She was out of the war.

The *Bunker Hill* was Admiral Mitscher's flagship; more than a dozen of his staff were among those killed, and most of his personal effects were destroyed. Mitscher and his surviving staff members were evacuated to the USS *Enterprise*. There, he continued to direct the task-force operations as the divine wind became a fire storm. He would have to move again.

Some notations from Dr. Williams's "Chronicle" described the scene:

. . . Flame and smoke rise one thousand feet from the *Bunker Hill,* the midships and the whole seas is shaken repeatedly by explosions. She goes dead in the water—Several DD's go alongside despite smoke and flame that envelope them to give aid. The *South Dakota* (battleship) is firing on more bogies. Many men in the water on rafts and jackets go by. We stand by for one and [a] half hours and during that time black billowing smoke lessens and turns grey and we get a report that the fire is under control. We hear that the casualties were roughly 265 so far. . . .

Replacement carriers were on their way from stateside, but the number available was growing smaller. To date (11 May), nineteen carriers had been damaged since January, almost half of them so seriously that they would see no further action in the war.

Kikai continued to be one source of the kamikaze problem, but some measure of success had been achieved. From VBF-12's AAR:

On 11 and 12 May in addition to the patrol herein reported (Bolduc and Witmer), VBF-12 made routine patrols and CAP's to Kikai as did VF-12. When loaded with bombs and/or rockets, attempts were made to hit underground revetments revealed by photos.

Results could not be observed. Following the first strike of VF, VT, and VB of 9 May, photos revealed the field inoperational and each patrol including this one has reported no attempt to fill up bomb craters.

Success at Kikai, however was overshadowed by another loss by the air group:

The second disaster of its kind befell the Air Group on 12 May. Commander Ralph A. Embree, had replaced Commander Charles L. Crommelin as Air Group Commander Twelve when the latter was lost over Okinawa. Commander Embree had directed a support strike (at Okinawa) and was observing damage inflicted preparatory to leaving the target when his plane was caught by a single burst of heavy anti-aircraft.

ARM3c Robert E. Martin of VT-12, Tyler, Texas, observed the loss from a TBM circling the target area:

Commander Embree had just strafed the area to show us precisely where he wanted our bombs placed and was circling as we prepared to make our run, when bam! a single burst of AA fire cut his Hellcat in half. I could see his limp body fall free and his chute just streaming. It did not open . . . he didn't have a chance.

Commander Embree lacked the charisma of Crommelin, but no one ever doubted his courage or tenacity. He had been a dive-bomber pilot during the North African Campaign, and his dive-bombing skills were legendary. ARM1c Alfred R. Smith remembered him vividly: "I always thought he liked enlisted men, but he wouldn't let them know it. Not a conversationalist, he was all business, 'Good morning Smith.' Three or four hours later, 'See you later, Smith,' but he had a wonderful smile."

Smith had been his gunner until Embree became air-group commander and switched to F6Fs. They had trained together for seven months prior to coming aboard the *Randolph*. This had not been a good cruise for Embree. His SB2C went into the barrier on 18 February, and he suffered second-degree burns around his face and wrists. Shortly thereafter, his plane was hit by AA fire, but he made it safely back aboard. This third episode was his final flirtation and ended in death.

Ens. Roy Bruce, formerly of VB-5, recalled a visit with Commander Embree while he was recuperating from burns suffered in a barrier crash on 18 February:

> I shared my love for dive-bombing with the commander on the occasion of an evening visit with him. He asked my opinion of his mahogany carvings of wild animals. They were simple in form, but skillfully hewn with a pocket knife! I told him—honestly—that I was not an expert, but I was envious of his talent.
>
> Upon his death the carvings should have been with his personal effects and returned to his widow. I found out years later—they had not.

Lieutenant Commander Pawka, commanding officer of VBF-12, became air-group commander, and Lt. Ruben Denoff, executive officer, took his place as squadron commander. Lt. A. B. "Chick" Smith became executive officer. Pawka brought the same brand of aggressiveness and innovation as his predecessors. Lt. (j.g.) Bill Drews, Bethesda, Maryland, of AG-12's staff:

> I remember the night several of our crew installed a wing-pod radar on Pawka's fighter at his request so he could spot enemy planes at a greater distance. This particular gear was not designed for this application, nor was it wired to accommodate it. However, we made it work. When he returned from the next mission, he reported the gear didn't work for him. So we examined it carefully to find out why. After much testing we found that an enemy bullet had penetrated the main cable. That radar pod did him absolutely no good, except that it may have saved his life.

The continued enemy air attacks against the task force and invasion forces at Okinawa were not unexpected. Task Force 58 had considerable measure of success interdicting these raids from the north, most of which were now believed to be originating in Kyushu. The British were having some success at intercepting enemy flights coming from Formosa. However, both U.S. and British task forces suffered kamikaze attacks from these two sources. The British carriers that were kamikazied suffered less damage against their steel flight decks than the U.S. carriers, which had steel framework and teak-wood decks.

To thwart these kamikaze attacks, the decision was made again to launch raids against Kyushu facilities to destroy enemy aircraft at the source. Two days, 13 and 14 May, were devoted to these strikes.

Both fighter squadrons, VF and VBF, were assigned targets in the northern and northwestern ends of Kyushu. The round-trips were more than 450 miles, with more than half of it over land. No enemy airborne aircraft were encountered, but the antiaircraft fire was extremely intense. VBF-12 was assigned Omura Airfield but was allowed only one dive-bombing run as a precaution against using too much fuel on such a long flight. It was an unfortunate requirement as photos revealed some two hundred aircraft in all, with forty of them on the airfield. VF-12's targets of Waifu, Kikutomi, Kumamoto, and Kicuchi had mostly small training planes visible. The antiaircraft fire at Kikutomi for defense of an adjacent aircraft factory was so intense that the aircraft targets were not considered worth the risk. No attack was pursued on this field.

On the return flight along the western coast of Kyushu, strike aircraft encountered twenty-eight fast torpedo boats. They were suspected as being part of the new kamikaze—the Special Sea Attack Force. This organization was deploying fast plywood boats armed with a depth charge on the bow to be rammed against Allied invasion ships. Members of the flight left eight boats dead in the water.

The fighter squadrons also had some CAPs assigned in addition to the strikes. Lieutenant McWhorter was on one of these CAPs over the task force on 13 May:

> Another highlight of this cruise occurred when my flight was vectored out to intercept a high bogey, a single-engine Myrt, that I shot down at twenty-five thousand feet. It was my highest victory, compared to my lowest one, a Betty twin-engine bomber that I shot down about ten feet above the water on my previous combat cruise. Shooting the Betty down also earned me the nickname of "One Slug" because after returning to the ship, it was found that I had expended only eighty rounds of .50-caliber ammunition, and that included a test-fire burst of all six guns shortly after takeoff.

The intensity of combat flights is reflected in the following letter from Ens. Glenn Chaffer of VBF-12, Bridgeport, Connecticut, to his mother and father about his activities during the afternoon flights of 14 May:

June 9, 1945

Dear Mom and Pop:

You have said that you would like to hear about some of my experiences. Well, I'll tell you one I had over ■■■■■. It isn't exactly typical, but it isn't far from the average.

In the morning I flew a four hour combat air patrol and there was no enemy action encountered. We landed (back on the carrier), had lunch and got briefed (instructions on objective) on the airfield at ■■■■. It is on the ■■■■ side of the island on the ■■■■ and directly between ■■■■ and ■■■■. It was about ■■■■ miles from our takeoff point and at about 1400 we took off. My division leader is skipper of our squadron and I flew wing on him. There were sixteen of us all told and the skipper of [the] squadron took a course around the southern end of ■■■■ and up the western coast. We met one lone F6F coming down the coast but no enemy planes were encountered. We flew to a point just south of ■■■■ Naval Base where I was to detach from the group to take pictures of the base as there were supposed to be enemy ships there. I was to take the pictures as my plane was equipped with a package camera for just that purpose. I broke away from the formation at fifteen thousand feet and about seven miles away and proceeded in.

They were aware of our coming and had the whole area smoke screened. There must have been two hundred smudge pots which completely covered the area so I was just going to take a picture of the smoke screen and withdraw. I got in where the camera was effective, took my pictures and started back. They fired two or three bursts at me but were off on range and the shells burst about one hundred yards short of me. They didn't get another chance as I was gone like a scared rabbit. I reformed with the group and we made a pass at ■■■■. We all had rockets and fired them at the hangars and repair shop. It is a huge airfield—the biggest I ever saw and the most heavily defended. In the dive it appeared as though the whole ground were afire with the flashes of ack-ack. Mostly 40-mm and smaller, but plenty of five-inch bursts. They had my division leader "boresighted" and put a burst where the skipper [had] been eleven different times. I was directly behind him and the shells were bursting between him and me. We pulled out at two thousand feet and retired across the strip of land out to the bay. Going about 350 knots and wishing for more. One of my rockets had "hung-up" and I got permission to fire it at a lugger in the bay. Another boy in my division and myself went down and I found out later from the division leader that I had hit the lugger on the water line. We strafed him twice and left him dead in the water. He didn't burn, however. Meanwhile, the other twelve planes had seen a tanker anchored in the bay and left him afire with a big hole in the stern that A. B. Campbell (I think it was) had put there with a rocket. We started our rendezvous.

Dutch (Lutz) and I were low from the strafing [of] the small lugger and started climbing to rendezvous with the rest of the group. Dutch spotted some small craft in the harbor, hard to see because of their size. I went down to take pictures of them as I didn't think they were military targets. We found to our surprise that they were boats, hell bent to get to the opposite shore. There were about twenty-five of them. They were hard as hell to hit (small and very fast) and you had to go down to less than one hundred feet to hit. Most of us were so low we left wakes on the water. We thought they would blow up when hit but they evidently didn't have torpedoes aboard as we burned seven of them and left five more dead in the water.

While this was going on two Jap planes were circling above us. They didn't attack—just waited for the replacements they evidently had radioed for. Pretty smart. We were pretty low on gas by this time and couldn't afford to tangle with enemy planes, so the four with the most gas climbed up to get the planes. The Japs always kept out of range and we started home. I had eighty five gallons of gas left and jettisoned my belly tank and wondered how else I could lighten the plane. We can burn as much as ▬▬▬ gallons of gas an hour or as little as ▬▬▬ if we go very slow under good conditions. I figured I could make it if nothing happened. The Japs were still following us waiting for help. I smoked five cigarettes and sat in a pool of sweat and probably other excretion just waiting for those Japs to come. Dutch's plane cut out and we thought he was a goner but the engine caught again and I flew with him as I had a raft I could jettison if he went in. The raft was just so much more drag and I wanted to get rid of it but knew I wouldn't if anyone had a chance of using it. So we just flew home and sweated.

We radioed the combat air patrol and they came out and took the Japs off our tail so all we had to do was to find the carrier. About "three days" later we spotted it and made a very unorthodox straight in approach and landed. I had seventeen gallons of gas left. We didn't lose a man and the mission was very successful. The flight lasted ███████ hours. I had lost eight pounds on that flight and ate two dinners and hit the sack. I dreamed about Muzz and I being married. Up at 0400 the next day, minus two pounds. Food and sleep are marvelous. We flew more hours than we slept and that is why we're here for a rest. I am now resting so I'll close now.

All my love,

Son

LETTER CENSORED THIS DATE 6/11/45

In spite of intense antiaircraft fire at target airfields on northern Kyushu, all aircraft returned safely to the carrier, having completed their assigned tasks. The next day, 14 May, not so. A combined strike of all Thunderbird squadrons—VF, VBF, VB, and VT—was scheduled against Usa Airfield on northeastern Kyushu. The strike "materialized into a general practice of training exercises, during which the target was bombed, a rescue CAP was maintained, shipping was strafed, and a Dinah shot down" (according to the VF AAR). All these "exercises," combined with the number of planes shot down by CAP over the task force, indicated that this was one of the most intense enemy air attacks since the middle of March when the *Franklin* was devastated. In addition, one of the most daring rescues in naval aviation annals was orchestrated.

Shortly after midnight on 14 May there were enemy aircraft snooping near the task force, a sure sign of a busy schedule ahead. At first light the strike against Usa Airfield was launched. Shortly after 0630 the first bogeys descended on the task force.

A three-plane division led by Lieutenant Jemison of VBF-12 intercepted some of the bogeys orbiting at twenty thousand feet. As two Zekes peeled off toward the task force, Lieutenant Jemison and his wingman, Ensign Johannsen, shot them down. A short time later Johannsen shot down two more. The remainder of the group of Zekes departed northward.

Ensign Chappell, the fourth man in Jemison's division, was unable to get to altitude because of mechanical problems. He joined with another CAP at a lower station and shot down a Zeke and a Judy.

One enemy aircraft did get into the task force and dove into the flight deck of the *Enterprise*. This was her sixth hit since 1942 and her third in as many months. Ens. M. W. "Mickey" Smith of VBF-12, Barnsville, Georgia, witnessed the hit:

> Our flight was on first-standby combat air patrol. General quarters sounded. The task force was under attack. We ran topside to our planes and taxied to the catapults. I was to be the second plane off. One magneto would not check out while I was on the catapult. On the second try the magneto checked out, and I was the third plane launched. While still on the flight deck I saw a kamikaze hit the carrier *Enterprise* off our starboard side (even with us) about four thousand feet away. I could see the elevator blown approximately three hundred feet into the air.

Ensign E. Phil C. Anderson was a member of Lt. A. B. "Chick" Smith's division, launched from Condition One. They were vectored out immediately to the west and contacted two Zekes about thirty miles from the force. The division was split into two sections to intercept the enemy aircraft. According to Ensign Anderson:

> Suddenly, we were given the signal to start our engines and were catapulted. Just after we became airborne the ship radioed, "Vector 250, gate," which meant get our buns out there as fast as you can go. Within minutes we spotted two bogeys about two o'clock down. The ship's radar controller had put us on a perfect gunnery run.
>
> I then remember calling in and saying, "Cudgel Base, this is Hoosier 13-3, splash two bogeys." A lot had happened in a short space of time.

When we landed, it seemed like the plane handlers came out applauding. Whether they were told we had shot down two kamikazes or not, I don't know, but it seemed like it.

The two other members of Lieutenant Smith's flight also had kills. Ensign Hayes destroyed one Zeke, and Ensign Smith destroyed another.

By 0800 the attack on the carriers increased in intensity. Two additional kamikaze aircraft penetrated the ships' CAPs and were splashed by ships' gunners.

Attacks by enemy aircraft were considered to be kamikaze because during their approaches to the fleet none were seen to take any evasive action when the CAP got behind them. However, the CAPs stationed at Okinawa experienced a little more evasive actions by kamikazes. Lt. R. O. Drewlow of VBF-12, stationed north of Okinawa with his division, tallyhoed one Zeke above. Once he reached that altitude, the Zeke did a split "S" to evade its attacker. Ensign Gadbois shot him down. A short time later Ensign Sankey of the same division splashed a Judy.

Approximately one hour had elapsed since the dawn launch as Commander Pawka led sixty Thunderbird fighters and bombers over Bungo Strait—ironically the same strait through which Admiral Yamamoto had taken the Japanese fleet en route to attack Pearl Harbor. Departing the Pacific, Pawka veered slightly to port and immediately began receiving AA fire over land. Antiaircraft fire increased as the formation approached Usa Airfield near the Inland Sea coast. The field was a large square mat with many hangars and workshops. The AA intensified as our fighters dove from twenty thousand feet, and they strafed and fired rockets to suppress it for the vulnerable torpedo bombers on their glide-bombing runs.

Lieutenant Frith, leading the dozen dive-bombers, was able before diving to steal a glance at the scene being wrought below by our fighters and torpedo bombers: "Explosions sent fire and smoke from hangars, buildings, and ammo- or gasoline-storage facilities."

Flying on Frith's right wing, Ensign Morris continued the description of the attack:

The lieutenant peeled off to starboard, opening bomb-bay doors and dive brakes as he cleared the formation. I followed, rolling into a seventy-degree dive—the unique experience of dive-bombing. Phegley, my rear-gunner radioman, began calling out our altitude every thousand feet. As he called out seven thousand, the entire plane shook with a loud bang, and I knew I'd been hit. I jettisoned the bomb load on a hangar, closed the bomb-bay doors and dive brakes while in the dive to gain speed. My plane gained so much speed that we overtook Frith in a hurry, and he knew I was in trouble even as I told him I was hit in the engine. A long trail of black smoke said it all.

Frith chased Morris out to the water north of Usa Airfield, relieved to see he was still gaining altitude from the excess speed built up in his dive, but moments later Morris announced he was losing power and oil pressure was zero.

A few more miles north would take them past the volcanic peninsula on their right. However, Morris was losing altitude, so the primary objective was to clear the small island of Hime Shima, but not by too much so as not to ditch too close to the busy shipping lane a mile or so north.

Ensign Morris and Aircrewman Phegley had practiced the ditching routine many, many times. Phegley prepared to grab the packaged life raft out of the stowage compartment between the pilot and gunner. With a dead engine, it wouldn't be long.

Frith watched as Morris's SB2C glided lower and lower, barely skimming the water, until the tailhook left a long, fine wake. Then the "beast" lurched into the water, creating a huge spray before settling into the white foam created when the hot engine hit the cold water. Despite the circumstances, it was a good water landing. The aircraft appeared so stable, resting in the water, that a less experienced observer might be fooled into thinking it would float indefinitely. However, the most the crew could hope for would be forty-five seconds. Both crewmen knew that.

John Morris described the last moments of his landing just north of Hime Shima:

We were skimming along very close to the water at 130 knots. As the plane began to slow, I eased back on the stick and stalled out a few feet above the water, then settled a bit and hit. We both stepped out on the port wing, Phegley grabbing the raft, then handing it to me, as we had practiced—just before the plane nosed down without any warning and sank.

Standing on the trailing edge of the wing, near the fuselage with the raft in my arms, I stepped in the water, but couldn't get clear of the fuselage as it slid past me. Then something caught a strap on my life jacket. Suddenly I was being dragged under water—still holding the raft—frantically tugging on the strap pulling me deeper with the plane. Finally, my feet touched the fuselage, and by drawing myself up closer I was able to push against it with all my strength. That last desperate effort worked. The strap gave, then broke, freeing me to shoot to the surface.

Phegley had taken the food and water container and jumped clear of the plane as it started down. The life raft package and the food and water container were tied together by a ten-foot piece of line. Phegley had looked around to see what was around him when suddenly the food and water container was ripped from his grasp and disappeared under the surface.

The aircrewman had no idea what a close call Morris had endured but was quickly at his side, groping for the toggle to inflate the raft. It worked, and soon they were aboard, sifting dye marker onto the water so that friendly planes could see them.

Morris was totally exhausted, mentally and physically. He struggled to get his breath after his ordeal. For the first time in almost two hours, he and Phegley had little to do except appraise their situation, wring out their flight suits, and occasionally use the small aluminum paddles to maintain their position relative to Hime Shima Island and the shipping channel, where intercoastal tankers constantly plied a mile north of the their raft.

Their situation was in stark contrast to the exhilaration of the dive-bombing attack and the total concentration required to bring the "beast" down on the water intact. The stress of being snagged—like a bass on a fishing line—to the plane during its plunge toward the depths of the Inland Sea just a few minutes before had added to that exhaustion. Their experience had drained both men, and it wasn't over.

It was quiet here, except for the water lapping at the life raft and the comforting purr of the Hellcats as they circled at a distance.

Morris and Phegley discussed the possibilities of rescue. The relative calm suddenly became threatening when one small tanker diverted from the channel toward the airmen.

Once Frith saw that Morris and Phegley were safely in the raft, he called Pawka and apprised him of the situation, joined his formation, and departed for the task force. Pawka sent two divisions to protect the downed men, Lieutenant Commander Michaelis, commanding officer of VF-12, and Lieutenant Bolduc of VBF-12. Pawka also relayed the situation to the *Randolph* and requested seaplanes for a rescue attempt.

Michaelis stationed Bolduc at seven thousand feet, took station at four thousand feet, and sent his section leader, "Junior Garrison," down to five hundred feet to discourage any mischief from the sampans and luggers, which were scattering like a swarm of hornets. A threatening situation was not long in materializing—a small intercoastal tanker turned from the shipping lane and headed toward the life raft. Michaelis had issued instructions not to attack any shipping unless it strayed out of the shipping channel toward the raft. When the tanker turned toward Morris and Phegley, Michaelis's division began strafing the ship in an effort to turn it away. The initial attack didn't deter the tanker, which by now was within one half mile and only slightly hurt.

Ens. Jim Funsten, Bolduc's section leader, announced he still had a bomb and was given permission to use it against the tanker. His bomb hit close aboard but failed to detonate. Then Funsten's wingman, Ens. Frank W. Ness, said he also had a bomb that he had been unable to drop at Usa Airfield. Bolduc instructed Ness to make sure it was armed and release it from about one thousand feet. Ness set a long, shallow glide-bombing run and jettisoned the bomb with the emergency-release system. The bomb hit a little short of the tanker but exploded.

Morris and Phegley watched the bomb leave the Hellcat and arc toward the tanker, now within three hundred yards of the raft. It hit at almost the same location as Funsten's, but this time the tremendous explosion almost lifted the tanker's stern out of the water. The airmen felt the blast and had visions of Jap survivors being in the water nearby. The tanker's skipper elected to leave rather than pursue his quarry. The tanker was last seen trailing oil, smoking near the stern, and spewing steam from the aft section. Finally, it was beached on the northeastern shoreline.

It was now about 0745. Task Force 58 was fighting off the early kamikaze attack. The light cruiser *Astoria* had been alerted to get two OS2U Kingfisher aircraft ready for a possible rescue mission to the Inland Sea.

The following TBS message from Commander Task Group 58.3, Rear Admiral Sherman, illustrated the level of concern commanders had for their pilots in trouble:

From: CTG 58.3 Date 13 May 45
    Action: Astoria/Randolph/Essex Time:132335
    Info: CTU 58.3.3
    ASTORIA STANDBY FOR RESCUE OF 2 SURVIVORS IN RAFT DISTANCE 25 MILES BEARING 115 FROM POINT TOLLGATE X RANDOLPH PROVIDE 4 VF ESCORT X 4 ADDITIONAL RANDOLPH VF WILL PROCEED DIRECT TO DOWNED PILOT AND RELIEVE VF NOW ORBITING RANDOLPH ADVISE WHEN ESCORT WILL BE READY X ESSEX VF SWEEP NO 2 WILL PROCEED WITH RESCUE FLIGHT AND COVER THE RESCUE X AFTER PILOTS ARE PICKED UP THE 8 RANDOLPH VF WILL RETURN WITH THE KINGFISHERS X ESSEX VF SWEEP THEN PROCEED TO SWEEP ASSIGNED AREA

Lieutenant Commander Michaelis would have been pleased had he known what elements were being brought to bear in this rescue effort deep in enemy territory. His comment regarding the aborted rescue of Lieutenant Toliver on 17 February would surely have come to mind.

Two OS2U Kingfisher rescue planes were launched, piloted by Lt. Charles Tanner and Lt. (j.g.) Donald Comb. Both pilots had made several dramatic rescues—but not under these circumstances. Comb, Edina, Minnesota, narrated:

When we received orders to launch aircraft for this rescue and found out where we were going and to have fighters for escort, I was so excited and nervous that I was wondering if I would be able to fly a seaplane, much less into the Inland Sea, the heart of the Jap homeland.

Comb did not have too long to contemplate the flight destination because they were given the order to go within fifteen minutes after being notified.

We launched both seaplanes in about fifteen minutes. Once in the air, after being catapulted, I did manage to calm down quite a bit. Tanner helped a lot—he was very reassuring. We flew under one thousand feet and noticed antiaircraft batteries in the [Bungo] straits between the islands of Kyushu and Shikoku, but they did not open up on us on the way in.

Aboard the *Randolph,* Lieutenant McWhorter and his division, Ensigns Bill Wolfe, Stony Carlson, and Bill Townsend, were briefed by ACI on where to rendezvous with the two Kingfishers. McWhorter's division was to escort them three hundred sixty miles—round-trip—at least a four-hour flight at the Kingfisher's ninety-mile-per-hour speed. The four-hour estimate did not allow for head winds or time needed to rescue the downed airmen.

The other division of fighters was catapulted after McWhorter's to proceed directly to the rescue site. The word "pronto" was added to their briefing instructions. Lieutenant Gus Gray and Ensigns Gene Sears, Bud Christie, and George Collins were launched within minutes, to complete an umbrella of coverage over the downed airmen.

By 0915 Michaelis, concerned he'd not heard definite word from the *Randolph* about relieving air cover, calculated that he had enough fuel for another hour and a half and still have enough to get back. Any planes low on fuel were instructed to return by twos and threes.

Pawka, en route home with the strike group, made a general transmission to any friendly planes within range: "Any planes already airborne, whose mission allows, proceed to a point twenty miles northeast of Usa Airfield and relieve fighters on station over survivors." The VF-12 AAR described another part of the rescue incident:

A Dinah [a twin-engine high-performance reconnaissance air-craft] was tallyhoed about three thousand feet above flying in an easterly direction. Lieutenant Commander Michaelis and his wingman, Ensign Lee Furse, climbed up and overtook it using water injection. Both pilots pressed home the attack and have split credit for the kill. Furse was enthusiastic, "It was a team effort. Mike smoked him (the left engine) and I blew him away."

Lieutenant McWhorter's division had been over the Kingfishers for more than an hour. McWhorter commented on the situation: "Since the seaplanes' cruising airspeed was only ninety knots or so, and even though we had our engine rpm's down to 1200, we still had to make continual 'S' turns to stay over them." McWhorter's division still had almost an hour of S turns before reaching the downed airmen.

Bolduc had moved north of the downed airmen, where he made a horrible discovery. He reported: "Two Jap destroyers heading south in the channel toward the survivors. They're about fifteen miles from the raft and making more than twenty knots." Michaelis promptly relayed this information to the *Randolph* and got an immediate reply: "The *Astoria* has launched two Kingfishers as rescue planes, and they have an eight-plane escort." The situation was getting tense for Michaelis. His flight was now getting low on fuel, and his supply of ammunition was not going to last very long against well-equipped Japanese destroyers.

Following the launch of early-morning strikes on Usa Airfield, a four-plane division, under Lt. Lane B. Bardeen of VF-12, was launched on a photo-reconnaissance sweep to survey damage inflicted by raids on Kyushu that morning. The flight had started briskly as shortly after takeoff Ens. C. O. McDaniel shot down a Nick about twelve miles from the task force.

Bardeen heard the messages from Lieutenant Commander Pawka requesting assistance from any aircraft in the vicinity. Bardeen's flight team had enough fuel to stay on station over the raft for two hours and still have enough to get home. Hearing Bolduc's call describing the threat from the two DDs, Bardeen headed for Usa in a hurry.

Michaelis headed toward the destroyers. He saw their wakes first, through the haze that hung over the southern edge of Honshu. Then out of the haze the hulls and superstructures became visible. Judging from their speed and distance from Morris and Phegley, he estimated they would leave the ship channel toward the raft in about eleven minutes. It was now 0945.

Michaelis transmitted his attack plan to Bolduc: "Take your team over to the southeast side of the cans. I'll hit them from the southwest, and will give you the signal to attack." Bardeen's division arrived on the scene just as Michaelis was about to make the coordinated attack with Bolduc on the destroyers. Bardeen was only too glad to assist. The diversion caused by attacking aircraft was just enough at the right time, and the destroyers could not get to Morris and Phegley without turning around and going back in the face of the stinging .50-calibers from the F6Fs, a maneuver they decided against. They had passed within gunnery range of the men in the water but had been so busy with the fighter planes that no shots were ever directed at the downed airmen.

It was now 1015, and Bardeen's photo team could maintain air cover, so Michaelis sent Bolduc's team and his own second section back to the task force. Two F4U Corsairs from the *Essex* joined the covering aircraft at 1025. Shortly thereafter McWhorter called that his ETA was 1125. With the situation well in hand, and no unfriendly aircraft in the area, Michaelis and Furse shoved off. It was 1045. None of the sampans or luggers had returned to harass Morris and Phegley, and even the aerial gunfire had ceased. The airmen settled in for their fourth hour adrift in the Inland Sea. They hadn't been fired on, although some bits of shrapnel had fallen near them. They weren't sure of the source but hoped it wasn't from the lighthouse on Hime Shima because they were still within its range. They were sure—with all the activity going on—that the task force hadn't forgotten them (in spite of the fierce kamikaze attacks that crippled the *Enterprise*). Although it was comforting to see the F6Fs, that safe feeling did not last too long, for suddenly the aircraft left, and an eerie quiet descended on the men in their raft.

They were alone with their thoughts.

Ensign Morris described the feeling:

There were a couple of times when a deep sense of depression overcame me. The first was the realization that I was going to crash-land. I wondered why me? There was a sudden realization that I would never see my parents again, never get married, and never have a family. That depression was short-lived as the water landing took up my attention. The other time was when all the planes that had been over us suddenly disappeared. The sudden quiet set in motion a sense of abandonment and what to do next.

We decided to stay right where we were and keep the water dye marker visible as long as we could.

They knew that everything was going to be all right when Phegley—looking eastward—saw two tiny specks on the horizon with a division of F6Fs circling them.

Tanner and Comb landed near Morris and Phegley and proceeded with the pickup as if it were routine. It was fairly routine except for the location, literally in the heart of Japanese territory. They had made similar rescues before but out at sea or where it was not quite so crowded or accompanied by sporadic rifle fire from the shore.

Tanner idled his engine. With the plane headed toward the life raft, he got out on the wing with a coil of rope. As the plane slid by the raft he threw the line across the raft, and Morris and Phegley grabbed it. Using a rope ladder, he assisted Morris up and into the rear cockpit, then released the raft with Phegley.

Comb approached the raft in the same manner and had just managed to get Phegley up and into the rear cockpit when the engine began to sputter. He jumped forward to the cockpit but too late, and the engine died. It is started by using a shotgun-like shell that is fired into an engine cylinder. Comb placed a round in the starter gun and fired it. The prop turned several times. The engine did not start. He loaded the second shell and fired it—same results. On the third try the engine started, much to the relief of the aircraft's occupants. Later, Comb discovered this shot was the last one he had.

Once airborne and under the protection of the Hellcat escort, Morris and Phegley settled back for the flight back to the task force under the comfortable guardianship of Lieutenant McWhorter and his division. Morris recalled, "I looked back as we were leaving. That small yellow life raft prompted a thought: What a trophy and conversation piece that would be for the mantel."

Comb continued his description of the flight:

On the return trip through the (Bungo) straits, the Japs did open fire on us. Bursts of antiaircraft fire were all around us. Tanner and I were flying low over the water, about five hundred feet, we thought that would be our best defense, and as it turned out we all made it, including our fighters overhead.

When we got back on board the *Astoria,* we all went down to sick bay for a checkup, and Dr. Slegle gave us a shot of Old Granddad to settle our nerves.

On board the cruiser, another one of those strange encounters of war occurred. While Morris and Phegley were in sick bay being examined by the doctor, they had a visitor, Capt. Gerald T. Armitage, officer-in-charge of the ship's marine detachment and a longtime friend from Morris's hometown, Haverhill, Massachusetts.

Morris and Phegley were found physically fit and were transferred by destroyer to the *Randolph.* They arrived in time for the evening meal the same day of being shot down.

Lieutenant Tanner and Lieutenant (junior grade) Comb were awarded Distinguished Flying Crosses for this rescue, by the direction of Admiral Mitscher "to make a suitable award."

Phegley's comment on the incident:

Then there was my "jockey," John Morris, a great guy. Nothing short of miraculous that John could break a [life jacket] snap that could stand hundreds of pounds of stress to save himself from a watery grave. Also, the questions of why the bomb on the fighter-bomber didn't drop when over the target but did drop OK when it was needed to turn the ship headed to capture or shoot us; the firing of the last cartridge before the engine would start on the rescue plane. All miracles!

As activities continued during 14 May, the VF-12 CAP shot down another Zeke, bringing the total of enemy aircraft shot down for the day to thirteen. A fighter sweep at Omura accounted for ten more destroyed on the ground with no losses, an amazing fact in the face of the intense antiaircraft fire encountered. From the VF-12 AAR:

As an enlargement of the AA defense of Omura it should be noted that the sixteen Hellcats were fired upon by heavy guns between ten and fifteen miles from the target on their approach. The bursts were accurate as to altitude, but fortunately a little off in deflection. This fire followed them into the target and out. All along the west coast sporadic bursts were observed during retirement.

The last sweep late that same afternoon was one of those flights no one likes to recall but cannot be forgotten. The sweep was scheduled as a final run on Omura airfield, but many problems arose. First, the flight leader's plane was found to be a "dud" after takeoff, and the replacement flight leader was hit at the first airfield, so he and his wingman returned to the ship. The sweep continued on to Sodohara, where one of the fighters, Ens. Robert Welty of VF-12, was hit, presumably by antiaircraft fire. He failed to recover from a strafing run. The crash site was marked by an explosion and fire on the eastern end of the town. No parachute was observed.

With most of the activity over the horizon out of sight of the ship, Dr. Richard Williams's "Chronicle" described the action as seen from the *Randolph:*

> 5/14—The Jap must have accumulated a few planes and means to use them today. Bogies at 9pm and 11pm last night. We go to torpedo defense. Again at 1am and 3am we go to ready guns. Snoopers and bogies closing and opening all night. At 4am they come in force and we open fire and splash two.

By this time the blare of general quarters had become somewhat routine, but "torpedo defense" was very serious business. Even the wailing of the bugle tattoo seemed more ominous. Air-group personnel made their way below the armored hangar deck to the officers' wardroom—on the double.

Below, we could visualize what might be going on topside when our long-range 5-inch guns opened up, and we could feel the lurching of the ship during its evasive twists and turns. However, we were still drawing coffee and enjoying small talk—that is, until the medium-range 40s began their steady bump-bump-bump, and we stole glances at Lieutenant Whiting of VB-12, his face coated with white oxide burn cream. Did he know something we didn't know?

Moments later, when the 20s (20-mm) opened up, *everybody,* meaning every body, hit the cold, hard steel deck—pronto! That meant only one thing, those bogeys were close.

Fortunately for us, that was the high, or low, point of the evening, depending on which way you want to look at it. No task-group ships were hit.

Ending

...lliams continued his narrative of the course of events on the following morning:

We have general quarters from 4–6am. Soon after securing for breakfast they come in again in force, singles and doubles low over the water from all directions at one time. One dives into the *Enterprise* just astern of us and blasts her flight deck and number one elevator and starts fires. She maintains full speed. The fire's controlled in thirty minutes. Burning planes are jettisoned. She can no longer operate aircraft but can at least support us with her guns. Admiral Mitscher was aboard. That's two ships shot out from under him. He and his staff are being transferred to the *Randolph* today and we become flag ship of Task Force 58. If they're really after Mitscher, then our turn is next. We now have the total of four CVs operating out of a potential of eighteen. The kamikazes are effective . . . many more Japs continue to come in. The sea is covered with yellow and black stinking smoke and the sky is mottled with Ak Ak. Many long plumes of the flame and smoke from falling planes. One splashes about fifteen hundred feet off our port bow and you can feel the heat of the explosion. The men below deck could hear the motor roar. The ships' guns down seven and planes down eleven this morning alone. One ensign got three. Boys returning from Kyushu say there is no airborne opposition. They have raised hell with factories, fields, and transportation while we serve as bait for the (Japanese) air force. One plane only from the *Randolph* was shot down by flak. It lands on the Inland Sea and the men are seen to get in a raft. Seaplanes from the *Astoria* are sent to rescue them. At 5pm we go to general quarters again. Three bogies close to six miles and then open. No further trouble this night. The seaplanes (OS2Us) return with the crew shot down unharmed. The first time the Americans have ever been rescued from the Inland sea. We stay at longitude 132 latitude 31 all day. Very close to Kyushu and throw heavy loads at the Jap all day. Got rid of one thousand bombs in these two days. This a record day, beating all other carriers. 199 sorties from *Randolph*. We head south at flank speed at night.

The *Randolph*'s action report recorded the main event of the following day:

The next day, 15 May, it was announced that the task force commander, Admiral Marc A. Mitscher, would transfer his flag to the *Randolph*. We went around the ship with fingers crossed. "Hope he doesn't bring the kamikazes with him," we said. Admiral Mitscher had been on the *Bunker Hill*. After she got hit he transferred to the *Enterprise,* staying there until she was likewise hit. When he came aboard our ship that afternoon he crossed from a destroyer in a boatswain's chair over the fantail. Our photographers took a picture of his arrival that later appeared in "Life" and "Time" magazines. He was smiling. The only gear he had left was a briefcase, which he carried. Maybe, despite our earlier feelings, the little Admiral brought us good luck, because we didn't get hit—not then, anyway. For two weeks we were flagship of Task Force 58. . . .

Dr. Williams also had recorded his impressions of that day in his diary:

5/15—Today we become U.S.S. *Randolph,* Flag Ship Task Force 58, Fifth Fleet, U.S. Navy. Admiral Marc Mitscher is piped aboard with a staff of sixty two personnel (including his chief of staff, Commodore Arleigh Burke). He is much like his pictures, small, wrinkled, wiry, looks sixty five, outstanding feature is his bright sharp glinting eyes. He is an admirable looking warrior. . . . The hospital ship U.S.S. *Modesty* takes on patients from the *Enterprise, Bataan, Wilkes Barre.* She looks funny, her clean white paint glistening in the sun, among all these dirty scarred drab gray monsters. . . . We transfer our casualties to the U.S.S. *Bountiful* and see the first white women since January. They all looked good.

5/16—Spend the entire day taking aboard ammo and supplies. We hear that the *Bunker Hill* had 556 dead, buried at sea, and fifty still missing and presumed dead. We hear that the marines are again moving on Okinawa and there are forty five thousand dead Japs with only fifteen thousand and ten miles to go. We narrowly avoided a catastrophe in the middle of the night. While at the movies we felt the ship shudder and shake and we later heard that it was due to an emergency full speed reverse to avoid collision with an AE [ammunition ship] with fifteen thousand tons of bombs. She was out of position and only an alert lookout saved us. We were nearly rammed astern when we reversed by the ship behind us. That ammo would have made angels out of all of us. We head north at dusk.

Three days later the support of the Okinawa campaign was continuing, as were our interdiction raids on the islands to the north. The interdiction raids were now extended as far north as Yaku Shima, almost within sight of the southern tip of Kyushu. On a sweep up the chain to Yaku and return to Tokuno Shima, VF-12 lost Ens. C. L. White to unknown causes as no antiaircraft fire was observed. White did not recover from a strafing run on two camouflaged aircraft at the edge of the airfield and crashed about two hundred feet offshore. A violent explosion was observed, and there seemed to have been no opportunity for him to bailout.

The Okinawa support operations continued to move on. Fatigue began to plague us and the planners. Miscues began to appear. One was related by Ensign Furse of VF-12:

The ship went to general quarters and launched aircraft while the ensigns were on deck taxiing planes into deck-spot positions. So eight flight leaders who were in the ready room ended up in one eight-plane group launched to chase an unidentified bogey.

I ended up shortly thereafter leading a flight of eight ensigns to Okinawa for ground support. We flew in to our standby point and circled, waiting for a support call.

Finally, it was time to return to the ship, and when I called to get relieved to return to the ship, they asked if we possibly had time to knock out a pillbox for the marines. We still had a full load of rockets and a lot of desire to use them, so I said sure.

We found the spot, destroyed the pillbox, and smugly headed back to the ship. We were late. It got dark, very dark. I was very concerned about finding the ship and more importantly getting aboard.

I did find the ship, and while making my approach I noticed when I received a turn command from the LSO that instead of the "roger" I thought I was on, he was giving me a "high," so I was able to let down enough to get a cut.

The LSO was using only lighted paddles with no suit, so you couldn't tell where he was in relation to the paddles, so a "high," "low," and "roger" all looked the same. One of our group needed ten approaches to get aboard.

Some other embarrassing errors were made, one in particular. Admiral Mitscher had been driven from two other damaged carriers, happily without personal injury. So far on the *Randolph* he seemed to be relatively safe. But, as Ensign Lindley of VF-12 explained, Mitscher was still in danger:

> I was the only man I know in the navy that ever knocked Admiral Mitscher down. One time we were manning planes. Everybody left the ready room, and for some reason I was a little bit late. The group went up the ladder, out onto the flight deck, and he was waiting at the top of the ladder to go below. As he started down and got down about one step, I was coming up with my head down in a half-run up the ladder, trying to catch up. I caught the admiral with my head and knocked him over onto his butt. He was just sitting there. I took one look at him and went out and got in my plane. Never did hear any more about it.

Daily activities continued for nearly a week when more tragedy struck, this time to the beleaguered night-fighter group. On 21 May Lt. (j.g.) Leadean Levis and Ens. David G. Howard collided while on a dusk patrol. Area searches for the next three days produced no evidence of survivors.

Strain and fatigue was beginning to show on the pilots and more visibly on Admiral Mitscher. On 28 May in an unprecedented act following a conference aboard the USS *Missouri*, Admiral Nimitz replaced Admirals Spruance and Mitscher with Admirals Halsey and McCain. Normally, a change of tacticians was made after a campaign is completed, not during an ongoing operation.

Admiral Mitscher had been tactical commander of Task Force 58 since January. He was exhausted after five months of almost continual and intense combat, of which ninety-two days had been at sea off Okinawa and Japan—a navy record. He had been forced from one flagship to another and had lost many of his staff. He was relieved on 29 May, and Task Force 58 became Task Force 38. At noon that day the *Randolph* departed the force with Mitscher aboard and transported him to Apra Harbor, Guam, arriving 31 May.

Apra Harbor is not very large. There is not enough room for a carrier of the *Randolph*'s dimensions to turn around. Once the admiral was delivered ashore, turning the ship around was done in a rather ingenious way. Our aircraft were parked and tied down securely along the flight-deck edges with their tails pointed outboard. All aircraft were manned and engines started, and contact was maintained with the ship by radio. The aircraft forward on the starboard side and those aft on the port side were then directed to run their engines up to full power. The thrust of these engines began to turn the ship slowly on an axis amidships, rotating it one hundred and eighty degrees and pointing it toward the mouth of the harbor. As she turned and began to aim at the entrance, these aircraft engines were stopped, and the aircraft on the port side forward and starboard side aft were directed to power up, thus stopping the pivot. Dubbed Operation Pinwheel, the maneuver was the brainchild of Captain Baker. It proved to be so successful that it was adopted by other carriers for small harbors, when no tugs were available and during emergencies.

The *Randolph* and Air Group 12 then steamed on to Tacloban, Leyte, in the Philippine Islands, for some well-earned rest and recreation. The ship dropped anchor in the San Pedro Bay anchorage of Leyte Gulf on 4 June.

There were recreational facilities on the island, but most of us seemed to prefer some quiet time aboard ship, just relaxing or soaking up sunshine. But the quiet did not last, as the *Randolph*'s cruise book related:

The afternoon of 7 June the ship lay quietly anchored in the Gulf. Some of us were on the flight deck, lying in spaces between the parked planes, sunbathing. An Army Air Corps P-38 twin-engine fighter was overhead making playful runs on us. About 1540 it pulled up a few thousand feet and then headed down toward us. Nobody paid much attention to it. We little suspected the pilot of that plane was going to misjudge his distance and what started out as his little joke was about to turn into a sickening tragedy. At 1544 the P-38 crashed [onto] the forward flight deck and glanced off into the water where it immediately sank. It left behind on the flight deck a raging fire. Fortunately, our planes in keeping with ship's policy were not fueled, but they burned just the same.

The sun-bathers in the area never had a chance. The fire was put out by capable action on the part of the men; our casualties were fourteen killed and eleven injured. We shuddered to think what would have happened if the P-38 had landed in the craft which was alongside us at the time unloading bombs! There would have been an abrupt end to our story.

This marked the second time we had been hit while in a supposedly safe anchorage. We began to feel we were safer in battle.

Flight-deck director ABM2c Glen W. Putney on the incident:

I was sitting on a tow tractor behind a 5-inch gun turret on the flight deck when two P-38s started circling and diving on various ships. One dived on us and came straight in at the number one elevator. We had several aircraft parked forward. Several crewmen were lying around, soaking up sun. One man from my crew was killed. We found a nose cone and part of a tail boom. Never did learn what happened to the other P-38.

This time Dr. Richard Williams, the ship's surgeon, was involved in the action and reported on it in an addendum to his "World War II Cruise Chronicle of the U.S.S. Randolph":

6/7/45—The *Randolph* was hit by a P-38. The ship's surgeon had been on the beach at a beer party and had boarded an LCI to return to the ship which was about fifteen miles offshore. The LCI made stops at various vessels on route and ultimately came alongside a battleship whereupon the Officer of the Deck shouted down asking if there were any personnel on board from the *Randolph*. The surgeon raised his hand and was asked to come aboard. Upon being identified as the ship's surgeon, the only surgeon in the *Randolph*'s company, the admiral on board the battleship broke out his barge and transported the surgeon straight away to the *Randolph*. Upon approaching the *Randolph,* and upon seeing an admiral's barge approaching, all kinds of bells began ringing and when the surgeon climbed the gangway there was the most impressive greeting party including the skipper of the *Randolph*. It was amazing to see the faces fall when the person climbing the gangway was a lowly Lieutenant (junior grade), somewhat disheveled, and unaware of what had taken place aboard the *Randolph*. By this time most of the casualties from the P-38 hit had been given first aid and had been transferred to a hospital ship. Those at the head of the gangway actually were awe struck because they had assumed that the surgeon was dead, the hospital group routinely using the forward port side of the flight deck as their place to lie in the sun and this was the precise spot that was hit by the P-38. As a matter of fact, a hospital corpsman first class was killed and another lost his leg in this incident. For many days thereafter when the surgeon was walking a companionway he would come upon people who would step aside and look in shock and say are you Dr. so and so, whereupon he would say yes, whereupon the person would say you're supposed to be dead.

Cdr. Ellery Clark, the damage-control officer, reflected on the hit:

. . . an Army P-38 stunted over "Randy," disregarded Captain Baker's instructions to cease, and then crashed the ship's flight deck forward, centerline, and killed area sunbathers. At that moment our hanger deck was filled with replenishment bombs, with the ammunition ship nearby. Gasoline poured from the plane through the flight-deck hole. Once again cool damage-control parties quickly surrounded the flames and limited then extinguished them. Our old friend and sometime companion, *Jason,* lived up to her previous reputation and this time repaired the flight deck in only four days. Again the ship was ready for action!

This former damage-control officer reflects upon these stirring and trying past naval events with a very deep sense of appreciation for the gallant WW II pattern that was "Randy's." It seems to be a lasting mosaic of fine ship's aircraft operations, both offensive and defensive; excellent defensive gunnery by Commander Lasell's department; good damage control; good fortune in not being hit during touch-and-go campaign operations; and the many near misses by enemy planes always being in favor of the ship.

Of most importance has been and continues to be the strong impression that God's blessing sailed with *Randolph.* Her many combat experiences show the ship, though twice damaged, was never put out of action when on the most important battle line. Regrettably, aviation and other losses were sustained, but in so-called reasonable numbers, based upon expected and actual mortality rates of all *Essex*-class carriers. My final conclusion is that

Randolph and her surviving wartime complement have been the grateful beneficiary of God's assistance.

Other carriers had not been so fortunate. Some had been damaged within sight of the *Randolph*. Certainly, she had been blessed, despite her "at-anchor" experiences.

Even as the *Randolph* was being repaired, she continued to rearm and resupply. Liberty and recreational activities continued on the beaches at the sparse facilities. Some of us found a wide range of activities, reminiscent of the days at Astoria, Oregon. However, "One visit to Tacloban was sufficient to satisfy all curiosity, and one whiff of the place made many wonder if it really had been necessary to capture the island" ("History of Bombfighting Squadron TWELVE").

Dr. Williams summarized other activities:

6/11—The damage is all repaired. The dead are all buried but some are yet to die and the wounds will never heal. The Army has admitted the P-38 was theirs and the pilot was transferring it to another field and it was his last flight. He was en route home. Today the results of the recent typhoon hove into the anchorage. The USS *Bennington* (CV-20) arrived with her flight deck destroyed all the way back to the after forward antenna. The deck drooping and dragging in the sea. We hear that the *Hornet,* the *Belleau Wood* and the *Pittsburgh* also got it. The *Pittsburgh* is broken in half and under tow. We hear that Halsey headed into the typhoon despite orders not to do so.

The captain announced that Air Group 12 was to be relieved and returned stateside. This bit of information was well received but also produced a strange confession from Ens. Harold N. Lindley of VF-12, the admiral-basher, concerning his stash of bourbon:

When we left the *Randolph* in the Philippines, I had five bottles left, which I sold at the head of the gangway for ten dollars a bottle. So I broke even.

The main purpose of the whiskey was to bolster my courage a little bit before going in on a target. I often wondered if the rest were as scared as I was.

The officers and men of Air Group 12 were relieved by Air Group 16 on 17 June and were transferred to the USS *Makassar Straits,* a small aircraft carrier, for transportation to Guam on the first leg homeward. We disembarked at Guam on 23 June to await additional transportation stateside. The USS *Kalanin Bay,* another small carrier and a repaired victim of the Battle for Leyte Gulf, arrived on 30 June to transport Air Group 12 and other personnel stateside. After six months of grueling shipboard life in the combat zone, lodging in a quonset in the murky backwoods of Guam wasn't the ideal way to relax. Frustration with the environment and the wait for transportation was inevitably a menu for trouble. The *Kalanin Bay* arrived just in time to rescue the group from Guam, the Guamanians, the military police, and various other government officials.

With the air group back aboard ship, calmer seas prevailed. Sedated by an exceptional diet of turkey, roast beef, chicken, and ham alternated daily, we didn't need long to slow down from the adrenalin-charged pace of the last six months. But our reputation apparently preceded us to Hawaii, for we were given little time to rummage around this island. The *Kalanin Bay* arrived on 11 July, refueled, and departed on 12 July.

Approaching the coast of San Diego late in the evening of 19 July, we received instructions concerning disembarkation for the following day. Among the times and procedures was buried the announcement that the U.S. Customs Service would inspect all luggage. After all, we had been in so-called foreign ports, namely the Philippines and Guam. Somewhere off the coast of San Diego where the *Kalanin Bay* circled during the night there is deposited in the Pacific many .30-.30–caliber carbine rifles and miscellaneous unlawful trophies.

During the Thunderbird's stay on Falalop Island, Ulithi Atoll, while the *Randolph* was being repaired, we had discovered barrels and barrels of preserved .30-.30 carbines. Belonging to "no one" in particular, they presented a perfect invitation to souvenir hunters. The Customs inspectors, however, considered them contraband, and messy explanations would be required.

The next morning, as instructed, all air-group personnel brought their duffle bags and carrying cases to the hangar deck for inspection by the Customs agents. When Customs arrived shortly after the ship docked, there on the hangar deck was Air Group 12's last coordinated effort. The duffle bags and suitcases were piled about fifteen feet high in the middle of the hangar deck. The Customs official took one look, paled, and said to hell with it or something to that effect. It took us a couple of hours to sort out the gear—except for one ingenious individual who put his alarm clock in his duffle bag and set the alarm for 1100. Didn't take him long to find his bag.

From that twentieth day of July, exactly six months after deployment, Air Group 12 just seemed to dissolve. Many pilots and enlisted men were sent to NAS Pasco, Washington, to reform the squadrons. Others were sent to new air groups forming on both the East and West Coasts, and still others to the training command, all to prepare for the possible invasion of Japan in the fall.

Japan's total capitulation on 14 August and subsequent surrender ended the war. Discharge was most common for officers and enlisted men, though many chose to transfer to the regular navy. Some of the aircrewmen applied for pilot training despite their harrowing experiences in combat.

The Thunderbirds' relationship with the *Randolph* had been, in many ways, like the navy's relationship with the civilian population. They both left the ship or port, disappeared over the horizon, did the job assigned them, and returned. The civilian population could only visualize what transpired from reports and sailors' descriptions of their experiences at sea. The ship's company could only visualize what transpired from reports and pilots' descriptions of their exploits. The civilians heard many stories. Likewise, the ship's company also heard of many activities. In all cases, what was heard and reported conveyed a sense of pride or embarrassment, jubilation or depression, about tasks that were completed successfully or not. As for the Pacific Campaign, in those first raids on Japan, then in the support of Iwo Jima and Okinawa, Air Group 12 left its mark. The enemy knew we had been there—as was reflected in this 14 June 1945 message from Commander Second Carrier Task Force, Pacific:

TO THE OFFICERS AND MEN OF AIR GROUP 12:
Soon now you will be going home on leave. You have earned it. This has been a tough campaign—how tough is shown by the loss of such gallant leaders as Charles Crommelin and Ralph Embree. But the record shows that despite what you were up against, you have done a magnificent job. You swept the Jap back to his homeland. You hit him hard with your strikes against Japan. You led the way at Okinawa, and you made it possible to secure the island by gaining and maintaining control of the air. Take pride in your record. It's a good one.

Well Done to every one of you. Goodbye and good luck.
/s/ J.S. McCain
Vice Admiral, USN
ComSECONDCarTaskFor

There has always been a feeling of accomplishment among members of Air Group 12, a feeling that our efforts contributed, in some measure, to the ultimate defeat of the Japanese Empire. Thus, the story of Crommelin's Thunderbirds, as reported in ships' logs, combat action reports, air-group and squadron AARs, and personal experiences related by those who were there, is now in and not lost to future generations.

✪ Epilogue

Okinawa was declared secure on 21 June, and Task Force 38 was relieved of support duty to become a persistent visitor to the islands of Japan. The force's constant raids were becoming more noticeable to Ensign Brown at Ofuna and Aircrewman Richards at Omari. What happened to them after Air Group 12 returned stateside provides some insight as to what the Japanese could have been planning to counter an invasion.

Brown: While [we were] at Ofuna there were daylight raids by carrier-based planes. Some of the bombs hit very close—in fact, so close that we could smell the odor of the burnt explosives. It was a strange feeling to be ducking for cover and, at the same time, hoping the attacks would continue and be more frequent. A new prisoner arrived on 7 August who had been shot down that day. He informed us through the grapevine that one bomb had destroyed a whole city. Of course, we thought he was off his rocker and hopefully would recover later.

Richards: We had three or four F6F raids. I think there was an airfield farther down, and when the navy came in, one of the first things you would see would be some TBMs doing a glide-bomb [run] on that airfield. Then evidently they sent some fighters over to make sure nobody got off the runways. The problem was that they didn't get to shoot anything, and they didn't want to go back to the carrier with a load. They'd look around for something to shoot up. Of course our camp wasn't marked, so they'd come down and shoot our camp up.

We didn't know the war was over. We had heard that the

Russians came in, but we didn't know anything about the A-bomb. One guard was telling us something about the *"ichi"* (one) raid. We were thinking one big raid. I remember we were all talking [that] they must have brought the European air force over here, all over this one city, because they were talking about this big raid. It was the A-bomb.

Brown: Fifteen August was a very tense day. They had the emperor's radio speech broadcast over loudspeakers so that all of the guards in the camp could hear. It was obvious from the demeanor of the guards what the emperor had said. We fully expected immediate reprisals, which did not happen. One of the guards who we disliked very much got drunk, attempted to commit hari-kari, botched it, and they took him to the hospital.

Richards: I remember that day. Everyone had to listen. Noon! Big speech. I know we did. We thought it was another pep rally to get them all excited so they'd fight on when the invasion came. They were all supposed to run to the beaches. We'd seen them have kids, old ladies, and girls with bamboo poles and pitchforks, and teaching them how to run. They were all supposed to run to the beaches when the landing came. That's what we thought, but then some of our people understood Japanese. They started running around, "Its over, its over!"

The guards sat around—nothing went on for ten days. They turned the camp over to us, and they stayed outside.

Brown: They told us to stay inside the camp for our own protection.

Richards: Yeah, they just stayed around. We didn't hear from the Americans. I remember I was inside, and we heard this plane, and we recognized the sound of the engine. We knew it was an American engine. We all ran out. When I got out I could just see him right off the water, and he went up the shoreline. He rocked his wings. He saw us and knew we were there. He circled around and threw a message in the camp. Remember the little weighted things? It said, "Hang on, massive help on the way, help coming." And then he threw some cigarettes out; and a couple of other fighters came over, and they threw cigarettes out, some candy bars, just whatever they had on them. But later on that day they must have been coming from the carrier because the fighters were coming over, and they had whole cartons of cigarettes and whole cartons of candy bars. Then the next day the PBMs came over, and they were throwing boxes of K-rations, wooden boxes, trying to slide them into camp. The next day a B-29 came through. He dropped the whole thing. Free drop, no parachute, nothing. Luckily, most of it hit outside, in the water. We were getting set up like a chain, passing the stuff in as well as we could, but, hell, there were big oil drums full of stuff. We were all sitting over there and had a can opener or something. We got a great big can, something like a big oil drum. We'd open a can of peaches and throw it in. Open another can and throw it in. It was like a big salad for everybody. We had some soup bowls they gave us on Omari—they gave us soup bowls and a spoon. So we would walk around with that bowl, scooping out of this massive fruit salad. Next day, I remember—or was it the next night—there was fog all over Tokyo Bay, so we didn't know what the hell was going on. As the day wore on, the fog started burning off, and someone said, "My God, there's an American destroyer out there! There's another one!" Pretty soon we realized the whole damn fleet was out there. Tokyo Bay. They had come through that night or that morning, I don't know when. How the hell are we going to get out there? And then later on in the afternoon we started yelling, "Boats, boats." There were some landing craft coming.

Brown: On 29 August Harold Stassen's unit came in after us and took us to the hospital ship, USS *Benevolence.* I was still on board in Tokyo harbor on 2 September and listened to the surrender on the radio. We were fed six meals per day with snacks in between, and my ninety-seven pounds started to go up. I was flown to Guam and spent a couple days in the hospital there.

Richards: I remember Harold Stassen; he was the one in charge of the landing. He came in there, and a Jap colonel came out. Do you remember that? He came out of the administration building, and he stood there. He said something about he couldn't do anything because he had no further word from the emperor.

Stassen said, "I don't give a shit if you have or not, I have orders from Halsey," and he said, "We're going in now."

These guys came in with submachine guns. They're standing there with him, and the colonel turned around and went back in.

I did hear Stassen say very quietly, "Get over there on the damn radio and tell them to get more people in here, quick."

I didn't get out until late that night. First of all they were taking out people who couldn't walk. There were a lot of people laid up, couldn't even move. A lot of them came in that day, the day the war ended. I don't know where you were at the time.

Brown: I don't remember. I don't remember where I was. I do remember getting on board the *Benevolence*.

Richards: I finally got to Hawaii. They didn't seem to find any record of me. They said, "Were you missing in action, dead, or something?" Couldn't find any record of me.

Both Ensign Brown and Aircrewman Richards were sent to Washington, D.C., for hospitalization before being discharged. Neither suffered any permanent injuries from their internment.

There is little known about those pilots and crewmen listed as missing in action. Brown and Richards are the only two from Air Group 12 known to have returned. The fate of others is only speculative, such as the case of Lt. J. E. "Buck" Toliver of VF-12, who was seen getting into his life raft, or Ens. William T. McAdams of VBF-12, who was also seen getting in his raft but who was seen taken prisoner. Lt. Bleeker P. Seaman, Jr., of VBF-12 was listed as missing in action on 16 February, the day before the loss of Toliver and McAdams. One clue has been found regarding these losses.

A United Press International news story published in the 7 December 1977 issue of the *Los Angeles Times* might provide an answer to what happened to Lieutenants Toliver and Seaman or Ensign McAdams:

Tokyo (UPI)—Japanese Authorities have released the names of seventeen American prisoners of war killed in the atomic bombing of Hiroshima in the last days of World War II. The names were taken from a Foreign Ministry list. In some cases, ranks, ages or serial numbers are unknown.

The article then identified army air corps and navy pilots and crew members. In addition, "One man is described as a U.S. Navy officer from the aircraft carrier *Randolph*."

The list continued, naming additional members of army air corps flight crews.

The aggressiveness and tactical talent exhibited by Commander Crommelin was perhaps an innate quality. However, he did have a leader that provided a pattern to emulate in Admiral Mitscher, Task Force 58 commander. Mitscher's tactical genius contributed as much to the navy's success in the Pacific hostilities as that of any other commander in that arena. His doctrine of recognizing the competence and experience of his subordinates, and of letting them operate under their own initiative within the simplest guidelines and of requiring a high standard of readiness at all times, was some of the basis of his success. His deep concern for his naval aviators—as he was one himself—elicited the maximum effort on the part of all hands. He also had a talent for listening to his subordinates and was always willing to entertain a new idea.

A pertinent example was the concerns of Commander Crommelin and Lieutenant Commander Michaelis about the aborted rescue of Lieutenant Toliver, and Crommelin's subsequent recommendation that the squadron whose pilot was in trouble should provide the coordination of that rescue. This recommendation was instituted to the fullest extent in the recovery of Ensign Morris and Aircrewman Phegley from the Inland Sea.

Admiral Mitscher was not intimidated by the Japanese, although he had a healthy respect for them, nor was he intimidated by his seniors. When he and his chief of staff, Arleigh Burke, returned to the United States after being replaced by Halsey, Mitscher sent Burke on to Washington to report in to the navy's most senior officer, the Chief of Naval Operations Adm. Ernest J. King—a protocol not normally followed in navy traditions. Mitscher went trout fishing instead, leaving only a sealed envelope with Burke just in case his presence was demanded. It wasn't, even by the chief of naval operations, who was known as a cantankerous old curmudgeon.

In September 1945 at the behest of the secretary of the navy, Admiral Mitscher was asked to outline his views on the postwar navy. The memorandum he submitted contained concepts that were integrated not only in the navy but later within all military services under the Defense Department. He observed that no future war would ever be fought without the use of the airplane; that more-sophisticated weapons systems were needed for both the airplane and the battleship, the latter to be relegated to last in line of support until a long-range weapon was available for it; that ground forces were important for invasion and occupation; that the military should demand the most for its money in terms of offensive weaponry; and that the nation should be conservative in its use of the nation's military manpower, which would have to be trained thoroughly to carry out future requirements.

In December 1945 Mitscher was tapped to form an Eighth Fleet on the East Coast for duty in the Mediterranean—a rather ominous task, as the prevailing attitude around the nation was a desire to "let down" after nearly four years of war. He accomplished the task by April and demonstrated his confidence in the completed task to no less than the president of the United States, Harry S. Truman.

Admiral Mitscher was assigned as Commander in Chief Atlantic Fleet in September 1946. In January of the following year he suffered a heart attack, and on 3 February ". . . this skinny little wrinkled man . . . the nemesis of Japanese air power . . . ," who looked nothing like a warrior in a baseball cap, passed away, leaving a legacy that will be studied and analyzed by many of his successors for years to come.

One final word on Cdr. Charles L. Crommelin from the pilot who flew with him more than any others in Air Group 12. From Lt. Al Bolduc of VBF-12, Crommelin's section leader, came a rather startling revelation:

The first fighter sweep over the mainland of Japan, we were approaching one of the fighter bases targeted for neutralizing 16 February when I spotted a Zero or Zeke at two o'clock, slightly above the division. It was less than a thousand feet ahead.

After pausing a moment or two, I called to Crommelin: "Commander, think we should go after the bogey at two o'clock?" We were overtaking it, and this guy was sitting there fat, dumb, and happy without a care in the world, or so he thought. Crommelin didn't say a word, but immediately eased over behind the Zeke and let him have a burst of all six .50-calibers, exploding the wing tank.

His Hellcat had been fitted with what was called a Chen package, which doubled the rate of fire of the six guns. The Zeke practically disintegrated.

It was an awesome display of firepower. Apparently, this installation was prone to burn out the gun barrels unless used conservatively. Few fighter pilots would tend to be that conservative, it's not their nature.

After the mission debriefing, Mangieri, Frank Ness, and I met in the VBF ready room to discuss the mission and try to evaluate what had transpired after spotting the Zeke—regarding Crommelin's inability to see clearly.

Almost everyone in the fighter squadrons knew about Charles Crommelin's early heroics over Marcus Island in 1943 and later over Mille Atoll in the Gilbert Islands when he was hit in the cockpit by AA fire. His face and upper body were slashed. With little or no vision in his left eye and a broken right wrist, he was barely able to fly one hundred miles to the *Yorktown* and land. Apparently, Commander Crommelin was able to memorize the eye charts in subsequent physical exams, for no one questioned his flying skills from that day on.

After discussing all the pros and cons, we decided that from then on we would be his eyes, and no one else would know the handicap he was flying under. And no one ever did, for he led a dozen or more strikes after being transferred to the *Hornet,* flagship of Task Force 58, on 13 March 1945.

Had Bolduc and crew been with Crommelin, could the collision south of Okinawa possibly have been avoided?

As for the *Randolph,* Dr. Williams's "Chronicle" elaborated on the main happenings as the war with Japan began to close down:

8/14—Refueled off Tokyo. Peace talk crams the air but no official word. . . .

8/15—Unconditional surrender. No word on the peace so we go to general quarters at 3am and proceed with our planned strike. The first strike goes off and drops its bombs on factories, rockets, ships and so forth. Splashes several Jap planes and returns intact. At 0800 the official word is released and our 2nd strike which is gone out is recalled. . . . There are many mines being sighted and there are many Japs who haven't gotten the word. Jap planes keep coming out all day. At 1000 hours we splash one in a suicide dive on the ship. Admiral Bull Halsey addresses the fleet and two bogies are splashed during his speech. We stay at general quarters all day and splash twenty Japs in all. Hell of a way to celebrate peace. But, with the recent loss of the *Indianapolis* and with (almost) 100 percent casualties, the torpedoing of the *Pennsylvania* two days ago, we're willing to remain alert. The men dislike

Halsey, adore Mitscher. Halsey is a blowhard, with his guts and armor protection of the *Iowa* we go right in there and fight. Our landing force is ready but doubt that it will be used. McArthur [*sic*] is appointed Supreme Commander so perhaps Halsey will take a backseat and won't ride the emperor's white horse with silver saddle. At dusk we head out for rendezvous of the entire Third Fleet to await orders.

8/29—Still supplying POW's. We dropped vitamins and medical equipment today. It is reported there is much avitaminosis among them. . . .

8/30—Fleet is at anchor. Landing is secure. The ships are open for ventilation. Lights and movies at night.

9/2—Peace is signed. We enter Tokyo Bay. Letters canceled bear this souvenir marked "Tokyo Bay CV15 2 September, VJ Day". . . .

9/4—Planes to the beach to carry requested gear to our men return with untold souvenirs. We get the best word of all today. Censorship is entirely lifted. We can write about anything. . . .

9/11—We arrive Pearl Harbor at 1630 hours . . . covering a distance of twenty nine thousand miles this cruise and a total of ninety three thousand miles since commissioning. . . .

9/20—Our marine landing force returns aboard the *Monterey.* Also in, are the *Missouri,* the *Bataan, New Mexico, Maryland, Idaho, North Carolina, Enterprise, Hornet.* Battleship row is full and proud just as prior to 7 December 1941.

10/1—Weigh anchor at dawn for Panama flying our first homeward bound pennant.

10/16—Transit the canal with *Wasp.* Liberty in Cristobal, Coco Sola, Colon.

10/21—At dawn we round Cape Henry and at 0831 we dock at pier 17 NOB, Norfolk, Virginia. Home, mid a terrific fanfare of all the horns, whistles and bells on all the ships in the area. This lady has returned from the wars to her place of origin.

Adm. Arleigh Burke, former chief of naval operations and one of the heroes of World War II, was aboard the *Randolph* as chief of staff to Admiral Mitscher after they had been forced off the *Enterprise.* Roy Bruce visited with Admiral Burke at his residence in Fairfax,

Virginia, to get his reflections of the time he was on the *Randolph*. From that interview in August 1991:

> The admiral met me in the lobby of the Virginian, where he and his wife of sixty-eight years now live in retirement. They had spent July Fourth commissioning the DDG *Arleigh Burke* (DDG 51), a new class of destroyers. Although he is slightly stooped, he has a very firm handshake, and I was surprised by the size of his hand that all but swallowed mine. In our discussion, I found him both serious and humorous, deep thoughts often being wiped away by the generous smile so familiar to all who know him. He appeared to light up as he related those days as Commodore Arleigh Burke, chief of staff, Task Force 58.
>
> "Admiral, do you remember leaving the USS *Enterprise* after having been bombed off of it and the *Bunker Hill?*"
>
> "Yes, I remember leaving with just the clothes on my back and not much else."
>
> "Do you remember what being on the *Randolph* was like?"
>
> "I don't remember the details, but I do remember that we [the entire staff of Admiral Mitscher] were a nuisance for any ship."
>
> "What kind of a leader was Admiral Mitscher to serve under?"
>
> "We were doing things that had never been done before, and we never knew what was next or what to expect [from the enemy]. He listened to everyone who had new ideas. He was a good listener . . . had a fantastic grasp of new concepts and would follow up on them. He was very precise about anything dealing with aviation or his aviators, and he demanded exactness, obedience from every element of the task group. He said we would be the aggressor and force the enemy to conform to what we did offensively . . . that we should put fear in their hearts and minds.
>
> "He was not a fatalist and knew the enemy was tough. The Japanese knew their limitations and were very good at what they did . . . would fight to the very end. Each of our air groups had its own style . . . within limitations—sifting intelligence constantly being fed to their ACI officers, then having to decide which was correct information.
>
> "Mitscher and I respected each other, but he definitely preferred aviators to line officers on his staff, and he made that very clear

from the day I reported for duty. He wouldn't talk to me at first, warning me only to stay out of the way."

I asked him to compare Admiral Mitscher and Admiral Halsey.

"Both were aggressive leaders. Halsey was impetuous, knew he was in command to attack. It was apparent to everyone Mitscher had more concern for his aviators and had extraordinary faith in what they could do . . . nothing was impossible."

"What about Admiral Burke?"

He responded that he had qualified for aviation, but then chose line officer duty. Even then, he said, he realized that aviation was the key to victory (this occurred in the 1920s). Stubbornness, he admitted, was his strongest point, although that quality was not what Admiral Mitscher saw in his chief of staff.

"What are your thoughts about the surrender on the USS *Missouri?*"

Admiral Burke paused reflectively, as though to summarize the interview: "The Japanese lost the war despite doing everything they could possibly do to win . . . despite tremendous sacrifices."

A fitting end.

✪ Appendix A:
Air Group 12 Personnel Deployed on USS *Randolph* as of January 1945

Air Group 12 Staff

Cdr. C. L. Crommelin, Coronado, California
Lt. O. C. White, Chicago, Illinois
Lt. J. D. Hare, Reedy, California
Lt. R. A. Morse, Tucson, Arizona
Lt. F. C. Kidd, Malden, Massachusetts
Lt. R. H. Anderson, Salt Lake City, Utah
Lt. (j.g.) W. A. Drews, Crowley, Louisiana
Lt. (j.g.) C. K. Wilson, Denton, Texas
P. D. Griffith, CPhoM, Long Beach, California
A. C. Fraser, ATCS, Madison, New Jersey
P. E. Thatcher, AMM2, Portland, Indiana
C. W. Harris, AOM3, Jacksonville, Illinois

Fighting Squadron 12

Ens. J. J. Abeler, St. Paul, Minnesota
Lt. P. H. Anderson, Miami, Florida
Ens. E. H. Ball, Sharonville, Ohio
Lt. B. L. Bardeen, Virginia Beach, Virginia
Ens. H. F. Barrett, Jackson, Michigan
Lt. R. H. Benson, Jacksonville, Florida
Ens. R. W. Bruce, Mobile, Alabama
Ens. W. D. Carlson, Detroit, Michigan
Ens. J. C. Cobb, Leesburg, Florida
Ens. S. H. Davidson, Franklin, Indiana

Ens. R. A. Davis, Pawtucket, Rhode Island
Lt. M. L. Detter, Burton, Kansas
Lt. P. N. DeVere, Morganton, North Carolina
Ens. J. M. Finley, Palo Alto, California
Ens. J. T. Fowler, Birmingham, Alabama
Lt. (j.g.) J. M. Franks, Macungie, Pennsylvania
Ens. L. E. Furse, Flint, Michigan
Ens. J. E. Gallagher, Moorhead, Minnesota
Ens. L. C. Garrison, Pratt, Kansas
Ens. L. O. Glidden, Dunning, Nebraska
Ens. H. M. Hardin, Wichita Falls, Texas
Ens. R. L. Hatcher, Carthage, Missouri
Lt. (j.g.) H. W. Hewlett, Cheyenne, Wyoming
Ens. J. A. Holloway, Register, Georgia
Ens. D. G. Howard Jr., Annapolis, Maryland
Lt. D. M. Hypes, Bell, California
Ens. W. E. F. Inzer, Colorado Springs, Colorado
Ens. E. Jindra, Cicero, Illinois
Ens. L. Levis, Marshalltown, Iowa
Ens. J. A. Lukes, San Francisco, California
Ens. D. L. Martin, Fountaintown, Indiana
Ens. W. L. Mason, Fort Wayne, Indiana
Ens. E. S. Masey, Kansas City, Kansas
Lt. G. T. Maxwell, Atmore, Alabama
Ens. S. W. McCabe, Lompoc, California
Ens. C. O. McDaniel, Rushville, Indiana
Lt. H. McWhorter III, Long Beach, California
Ens. J. A. Meacham, Reed Point, Montana
Lt. Cdr. F. H. Michaelis, New Symrna, Florida
Ens. R. F. Monaghan, Chicago, Illinois
Ens. R. A. Moore, Southington, Connecticut
Ens. R. I. Morgan, West Branch, Michigan
Ens. T. J. Northcutt, Atlanta, Georgia
Ens. E. L. Rafferty, Kansas City, Kansas
Ens. R. C. Ray, Kittery, Maine
Ens. W. A. Rosser, Atlanta, Georgia
Ens. W. L. Rund, El Cerrito, California
Lt. N. W. Sandler, Des Moines, Iowa
Ens. W. L. Smart, La Grange, Illinois
Ens. R. C. Sormanti, Providence, Rhode Island
Ens. F. Sullivan, Lakewood, Ohio
Lt. L. E. Thompson Jr., San Diego, California
Lt. R. D. Thompson, Tucson, Arizona
Lt. H. E. Vita, Long Island, New York
Lt. (j.g.) P. T. Wielert, Ocean Grove, New Jersey
Ens. L. O. Woods, Highland City, Florida

R. B. Ackler, ACEM, San Diego, California
L. A. Allen, AMM3, Fort Worth, Texas
E. I. Anderson, AOM1, East Orange, New Jersey
H. J. Beylotte, AMM1, Charleston, South Carolina
A. E. Bond, ARM1, Osceola, Nebraska
J. C. Campbell Jr., ACOM, Canton, North Carolina
J. B. Carroll, AEM3, South Boston, Massachusetts
T. H. Carroll, AOM1, Houston, Texas
W. R. Church, AMM2, Eaton Rapids, Michigan
W. F. Ciocys, ART2, Providence, Rhode Island
J. D. M. Clifford, AMM2, Hyde Park, Massachusetts
R. W. Eichhorn, PR1, Pittsburgh, Pennsylvania
E. J. Evans, S2, San Quentin, California
C. D. Ford, S1, Independence, Kansas
E. J. Hill, ACMM, Chula Vista, California
W. O. Hix, ACM, Imperial Beach, California
P. G. Holcombe, ART2, Trenton, New Jersey
C. B. Irons, AMM1, Gilmer, Texas
E. O. Johnson, ACRT, West Hartford, Connecticut
F. J. Koch, AMM2, West Los Angeles, California
F. O. Kopra, ART2, Pomona, California
W. C. Kottke, ART1, Minneapolis, Minnesota
J. E. Logsdon, AOM3, Connellsville, Pennsylvania
H. V. Mackey, AEM2, Springfield, Missouri
T. A. O'Donnell, Y1, Bromhead, Saskatchewan, Canada
E. Passmore, AOM2, San Diego, California
J. D. Pope Jr., ACMM, Elk City, Oklahoma
A. Remkus, PhoM1, Detroit, Michigan
L. L. Roach, AMM3, Indianapolis, Indiana
I. M. Sloan, S1, Phoenix, Arizona
J. E. Valinski, ARM1, Simpson, Pennsylvania

Fighting-Bombing Squadron 12

Ens. E. P. C. Anderson, Aurora, Illinois
Lt. (j.g.) W. Bair, Los Angeles, California
Ens. C. E. Barr, Natick, Massachusetts
Ens. P. J. Begin, Danvers, Massachusetts
Ens. L. T. Bernard, Lafayette, Louisiana
Lt. A. G. Bolduc, Franklin, Massachusetts
Lt. M. S. Byrnes Jr., Rensselaer, Indiana
Ens. A. B. Campbell, Stoughton, Massachusetts
Lt. (j.g.) D. A. Carmichael, Columbus, Ohio
Ens. J. M. Carpenter, Buckhannon, West Virginia
Ens. H. G. Chaffer, Easton, Connecticut
Ens. F. Chappell, Americus, Georgia

Ens. M. G. Christie, Buffalo, New York
Ens. L. L. Colin, Tarentum, Pennsylvania
Ens. G. G. Collins, Alexandria, Virginia
Lt. R. H. Denoff, Chicago, Illinois
Lt. R. W. Drewelow, Omaha, Nebraska
Ens. J. C. Funsten, Charlottesville, Virginia
Ens. R. O. Gadbois, Providence, Rhode Island
Ens. P. Glasser, Long Beach, California
Ens. B. L. Glover, Kansas City, Missouri
Ens. R. E. Goerke, St. Joseph, Missouri
Lt. (j.g.) L. G. Gray, Tonkawa, Oklahoma
Lt. (j.g.) R. K. Green, Whiting, Indiana
Ens. W. C. Grigsby, Bristol, Virginia
Ens. B. R. Hayes, Brooklyn, New York
Ens. R. T. Higgins, Monett, Missouri
Ens. C. R. Hintz, Palisades Park, New Jersey
Ens. J. E. Howard, Beacon, New York
Lt. (j.g.) P. J. Husting, Crawfordsville, Indiana
Lt. W. R. Jemison, Charleston, West Virginia
Ens. H. P. Jenerick, Cicero, Illinois
Ens. D. K. Johannsen, Melvin, Illinois
Ens. C. R. Leonard, San Angelo, Texas
Ens. H. W. Lindley, Milford, Connecticut
Ens. H. C. Lutz Jr., St. Louis, Missouri
Ens. J. Mangieri, Abingdon, Illinois
Ens. E. K. Manhold Jr., Erie, Pennsylvania
Lt. L. A. Menard Jr., Daytona Beach, Florida
Lt. (j.g.) R. J. Miller, West Chester, Pennsylvania
Ens. T. G. Morehead Jr., Memphis, Tennessee
Lt. (j.g.) T. W. Morsman, Omaha, Nebraska
Ens. F. W. Ness, South Weymouth, Massachusetts
Lt. Cdr. E. J. Pawka, Alexandria, Virginia
Ens. J. T. Ray, Clare, Michigan
Ens. J. D. Samelson, Lake Forest, Illinois
Ens. W. K. Sankey, Detroit, Michigan
Ens. J. A. Schipper, San Mateo, California
Ens. C. C. Schmidt, Corfu, New York
Ens. G. B. Sears, Richmond, Virginia
Lt. A. B. Smith Jr., Gastonia, North Carolina
Ens. M. W. Smith, Barnesville, Georgia
Ens. A. C. L. Splittgerber, Wisner, Nebraska
Lt. (j.g.) J. K. Steel, Wilmette, Illinois
Ens. D. O. Tillery, Elgin, Illinois
Lt. R. M. Witmer, Chambersburg, Pennsylvania

W. J. Baldwin, AMM2, Uncasville, Connecticut

D. T. Barton, ART1, Jamesport, Missouri
C. R. Chambers Jr., ACMM, Ventura, California
A. M. Cusdorff Jr., PhoM2, Philadelphia, Pennsylvania
B. R. Hidle, AOM1, Bonifay, Florida
R. C. Lace, ACRT, Cleveland, Ohio
R. D. Lovell, ACMM, Ball, Louisiana
W. C. Lyles, Y1, Ocala, Florida
P. R. Merrill Jr., ACRM, Preston, Idaho
W. J. Moessner, AOM3, Allentown, Pennsylvania
A. J. Muscle, AOM2, Highland Park, New Jersey
H. Pistole, ACOM, Bellflower, California
W. P. Ryan, AEM2, Chicago, Illinois
M. E. Sayre, S1, Portland, Oregon
C. P. Scott, AMMP2, Downeyville, California
A. H. Shaw, PR1, Philadelphia, Pennsylvania
W. P. Short, ACEM, San Diego, California
T. D. Ward, AMMC, Fort Worth, Texas
G. D. Whitthaus, AMMH2, St. Louis, Missouri

Torpedo Squadron 12

Ens. M. F. Able Jr., Grafton, West Virginia
Ens. H. M. Allen Jr., Citroneir, Alabama
Lt. (j.g.) R. W. Banta, Summit, New Jersey
Ens. W. J. Blair, Mt. Lebanon, Pennsylvania
Lt. K. R. Brizzee, Ogden, Utah
Lt. (j.g.) P. D. Dorratcague, New York, New York
Ens. J. A. Dotson, Dallas, Texas
Lt. Cdr. T. B. Ellison, Stockdale, Texas
Lt. (j.g.) J. W. Fles, Hawthorne, New Jersey
Lt. F. S. Franklin, Lancaster, Pennsylvania
Lt. (j.g.), D. M. Gordon, Jacksonville, Florida
Lt. G. F. Hames, Chicago, Illinois
Lt. C. Hamilton, Okemah, Oklahoma
Ens. W. H. Hazlehurst, Baltimore, Maryland
Ens. L. A. Holdren, Fort Dodge, Iowa
Lt. C. H. Jaep, Westmont, New Jersey
Ens. F. J. Keinath, Dundee, Michigan
Lt. D. A. King, Albans, New York
Ens. R. C. Lisle, Otis, Colorado
Lt. (j.g.) G. L. Lucas, El Dorado Springs, Missouri
Ens. C. H. Mundt, Bronx, New York
Lt. (j.g.) J. H. Newby, Bend, Oregon
Lt. (j.g.) H. M. Reedy, Port Hueneme, California
Lt. (j.g.) N. R. Smith, Lakewood, Ohio
Ens. J. L. Stirn, Spokane, Washington

Lt. (j.g.) J. R. M. Whelan, Brooklyn, New York
Ens. J. M. White, Portsmouth, Virginia
Ens. J. F. Zook, Detroit, Michigan

T. H. Abker, AOM2, Sioux City, Iowa
P. A. Alsbrook, AOM1, Selma, Alabama
R. H. Anderson, ARM3, Sioux Falls, South Dakota
M. W. Balken, ARM2, Culver City, California
J. E. Barber, ARM3, Waymart, Pennsylvania
P. J. Baughman, AOM3, York, Pennsylvania
R. E. Bisbee, ARM3, Macedonia, Iowa
B. B. Blevins, AOM3, Amber, Oklahoma
D. C. Boles, ARM3, River Falls, Wisconsin
M. E. Booth, AMM3, Nashville, Tennessee
G. D. Bothell, ACRT, Port Orchard, Washington
L. E. Brinson, AOM3, Muncie, Indiana
A. R. Buglione, ACOM, Waterbury, Connecticut
C. D. Chadwell, AOM3, Texarkana, Texas
B. B. Chipp, ARM3, St. Joseph, Missouri
L. L. Comstock, AOM1, Independence, Missouri
R. T. Cooney, ACMM, Los Angeles, California
M. Cummins, ARM3, Toledo, Ohio
C. M. Dake, PR1, Naches, Washington
C. P. DeMoss, AOM2, Hilmar, California
D. E. Downing, ARM3, Bells Gardens, California
F. Dreiger, AOM2, Lincoln, Nebraska
E. L. Ellefson, AM1, Washington Island, Wisconsin
R. W. Ensley, ARM2, Auburn, Washington
J. E. Fowler, ARM3, Charleston, West Virginia
M. F. Fox, AOM1, Iron Mountain, Michigan
J. T. Fuller, ART1, Middleton, New York
S. W. Hake, AMM1, Red Lion, Pennsylvania
J. D. Hayes, ARM3, Cascade, Iowa
G. J. Heilsberg, AMM3, Valley Stream, New York
H. A. Herbert, ARM1, New Orleans, Louisiana
R. Hill, Y1, Premont, Texas
G. O. Humphreys, AOM3, Oakland, California
G. R. Iiames, ARM2, Dayton, Ohio
M. L. Ingram, AMM1, Hingham, Massachusetts
G. J. Krigel, ACRT, Seattle, Washington
P. B. Kuyrkendall, AMM3, McComb, Mississippi
N. K. Larsen, ARM3, Sinclair, Wyoming
S. B. Lund, ARM3, Seattle, Washington
R. E. Martin, ARM3, Topeka, Kansas
W. L. Martin, ARM2, Longview, Texas
R. E. Masten, AOM3, Grand Island, Nebraska

H. L. McMahon, AOM3, Fairview, Illinois
E. M. Nowak, AMM3, Indian Orchard, Massachusetts
R. C. Overbaugh, AMM3, Catskill, New York
J. B. Pezely Jr., ARM3, Park City, Utah
P. V. Pond, AOM1, Wildwood Crest, New Jersey
H. L. Reece, AMM1, Oakdale, California
A. J. Smith Jr., ARM2, Lynwood, California
A. W. Sotherland Jr., ARM3, Brainero, Minnesota
R. R. Staszak, ARM3, Chicago, Illinois
J. K. Switzer, ARM3, Glendale, California
D. E. Thomas, ARM3, Altoona, Pennsylvania
L. E. Thomas, ARM3, Salt Lake City, Utah
R. J. Voelker, ARM3, St. Louis, Illinois
E. H. White, AMM2, Philadelphia, Pennsylvania
J. E. Wickham, AEM1, Flemington, New Jersey
D. J. Wood, ARM1, New Orleans, Louisiana

Bombing Squadron 12

Ens. R. R. Andreason, Long Beach, California
Lt. A. L. Bureau, Coronado, California
Lt. O. S. Burnette, Decatur, Illinois
Ens. J. L. Childress, La Fallette, Tennessee
Lt. G. W. DeVore, Cambria, Iowa
Ens. H. J. Edmund, Hawthorne, New Jersey
Cdr. R. A. Embree, Bellflower, California
Ens. C. L. Fisher, Junction City, Oregon
Ens. W. H. Frenger Jr., St. Louis, Missouri
Lt. J. R. Frith, Williamsport, Pennsylvania
Ens. G. A. Fye, Columbus, Indiana
Ens. C. L. Galbreath, Chanute, Kansas
Lt. C. T. Greenleaf, Lakewood, Ohio
Lt. J. F. Guyon, Louisville, Kentucky
Ens. H. A. Hammonds, El Paso, Texas
Ens. C. R. Hauth, Ebensburg, Pennsylvania
Ens. R. Hearn, Los Angeles, California
Lt. J. H. Johnson, Greenwood, South Carolina
Ens. G. A. Kernan, New Orleans, Louisiana
Lt. J. N. Lemon, Richmond, Indiana
Lt. A. J. Lindstrom, Los Angeles, California
Ens. J. A. Mackedie, Salinas, California
Ens. T. J. Miller, Durant, Oklahoma
Ens. J. Morris, Haverhill, Massachusetts
Ens. C. R. Potts, Burbank, California
Lt. V. F. Tucker, Philadelphia, Pennsylvania
Ens. J. F. Unverfurth, Perryville, Missouri

Ens. H. W. Wegener, Higginsville, Missouri
Lt. J. B. Whiting, Gainesville, Florida
R. A. Brubaker, ART1, Redlands, California
J. H. Caldwell, ARM3, San Gabriel, California
M. E. Cameron, AEM1, Limon, Colorado
L. G. Coleman, AMM2, Emporia, Kansas
C. Comko, ARM3, Monessen, Pennsylvania
T. P. Daly, ACMM, Alta Vista, Iowa
D. J. Del Grosso, ARM3, Detroit, Michigan
E. E. Erickson, PR1, Minneapolis, Minnesota
H. C. Githens, AM1, Oregon City, Oregon
W. F. Hale, ARM1, Derby, New York
R. L. Hall, ACRM, no permanent address
F. V. Hilbert, ARM2, Taylorville, Illinois
W. W. Hileman, ACRM, Meade, Kansas
J. W. Hogsett, ARM3, Lake Gem, Florida
J. E. Hudson, ARM3, Daisetta, Texas
H. D. Jones, ARM3, Princeton, Illinois
W. R. Judson, AMMI1, Chicago, Illinois
O. Little Jr., ARM3, Fed, Kentucky
E. J. May, AOM2, Forest, Mississippi
R. C. McCulley, AMM1, Los Angeles, California
T. R. McGinnis, ARM3, Charlotte, North Carolina
W. H. Morrow, ARM2, Hackensack, New Jersey
R. B. Neubig, ARM3, Minetto, New York
J. W. Noble, ARM3, Rosemead, California
P. E. Nugent, ARM3, Mount Ranier, Maryland
C. L. Phegley, ARM3, Ristoe, Missouri
L. D. Powell Jr., ARM3, Memphis, Tennessee
M. R. Schultz, ARM2, Wheeling, West Virginia
R. J. Schwarz, AOM1, Seattle, Washington
A. R. Simon, ARM2, Patterson, New Jersey
A. R. Smith Jr., ARM1, Marblehead, Massachusetts
J. G. Stevens, Y1, Mansfield, Ohio
R. M. Teal, ARM3, Vancouver, Washington
M. M. Tillmand Jr., ARM3, Memphis, Tennessee
M. M. Tottleben, ARM3, St. Louis, Illinois
W. G. Walters, ARM1, Harrington Park, New Jersey
R. B. Weston, ARM1, Skowhegan, Maine
L. R. Xethakis, ARM1, Erie, Pennsylvania

✪ Appendix B: Air Group 12 Personnel Losses, 1944–1945

Air Group 12 Staff

Cdr. C. L. Crommelin, Okinawa, 28 March 1945
Cdr. R. A. Embree, Okinawa, 12 May 1945

Fighting Squadron 12

Ens. D. G. Howard Jr., at sea, Okinawa, 21 May 1945
Lt. (j.g.) Sabe Legatos, Tokyo, 16 February 1945
Lt. (j.g.) L. Levis, at sea, Okinawa, 21 May 1945
Ens. D. L. Martin, Yap Island, Caroline Islands, 21 March 1945
Ens. W. L. Mason, at sea, Okinawa, 18 April 1945
Ens. W. Murray Jr., at sea, West Coast, 9 November 1944
Ens. F. A. Nittel, at sea, West Coast, 20 December 1944
Lt. N. W. Sandler, Tokyo, 25 February 1945
Lt. J. E. Toliver, Tokyo, 17 February 1945
Ens. R. L. Welty, Kyushu, 14 May 1945
Ens. C. L. White, Tokuna Shima, 18 May 1945
Lt. J. J. Wood, Kikaiga Shima, 2 May 1945
Ens. L. O. Woods, Kikaiga Shima, 14 May 1045

Fighting-Bombing Squadron 12

Ens. W. T. McAdams, Tokyo, 17 February 1945
Ens. W. N. McConnell, Tokyo, 17 February 1945
Lt. B. P. Seaman Jr., Tokyo, 16 February 1945
Ens. D. O. Tillery, at sea, Ryukyu Islands, 26 February 1945

Bombing Squadron 12

Ens. C. H. Brown, Tokyo, 16 February 1945 (POW—returned)
Ens. J. F. Glynn, Astoria, Oregon, 30 September 1944
Ens. W. Kolonik, Astoria, Oregon, 16 October 1944
J. Macina, ARM3, Astoria, Oregon, 30 September 1944
J. D. Richards, ARM3, Tokyo, 16 February 1945 (POW—returned)

Torpedo Squadron 12

Ens. H. M. Allen Jr., Ulithi, Caroline Islands, 10 March 1945
G. F. Brown, ARM2, Salton Sea, 20 December 1944
Lt. W. V. Colbert, Salton Sea, 20 December 1944
C. P. DeMoss, AOM2, Ulithi, Caroline Islands, 10 March 1945
D. E. Downing, ARM3, Ulithi, Caroline Islands, 10 March 1945
G. J. Frazier, AOM2, Chichi Jima, 18 February 1945
C. C. Hall, ARM2, Chichi Jima, 18 February 1945
Ens. F. E. Hall, Chichi Jima, 18 February 1945
M. W. Mershon, ARM3, Chichi Jima, 18 February 1945
J. E. Notary, AOM3, Chichi Jima, 18 February 1945
Ens. R. F. Rohlfing, Chichi Jima, 18 February 1945

✪ Appendix C:
Summary of Combat Activities of Carrier Air Group 12: 16 February through 31 May 1945

Date	Strikes-Sweeps (at targets)			CAPs[1]	Other[2]			Enemy Aircraft Destroyed[3]			Ordnance Expended[4]			
	VF	VB	VT	VF	VF	VB	VT	Air	Ground	Probables	Bombs (Tons)	Rockets (Nos.)	Napalm (Tons)	
Feb.														
10–15	—	—	—	64	4	14	—	—	—	—	—	—	—	En route
16	109	14	—	—	16	—	—	38	32	28	8.75	638	—	Toyko area
17	58	12	15	16	8	—	—	6	3	9	20	292	—	Toyko area
18,19	18	12	12	32	—	—	3	—	—	—	19	70	—	Chichi Jima
20–24	108	38	36	36	3	7	—	—	—	—	46.75	453	29	Iwo Jima
25	61	—	—	—	4	—	—	8	35	13	—	48	—	Tokyo area
26–28	—	—	—	—	6	—	14	—	—	—	—	—	—	Refuel
Subtotal	354	76	63	204	41	41	23	52	70	50	94.5	1,502	29	
April														
5–7	—	—	—	48	22	12	14	—	—	—	—	—	—	En route
8–10	—	—	—	299	73	16	—	—	1	—	—	175	—	Kikai(ga)
11	—	—	—	—	—	—	2	—	—	—	—	—	—	Refuel
12,13	—	—	—	141	7	—	—	2	—	—	—	—	—	Diato Jima
14,15	54	11	20	168	—	—	—	9	2	13	26	243	—	Okinawa
16	—	—	—	28	—	8	—	—	—	—	—	—	—	Refuel
17–21	54	63	69	393	8	4	—	16	1	2	101.5	419	12	Okinawa
22,23	10	9	12	124	—	—	—	12	—	5	17	69	—	Kikai
24	—	—	—	8	—	—	—	—	—	—	—	—	—	Refuel
25–27	72	—	—	81	—	—	—	—	—	—	16	217	—	Kikai
28–30	28	37	32	217	—	—	—	4	1	3	73	332	—	Okinawa
Subtotal	218	120	133	1,507	110	40	16	43	5	20	233.5	1,455	12	

May														
1–5	26	39	37	262	8	—	11	—	13	1	63	320	66	Kikai
8	—	—	—	8	—	—	—	—	—	—	—	—	—	Refuel
7–9	18	23	23	163	—	—	1	—	—	—	44	146	16	Kikai
10	12	—	10	80	—	—	—	—	3	—	11.25	60	—	Diato Shima
11,12	12	29	24	208	—	—	3	—	1	2	27	67	—	Okinawa
13	86	26	24	44	6	—	1	6	13	8	51	111	—	Kyushu
14	75	—	25	53	14	—	13	7	—	—	53	177	—	Usa
15,16	—	—	—	16	—	—	—	—	—	—	—	—	—	Refuel
17,18	16	8	9	192	—	—	—	—	—	—	11	433	—	Ryukus
19	—	—	—	8	—	—	—	—	—	—	—	—	—	Replenish
20,21	44	—	9	102	—	—	—	—	—	—	10	23	—	Okinawa
22	—	—	—	—	12	—	—	—	—	—	—	—	—	Refuel
23,24	19	3	12	96	—	—	—	—	—	—	20.3	94	—	Kikai
25	—	—	—	46	—	—	—	—	—	1	—	—	—	CAP only
26–31	—	—	—	180	—	—	28	—	—	—	—	—	—	En route
Subtotal	308	128	173	1,458	40	0	28	29	13	12	290.3	1,431	82	
Total	880	324	369	3,169	191	64	67	124[5]	88	85	618.3	4,388	123	

1. Includes all combat air patrols over task force, targets, and radar-picket vessels.
2. Includes antisubmarine patrols, searches, photographic flights.
3. Probables include unconfirmed enemy aircraft destroyed in the air or on the ground.
4. Not included: 780,000 rounds of 50-caliber ammunition expended by VF and VBF. Rocket numbers include both 3.5-inch and 5-inch HVARs.
5. Does not include enemy aircraft destroyed by the *Randolph*'s antiaircraft defenses. Tote board on hangar deck shows a total of 129.

Data combined from the USS *Randolph* Action Report 10–28 Feb. 1945 and USS *Randolph* Action Report 5 April through 31 May 1945. Office of Naval Records and Library.

✪ Appendix D:
Summary of
Kamikaze Activities

Japanese Naval Aircraft

	All Kamikaze (Estimate)	(Less) Philippines	Formosa, Iwo Jima, Okinawa
Sortied	2,314	760	1,554
Returned	1,086	180	906
Expended	1,228	580	648

Kamikaze Activities, Formosa, Iwo Jima, Okinawa (Estimate)

Type of Vessel	Sinkings		Damaged	
	Claimed	Actual	Claimed	Actual
CV	1	0	28	16
CVL	0	0	0	3
CVE	0	1	2	4
BB	10	0	6	10
CA	1	0	0	2
Cr	7	0	13	0
CL	0	0	0	2
DD	0	10	16	64
DE	0	0	0	19
DM	0	0	0	0
DMS	0	0	0	14
Misc.*	18	5	61	60
Total	37	16	126	194

* Includes transports, auxiliaries, LSTs, patrol craft, yard vessels, and unknowns.

Japanese Air Fleets*

	All Kamikaze, Okinawa Area
Sortied	1,809
Returned	879
Expended	930

* Figures include kamikazes and escorts.

Kamikaze Activities, Okinawa Area

Type of Vessel	Sinkings		Damaged	
	Claimed	Actual	Claimed	Actual
CV	1	0	25	8
CVE	1	1	2	4
BB	8	0	6	10
CA	1	0	0	2
Cr	7	0	13	0
CL	0	0	0	3
DD	8	10	16	63
DE	0	1	0	19
DM	0	0	0	13
DMS	0	1	0	14
Misc.*	18	4	37	61
Total	44	17	99	198

* Includes transports, auxiliaries, LSTs, patrol craft, yard vessels, and unknowns.
Source: Rikihei Inoguchi and Nakajima Tadashim, ex-kamikaze pilots. *The Divine Wind.* New York: Ballantine Books, Inc., 1958.

✪ Glossary

A/F—airfield

ABM2c—aviation boatswain's mate second class

Admiral's barge—35- to 40-foot motorboat with cabins fore and aft, distinguished from other motorboats by a black hull and white cabins

Aft—toward the rear of a ship or vessel

Aground—ship or vessel touching bottom when in too shallow water

Aircrewman—normally an enlisted man with a technical specialty as part of aircraft flight crew

Airdale—a reference to those who fly

Alongside—vessels close enough together to transfer personnel or materials

ARM3c—aviation radioman third class; an aircrewman

Artificial horizon—aircraft flight instrument showing aircraft's wing relationship to the horizon

ATCS—aviation electronics technician chief

Bandit—enemy aircraft or bogey

Battle station—assigned task for each of the ship's crew when under attack; highest state of readiness

Belly tank—external gas tank carried beneath the fuselage. The F6F carried a 150-gallon jettisonable tank to extend its range.

Blacking out—losing eyesight under excessive "G" forces and/or losing consciousness

Boatswain's chair—cagelike chair suspended by cables to transfer personnel between ships

Bogey—unidentified aircraft

Bore sight—to align several guns so that the projectiles will converge at a specific distance

Breeches buoy—life ring with legs and harness used as a boatswain's chair

Bridge—upper level of ship's superstructure used as the control station for the ship's functions

Bulkhead—wall

Canopy—aircraft cockpit enclosure, part of which is movable

Catwalk—narrow walkway suspended along each side of the flight deck for deck personnel working among aircraft

Chandelle—high-speed climbing maneuver of an aircraft, terminating at low speed with a dive in the opposite direction

Combing—doorlike opening in bulkhead, raised at floor and lowered from ceiling

Commissioning—ceremony placing vessel in active service with the U.S. Navy

Companionway—hallway or passageway

Cut—flag-waving signal across the throat used by the landing signal officer to tell the pilot to cut power and land; execution is mandatory

CV—large aircraft carrier; carried approximately one hundred aircraft

CVE—small escort aircraft carrier; carried approximately fifty aircraft

CVL—medium aircraft carrier; carried approximately seventy-five aircraft

DD—abbreviation for destroyer

Deck—floor

DFC—Distinguished Flying Cross

Dilbert—aviation-training character used to depict good or bad actions in flight operations; drawn for the Navy Department by R. C. Osborn

Ditching—landing and then abandoning an aircraft in the water

Dive flaps or brakes—drag device in dive-bomber wings to slow aircraft in a dive

Echelon—staggered flight formation with each aircraft slightly behind, left or right and higher or lower than the aircraft ahead of it

Fantail—lowest extended deck over the stern of the ship

Fathom—six feet (depth of water)

Fighter director—Individual controlling the pilot's flight path over the earth's surface; from radar information

Fire wall—protective wall between the pilot and the engine compartment; also, to full-throttle the engine

Flash cream—ointment applied to exposed skin to minimize injury from flash fires

G—abbreviation used to describe the force of gravity

Gallery deck—suspended deck in the hangar deck below the flight deck

Galley—kitchen

Gear—any movable item(s) used aboard ship

General Quarters—highest state of battle readiness, in which all ship's personnel are at their assigned stations for combat

Graveyard spiral—uncontrolled descending turn, a result of vertigo

Group leader—senior pilot and coordinator of several flight divisions in company

Hack—restricted to his quarters (way of disciplining an officer)

Hatches—vertical openings in bulkheads; can be closed with watertight doors

Head-on—aircraft approaching each other at the same altitude from opposite directions

Immelmann turn—a climbing turn to gain altitude and change direction

Jacob's ladder—round wooden cross pieces suspended by ropes on each side to form a flexible ladder

Jinking—causing the aircraft to follow an erratic flight pattern both in longitudinal and vertical movements

Jockey—aircrewman's lingo for the pilot

Joe pot—coffee pot

Knot(s)—nautical mile(s) per hour, approximately 1.18 mph

Landlubber—one unfamiliar with the sea

LCI—amphibious landing craft, Infantry

LCT—amphibious landing craft, tank

Leeward—downwind

LSI—amphibious landing ship, infantry

Lugger—small coastal steamer with sail

Magneto—electrical energy supply for aircraft engine

Man-overboard-drill—assembly of all personnel aboard ship for an accounting of members on board

Monsoon—seasonal period of heavy rainfall

Napalm—highly flammable jellylike substance

Naval—both Navy and Marine Corps units in company

Needle-ball-airspeed—basic flight instruments

OD—officer of the deck, functioning for the ship's commanding officer in routine matters of conning the ship

Officers' country—general area, usually forward, where officers' staterooms are located

Operation order—directive specifying tasks and timetables of several navy entities operating together

Orbit—an aircraft's circular path around or over some reference point

Overhead run—an intercepting flight path from above enemy aircraft

Parachute rigger—enlisted technician charged with the maintenance of the pilots' safety equipment and survival gear

Passageway—hallway

Picket—usually one or more destroyers located fifty to one hundred miles from the main force in the direction of the expected enemy approach

Port—left

Quarterdeck—area designated for conducting ship's business while in port

Rank—commissioned officers' titles

Rate—enlisted mens' titles

Ready room—pilots' briefing room and general-quarters station

S/E plane—single-engine aircraft

Scarf ring—semicircular ring in the rear SB2C cockpit; supports machine guns

Screen—group of destroyers surrounding larger combatants and carriers; a defensive formation against hostile aircraft and submarines

Section leader—second-senior pilot of a division

Ship's company—all personnel permanently attached to the ship. Air-group members are temporary.

Shore patrol—naval personnel assigned police duties ashore

Sick chick—aircraft with difficulty

Skipper—commanding officer

Sortie—movements of ships or aircraft toward some objective

Starboard—right

Stick—cockpit flight control for maneuvering the plane

Strategic command—campaign-area commander

Tactical command—immediate local command

Tail-end charlie—last plane in formation

Tallyho—voice radio signal calling attention to another aircraft; if unfriendly, a relative, "o' clock" position was given

Task force—all ships and/or groups of ships under a tactical commander

Task group—integral organizations in the task force

Topside—shipboard areas above the main deck

Truck lights—uppermost lights on a ship's superstructure

USO—United Service Organization; volunteer civilian organization providing recreational facilities for military personnel

Vector—direction to fly on the compass

Wardroom—officers' dining room

Watch—daily division of work at special stations

Water injection—addition of water to fuel to temporarily increase engine power

Wave-off—flag-waving signal by landing signal officer, instructing the pilot to add power and go around for another approach; execution is mandatory

Wing spar—main strength member of aircraft's wing

✪ Bibliography

Books

Bauer, Eddy, Lt. Col., USA. *Marshall Cavendish Illustrated Encyclopedia of World War II.* Brig. Gen. James L. Collins, USA, Chief of Military History, Department of the Army, (consultant/ed.). New York: Marshall Cavendish Corp, 1972.

The Bluejackets' Manual. 19th edition. Annapolis, Maryland: U.S. Naval Institute, 1973.

Costello, John. *The Pacific War, World War, 1939–1945—Pacific Ocean.* New York: Rawson, Wade. 1981.

Gangway. USS *Randolph* Cruise Book, 1944–45.

Guyton, Boone T. *A Test Pilot's Story of the F4U Corsair.* New York: Orion Books, 1990.

Inoguchi, Rikihei, and Nakajima Tadashim, ex-kamikaze pilots. *The Divine Wind.* New York: Ballantine Books, Inc., 1958.

Morison, Samuel Eliot. *Victory in the Pacific 1945.* Boston: Little, Brown & Co., 1968.

Potter, E. B. *Admiral Arleigh Burke.* New York: Random House, 1990.

Potter, E. B., and Arleigh Burke. *Bald Eagle.* New York: Random House, 1990.

Potter, E. B., and Chester W. Nimitz. *The Great Sea War.* New York: Bramhall House, 1960.

Potter, E. B. (ed.), and Chester W. Nimitz (associate ed.). *Sea Power, A Naval History.* Englewood Cliffs, N.J.: Prentice-Hall, 1968.

Preston, Antony. *Aircraft Carrier.* New York: Galahad Books, 1979. p. 84/85.

Sims, Edward H. *Greatest Fighter Missions.* New York: Harper & Brothers, 1962.

Tillman, Barrett. *Hellcat: The F6F in World War II*. Annapolis, Maryland: U.S. Naval Institute, 1979.

Vaccari, Mr. and Mrs. O. *A Concise English-Japanese, Japanese-English Dictionary*. Minato-Ko, Tokyo: Kasai Publication and Print Co., 1958.

Warner, Denis, and Peggy Warner, with Commander Sadao Seno, JMSFD (Ret). *The Sacred Warriors: Japan's Suicide Legions*. New York: Avon Books, 1984.

Yust, Walter, ed. *10 Eventful Years*. vol. 4., Encyclopedia Britannica. Chicago: Encyclopedia Britannica, Inc., 1947.

Historical Documents from the Naval Historical Center, Navy Department

Aircraft Action Reports of Air Group TWELVE, 16 February through 25 February 1945. C. L. Crommelin, Commander Air Group TWELVE, to CinC, United States Fleet, 3 March 1945.

Aircraft Action Reports of Air Group TWELVE, 5 April to 31 May 1945. E. J. Pawka, Commander, Air Group TWELVE, to CinC, PacFlt, 10 June 1945.

Action Report, USS *Randolph* (CV 15), 10 February to 28 July 1945. First War Cruise—Tokyo and Iwo Jima.

Action Report, USS *Randolph* (CV 15), 10 February to 1 March 1945.

Action Report, USS *Randolph* (CV 15), 5 April to 31 May 1945.

Carrier Sense. Aviation Training Division, Office of the Chief of Naval Operations, OPNAV 33-NY-22, NAVAER 00-80Q-23, October 1944.

"Fighting Squadron Twelve (VF-12)." A Narrative, 20 July 1944 to 20 July 1945.

"History of Bombfighting Squadron TWELVE." A Narrative, January to July 1945.

Log Book of the USS *Franklin* (CV 13), 19 March 1945.

Log Book of the USS *Randolph* (CV 15), 1 January 1945 to 31 May 1945.

Log Book of the USS *Yorktown* (CV 10), February 1945.

Pamphlets

"Memories." A History of Air Group TWELVE, April 1944 to July 1945.

Schipper, Jack. "BombFitronTwelve." R. H. Denoff, July 1967.

Williams, Dr. Richard. "The World War II Chronicle of U.S.S. Randolph/CV-15." Self-published pamphlet and addendum.

Biographical Information

Michaelis, Michael. Interview by Roy W. Bruce, 1989, and letter to Roy W. Bruce, 1991.

Minter, Charles. Letter to Roy W. Bruce, 1991, and memorandum to Charles R. Leonard, 7 February 1994.

Naval Historical Center, Archives Branch, Biographical Section: Felix
  Baker, Charles L. Crommelin, Ralph Embree, Noel Gayler.
Pawka, Edward. *The Hook.* (Spring 1987) 10.

Newspapers

Foley, James, for Reuters. "Surviving Kamikaze Pilots in Dilemma," *Los
  Angeles Times.* (25 March 1981).
"U.S. War Prisoners Killed By Hiroshima Bomb Listed," UPI, *Los Angeles
  Times.* (7 December 1977).
The *Richmond Times.*

Interviews

Burke, Arleigh, Adm. USN (Ret.), by Roy W. Bruce, Fairfax, Virginia, July
  1993.
Harris, Richard W., by Charles R. Leonard, Austin, Texas, March 1989.
Richards, Jack, by Charles H. Brown, 21 July 1990.

Letters

Anderson, Rees H., to Roy Bruce, 2 May 1992.
Bernard, Lowell T., to Charles R. Leonard, 24 March 1990.
Bolduc, Alfred G., to Roy W. Bruce, 11 March 1991, with enclosures on 14
  May 1945 rescue.
Byrnes, Matthew S. "Bob," to Charles R. Leonard, 11 October 1989.
Carmichael, Dan A., to Warren McConnell, 21 April 1988.
Chaffer, H. Glen, to Roy W. Bruce, 22 April 1991, with copy of letter to
  parents of 9 June 1945.
Clark, Ellery, Capt. USN (Ret.), to Roy W. Bruce, 5 December 1989, with
  enclosure, "USS *Randolph*'s Two Hits."
Comb, Donald, to Roy Bruce, 25 August 1992.
Fraser, A. C., ATCS, USNR (Ret.), to H. Glen Chaffer, 11 February 1989.
Furse, L. E., to Roy W. Bruce, 2 September 1987 and 8 November 1989.
Hauth, Charles R., to Roy W. Bruce, 13 January 1990.
McWhorter, Hamilton, to Roy W. Bruce, 2 October 1989 and 6 April 1993.
Minter, Charles S., Jr., Vice Adm. USN (Ret.), to Roy Bruce, December 1990.
Morris, John, to Roy W. Bruce, 20 October 1987, and to Charles Leonard,
  25 February 1994.
Pawka, Edward J., to Roy W. Bruce, 28 September 1989, and to Charles R.
  Leonard, October 1989.
Phegley, Cletis L., to Roy W. Bruce, 7 September 1988.
Putney, Glen W., to Roy W. Bruce, 6 October 1989.
Stanway, Carl, to Roy Bruce, 9 April 1994, on VPB-18 rescue, 13 April 1945.
Schipper, Jack, to Charles R. Leonard and Roy W. Bruce, 14 October 1989.
Smith, Armistead B., Capt. USN (Ret.), to Roy W. Bruce, 5 February 1991.
Splittgerber, Allen C., to Charles R. Leonard, 17 October 1989.

Most Memorable Experiences

Anderson, E. Phil C.

Applegate, Frank, "Rescue of Ensign Salvaggio" and "At Sea Rescue."

Bernard, Lowell T., 8 September 1987.

Bolduc, Alfred G., "Surprise on Replenishment Day," "Lady Luck Strikes Again," "Shoot Out at Kikai," and "RAPCAP 90 Miles NNE of Task Force 58."

Booth, Merrill E.

Collins, George C., 25 September 1978.

Cummins, Marcus, 17 September 1989.

Davidson, Stanley H.

Finley, Jay M., February 1989.

Galbreath, Chuck L., 15 September 1987.

Hauth, Charles R., 13 January 1990.

Hintz, Carman, December 1988.

Lindley, Harold N., 5 May 1988.

McGinnis, Ted R., Cdr. USN (Ret.).

McWhorter, Hamilton. Cdr. USN (Ret.), "Some Combat Memories."

Meacham, James A., 10 November 1989.

Monaghan, Robert F.

Northcutt, Thomas J.

Nugent, Paul E.

Remkus, Tony.

Smith, Alfred R., 10 October 1989.

Smith, M. W.

Staszak, Robert R.

Wegener, Harold, 8 September 1987.

Witmer, Robert M., Capt. USN (Ret.).

✪ Index

✪ About the Authors

Roy Wallace Bruce, a native-born Washingtonian, worked in the Naval Gun Factory until joining the navy's V-5 Program in August 1942. He chose dive-bombing after being commissioned and "winged" at Pensacola in February 1944 and reported to Bombing Squadron 5 at Naval Air Station Alameda. When the navy doubled the number of fighters aboard its carriers in response to Japanese kamikaze attacks, Bruce volunteered to switch to fighters and was transferred to Air Group 12 under Charles Crommelin. Bruce flew in the first carrier strikes on Tokyo, in ground-support missions over Iwo Jima and Okinawa, and in fighter sweeps over Kyushu to destroy kamikaze facilities. He was awarded the Distinguished Flying Cross and four Air Medals. After the war, he flew fighters and attack bombers in the Naval Air Reserve, retiring in 1962, and pursued a career as a technical illustrator and art director. He organized the first reunion of Air Group 12, held aboard the USS *Yorktown* in 1987.

Charles R. Leonard was born in Dallas and raised in San Angelo, Texas, where he attended San Angelo Junior College (now Angelo State University). Entering the navy as a seaman second in World War II, he transferred to the aviation cadet flight program, completing training at Pensacola, Florida. He was commissioned an ensign and designated a naval aviator in 1944 and elected a navy career, retiring in 1963. After having ventured out as a livestock farmer, real-estate broker, insurance agent, and abstractor, he returned to college and completed a bachelor of science degree with majors in journalism and business administration at the University of Texas at Austin in 1969. A ten-year stint as a high-school naval-science instructor rounded out his career until retirement. Subsequently, he has pursued a vocation as a freelance writer.

The **Naval Institute Press** is the book-publishing arm of the U.S. Naval Institute, a private, nonprofit society for sea service professionals and others who share an interest in naval and maritime affairs. Established in 1873 at the U.S. Naval Academy in Annapolis, Maryland, where its offices remain, today the Naval Institute has more than 100,000 members worldwide.

Members of the Naval Institute receive the influential monthly magazine *Proceedings* and discounts on fine nautical prints and on ship and aircraft photos. They also have access to the transcripts of the Institute's Oral History Program and get discounted admission to any of the Institute-sponsored seminars offered around the country.

The Naval Institute also publishes *Naval History* magazine. This colorful bimonthly is filled with entertaining and thought-provoking articles, first-person reminiscences, and dramatic art and photography. Members receive a discount on *Naval History* subscriptions.

The Naval Institute's book-publishing program, begun in 1898 with basic guides to naval practices, has broadened its scope in recent years to include books of more general interest. Now the Naval Institute Press publishes more than seventy titles each year, ranging from how-to books on boating and navigation to battle histories, biographies, ship and aircraft guides, and novels. Institute members receive discounts on the Press's nearly 400 books in print.

For a free catalog describing Naval Institute Press books currently available, and for further information about subscribing to *Naval History* magazine or about joining the U.S. Naval Institute, please write to:

Membership & Communications Department
U.S. Naval Institute
118 Maryland Avenue
Annapolis, Maryland 21402-5035
Or call, toll-free, (800) 233-USNI.